Imperial China's Last Classical Academies

CHINA RESEARCH MONOGRAPH 42

INSTITUTE OF EAST ASIAN STUDIES
UNIVERSITY OF CALIFORNIA • BERKELEY
CENTER FOR CHINESE STUDIES

Imperial China's Last Classical Academies

Social Change in the Lower Yangzi, 1864–1911

BARRY C. KEENAN

A publication of the Institute of East Asian Studies, University of California, Berkeley. Although the Institute of East Asian Studies is responsible for the selection and acceptance of manuscripts in this series, responsibility for the opinions expressed and for the accuracy of statements rests with their authors.

Correspondence may be sent to:
Joanne Sandstrom, Managing Editor
Institute of East Asian Studies
University of California
Berkeley, California 94720-2318

The China Research Monograph series, whose first title appeared in 1967, is one of several publications series sponsored by the Institute of East Asian Studies in conjunction with its constituent units. The others include the Japan Research Monograph series, the Korea Research Monograph series, the Indochina Research Monograph series, and the Research Papers and Policy Studies series. A list of recent publications appears at the back of the book.

Library of Congress Cataloging-in-Publication Data

Keenan, Barry C., 1940—
Imperial China's last classical academies : social change in the lower Yangzi, 1864–1911 / Barry C. Keenan.
p. cm. — (China research monograph : 42)
Includes bibliographical references, glossary, and index.
ISBN 1-55729-041-5
1. Education—Social aspects—China—Yangtze River Region—History—19th Century. 2. Education—Social aspects—China—Yangtze River Region—History—20th century. 3. Confucianism and education—China—Yangtze River River Region—History—19th century. 4. Confucianism and education—China—Yangtze River Region— History—20th century. I. Title. II. Series: China research monographs ; no. 42.
LC191.8.C52Y365 1994
370.'951'2—dc20 93-34749
CIP

Cover: A historical reconstruction of student rooms at Southern Quintessence Academy (Nanjing shuyuan) in Jiangyin town, Jiangsu province (photo by Barry C. Keenan, December 1982)

Second printing, 2001

Contents

Abbreviations

FWGD	*Fuwu gongdu*
FZ	*fuzhi*
JDSL	*Jindai Zhongguo shiliao congkan*
JJZZ	*Jingji zazhu*
JSJYGB	*Jiangsu jiaoyu gongbao*
JSJYZH	*Jiangsu jiaoyu zonghui*
JSXW	*Jiangsu xuewu gongdu*
JYXZXZ	*Jiangyin xianzhi xuzhi*
QDZJ	*Qingdai zhuanji congkan*
QSG	*Qingshi gao*
SHSTZG	*Shanghai shi tongzhi guan qikan*
XZ	*Xianzhi*
YFTXJ	*Yifeng tang wen xu ji*
ZWDCD	*Zhongwen da cidian*
ZWZQJ	*Zeng Wenzheng gong (Guofan) quanji*

Foreword

In her now classic study of the Tongzhi period (1862–1874) published more than thirty-five years ago, Mary Wright showed how the Qing government and its regional viceroys restored Confucian political order to the war-torn provinces of the Yangzi Valley after the defeat of the Taipings.[1] By her account the Tongzhi Restoration rested upon dual cultural foundations: the resumption of civil service examinations and the opening of local academies. Barry Keenan's finely scaled rendering of the Confucian educational revival in the Yangzi delta not only takes us beyond the Tongzhi Restoration down to the Xinhai Revolution; his book also draws us into those very institutions—Nanjing's Zhongshan Academy, Jiangyin's Southern Quintessence Academy, and so forth— whence reform and revolution emerged.

One major consequence of the Taiping Rebellion, once the conflict was over, was the release of "the pent-up aspirations of a wartime generation with commercial capital and managerial skills" (18). Some of these scholars (*shi*), who were not official degree-holding gentry (*shen*), had found a place for themselves as private secretaries in the "tent governments" (*mu-fu*) of Zeng Guofan (1811–1872), Li Hongzhang (1823–1901), Zuo Zongtang (1812–1885), and other governors or governors-general who led the Restoration in the provinces.[2] Most *shi*, however, were ready to serve at the local level as faculty members of the new academies that mushroomed in southern Jiangsu from 1862 to 1900.

As Keenan emphasizes, two different kinds of academies flourished. One, which was initially favored by Zeng Guofan, was seen

---

1 Mary Clabaugh Wright, *The Last Stand of Chinese Conservatism: The T'ung-chih Restoration, 1862–1874* (Stanford: Stanford University Press, 1957).

2 Kenneth E. Folsom, *Friends, Guests, and Colleagues: The Mu-fu System in the Late Ch'ing Period* (Berkeley: University of California Press, 1968); Jonathan Porter, *Tseng Kuo-fan's Private Bureaucracy* (Berkeley: Center for Chinese Studies, University of California, 1972).

as a training institution for the new postbellum elite of self-strengtheners. Zeng was committed to founding local academies because he believed that training scholars to pass the state examinations and serve as government officials was the best way to abet a restoration of Confucian rule. Early on, therefore, Zeng stressed recruiting practically minded teachers and appointing academy directors who could teach the eight-legged (*bagu*) style of examination prose.

In contrast, the second sort of academy eschewed examination preparation. Favored by more conservatively oriented officials such as Woren (d. 1871), these schools were to be ethical communities staffed by elite teachers who could develop moral talent by their own virtuous example.

The gap between these two different pedagogical models was initially bridged by Zeng Guofan himself. Zeng's aspiration to promote the functional training of administrators was matched by his admiration for ethicists such as Tang Jian, who had been promoting a recommitment to Cheng-Zhu Confucianism within his Beijing coterie since the early 1840s. Much has been made by other historians of Zeng Guofan's xavierian self-discipline, and especially of his keeping a diary in order to check bad habits and cultivate good behavior.[3] Keenan shows that this intense practice of Neo-Confucianism was part of a "parallel promotion of material and moral rearmament" (35) in Zeng Guofan's circle, as well as a desirable habit to be imposed upon students in the academies that Zeng and others sponsored after 1864.

Although mid-Qing academies (*shuyuan*) were strictly under directors of study, they were traditionally identified with the local gentry—an identification that was reinforced by the widespread revival of "statecraft" (*jingshi*) thinking during the 1850s and 1860s. Keenan is one of the first historians to emphasize how strongly officials like Zuo Zongtang and Zeng Guofan distrusted the self-interested local gentry and how the two viceroys tended to identify county-level academies with the private interests of an expanding southern elite. Consequently, they favored keeping the highest-level *shuyuan* under strict official control funded by the public purse. At the Southern Quintessence Academy in Jiangyin, private funds were rejected in favor of the provincial director of education's support, and at Zhongshan Academy in Jinling (Nanjing), expenses were covered

---

[3] See, for example, Hellmut Wilhelm, "Chinese Confucianism on the Eve of the Great Encounter," in *Changing Japanese Attitudes toward Modernization*, ed. Marius B. Jansen (Princeton: Princeton University Press, 1965), pp. 282–310.

by the circuit intendant's office. Both academies refused to offer classes in *bagu* examination prose and instead required monthly essay contests richly rewarded with cash and wine prizes. The contests were used to keep only the very best students, whose tenures were not fixed.

A major contribution of Keenan's study of Jiangsu academies is the further revelation that a number of the most elite colleges were primarily founded to reinvigorate a syncretic classical learning in order to stem the tide of Westernization and commercialization emanating from the treaty ports. This was especially evident in the case of the Southern Quintessence Academy, which was modeled upon Ruan Yuan's (1764–1849) residential academies in Guangdong and Zhejiang. Under the influence of Director Huang Yizhou's "revitalized classical pedagogy" from 1885 to 1898, students at Southern Quintessence "master[ed] a non-vocational curriculum" in order to return to the moral concerns of Cheng-Zhu learning (76). Ceremonially honoring the spirits of Zheng Xuan (127–200) and Zhu Xi (1130–1200), the students and professors deliberately narrowed the distance between Han and Song learning, so that the originally quite separate coteries of Ruan Yuan and Woren "were becoming increasingly conceived to be within the same spectrum of opinion" (85).

The post-Taiping revival of classical learning in the lower Yangzi valley's academies included tremendous publishing efforts, such as Wang Xianqian's (1842–1918) compendium of classical commentaries, the *Huangqing jingjie xubian* (1,430 vols.), continuing the effort started by Ruan Yuan and his students in the 1820s in Guangdong. The scholars who helped put such compilations together were unusually gifted literati who evolved into the brilliant "national learning" intellectuals of the Republican period. Keenan cites the example of a list of 119 Southern Quintessence alumni, of which 24 were singled out in 1958 by Hu Shi as being nationally prominent intellectuals, including a number of leading classicists.

Yet most of the Jiangsu academies' graduates ultimately constituted a deeply discontented elite. The price of the Tongzhi Restoration leaders' avid passion for academies was thus "the social problem of how to meet the employment needs of a steadily increasing local educated elite" (28). Keenan's finding that the very success of the late-nineteenth-century Tongzhi Restoration guaranteed the social restlessness of the early-twentieth-century reform movement, moreover, accompanies the observation that while the classically oriented academies produced a small number of brilliant intellectuals active in the Republican period, these were not the local elites that eventually led the 1911 Revolution.

Instead, there was a major shift in elite academic formation after 1894–1895, with fundamental changes from the top down in curriculum and pedagogy. Under the influence of Viceroy Zhang Zhidong's (1837–1909) yamen in Wuhan, elite schools such as Zhengmeng Academy began relating moral principles to political issues on the one hand, while promoting military drills, social sciences, engineering, and Western language instruction on the other.

Keenan dates the pivotal turning point from neoclassical to Sino-Western education to 1901, when the public academy in each provincial capital became a university-level institution (*da xuetang*), when prefectural academies were made middle schools, and when county-level academies became elementary schools. At that same moment, "the generation who staffed the revival of classical academies passed from the scene" (104). In their place, members of the new lower Yangzi educated elite founded new schools under local bureaus of education and then went on after 1906 to become official members of new Offices to Encourage Education (Quanxue suo), gaining seven-button bureaucratic rank as educational managers with the complete endorsement of the imperial government.

The full implications of the "irrepressible organization taking place among Jiangsu's local educated elite" (96) between 1906 and 1911 are open to dispute, but what Keenan makes clear in this fascinating study of cultural revival, social ascent, and political turmoil at the end of the Qing is that the unintended consequence of the Tongzhi Restoration was a swelling of the ranks of the local educated elite. That profusion in turn accounted for much of the agitation leading up to the Revolution of 1911. As Keenan shows, there were numerous instances of financial malfeasance, of pettifoggery, and of administrative abuse on the part of the local gentry running Jiangsu's academies, while peasants and townsmen rioted against the taxes imposed to support the new schools and disaffected students went on strike to keep their elite academies from being transformed into training schools for primary- or middle-school teachers. It was no accident, in the end, that so many Nationalist and Communist revolutionaries, including Mao Zedong himself, came out of the very normal schools into which many of these central China academies evolved.

Frederic Wakeman, Jr.
Berkeley, 1994

Jiangsu

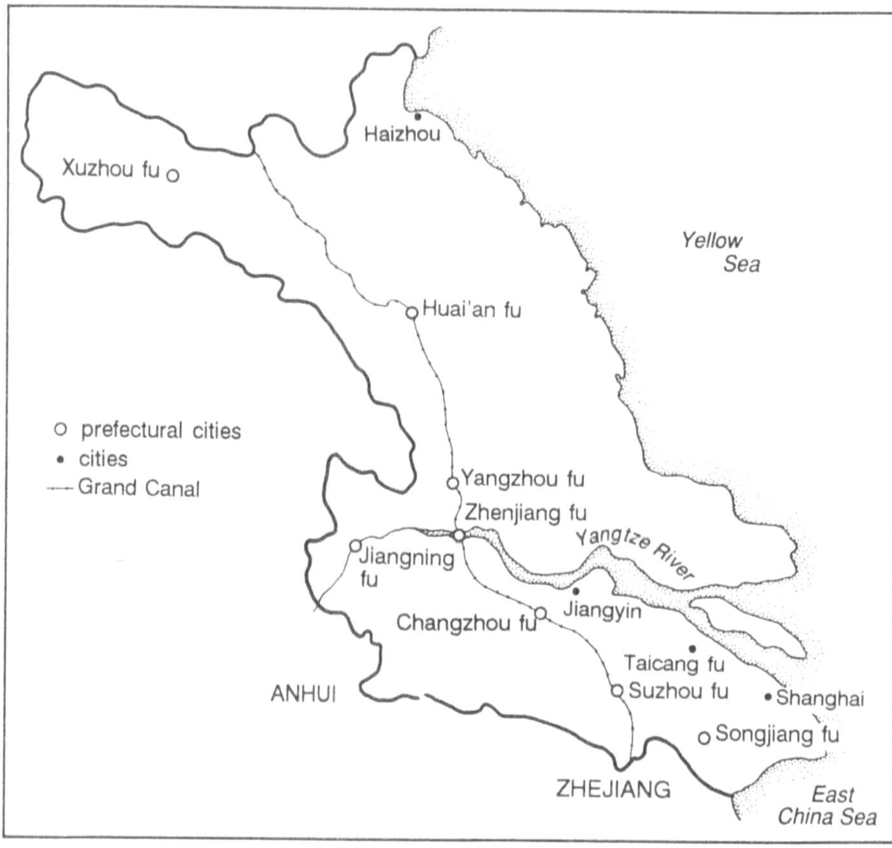

SOURCE: Adapted from David Faure, *The Rural Economy of Kiangsu Province, 1870-1911* (Hong Kong: Institute of Chinese Studies, Chinese University of Hong Kong, 1978), p. 366.

Introduction

The Taiping Revolutionary Movement was suppressed by forces loyal to the Manchu Qing dynasty in 1864. The suppression was a bloodletting, spread out over fourteen years from 1850 to 1864, as violent as the anger directed at the local social elite by the Taiping peasant movement itself. Like the Civil War in the United States, the victory was uncontested in China, but it left the nation a demanding agenda of economic, social, and political reconstruction.

After 1864 national priorities focused upon rebuilding the institutions of the central government. In the period preceding the seismic political shock of defeat by Japan in 1894–95, education was singled out for expansion at the village, county, and provincial levels. In Jiangsu province, for example, where Taiping destruction was heavy, local officials took the initiative in restoring former academies and then in expanding the number of academies as well as public charitable schools. County magistrates, prefects, and subprefects were given credit in official gazetteers for establishing almost all of the new academies. It is clear, however, that gentry contributions were also important in allowing these officials to maintain the lasting endowments in land or the interest-bearing accounts in pawnbroker-banks used for the annual academy budgets.[1]

Local elite activism in education involved local gentry and expanded in the mid-nineteenth century in part because of the national suppression of the Taiping Revolutionary Movement.[2] Local defense associations had enhanced the power of the local elite in the Lower Yangzi by the end of the Taiping suppression, and the

[1] Okubo Eiko, "Shindai kosetsu chihō no shoin to shakai," 239–246; Benjamin Elman, "Imperial Politics and Confucian Societies in Late Imperial China," 392–402; idem, *From Philosophy to Philology*, 119–130.

[2] Mary Rankin, John K. Fairbank, and Albert Feuerwerker, "Introduction: Perspectives on Modern China's History," in *The Cambridge History of China*, ed. John Fairbank and Albert Feuerwerker, 13:53–59.

reconstruction agencies set up after the war opened many new opportunities for local elite leadership.[3] Financial support came from the special *lijin* tax exacted on goods traded. This commercial tax began in Jiangsu, because of the need for revenue to finance the war and reconstruction, and gradually spread throughout the country. Initially volunteered by merchants, the tax was used in Jiangsu for the thirty years after 1869 primarily to cover local provincial expenses.[4]

Even before the outbreak of the Taiping Revolutionary Movement, Lower Yangzi society experienced a level of gentry management unusual in China. By the end of the eighteenth century commercialization of sections of the region had created the need for local public service activities. These activities often involved the collaboration of merchants[5] and were carried out by the Lower Yangzi educated gentry with the sanction of the state. Because financial exigency prevented the Qing state from expanding local government to meet the new local needs created by the steady urbanization, commercialization, and rising population densities of the eighteenth century,[6] the gentry naturally increased their role in the local management of public services. In the coming nineteenth century, gentry management was poised to expand as repeated crises rendered the official bureaucracy increasingly unable to address local needs.

The financial necessity for some collaboration between officials and gentry in founding and maintaining Qing academies provided all academies some independence from complete official control and thus prevented excessive political domination of these institutions. Academy directors were not classified as officials, and, once appointed, they worked of necessity within the realities of the local society in which they lived. Much local variation resulted, even in enrollments—which might vary from a minimum of ten students to just over a hundred. At any given time, the quality of an academy depended upon the financial support from official and private sources in the region and upon the reputation and energy of the chosen academy director.[7]

---

3 Philip Kuhn, *Rebellion and Its Enemies in Late Imperial China*, 211–225.

4 Susan Mann, *Local Merchants and the Chinese Bureaucracy, 1750–1950*, 108.

5 Ibid., 21–25; Joseph Esherick and Mary Rankin, *Chinese Local Elites and Patterns of Dominance*, 330–334.

6 Rankin, Fairbank, and Feuerwerker, "Introduction," 50–53. See also Mary Rankin, "The Origins of a Chinese Public Sphere: Local Elites and Community in Late Imperial China," *Études Chinoises* 9.2 (Autumn 1990): 3–35, 54–58.

7 Alexander Woodside, "State, Scholars, and Orthodoxy: The Ch'ing Academies, 1736–1839," in *Orthodoxy in Late Imperial China*, ed. Kwang-ching Liu, 166–171.

The expansion of education after 1864 may be compared to the expansion of other local elite activities that were related to *lijin* tax collection. The Tongzhi Restoration explicitly mandated that provincial officials found academies.[8] The administration of *lijin* taxes, like these academy foundings, began in principle as a governmentally delegated authority. But neither *lijin* taxes nor academies were more than quasi-official in practice. In the Lower Yangzi, tax collection and academy financing eventually employed thousands of gentry managers.[9] Some academies even received essential financing directly from *lijin* collection, especially when solicited donations from lower officials and gentry proved inadequate.[10] In the crisis-ridden final fifty years of the Qing dynasty, this unclear point of contact between gentry activity and bureaucratic official power was often yielded to local elite management.

County magistrates, prefects, daotais who managed several prefectures, or provincial governors could all finance and oversee academies. Students selected were generally successful *shengyuan* (government student) candidates who had passed the lowest degree in the civil service examinations. They spent on average three years at an academy, hoping that their study there would help them pass the provincial-level examinations and guarantee official appointment to a bureaucratic post, assuring them job security. But more commonly, the academy-educated rejoined the local elite. These young men then comprised a highly educated layer at the top of the *shengyuan* stratum of the local elite, but with no certain jobs.

Women were excluded from lower degrees and from classical literacy more generally. Somewhat like Latin in medieval and early modern Europe, mastery of classical Chinese was an initiation rite that defined a distinct social elite and determined access to all high-level posts presuming fluency in classical Chinese. When these barriers were gradually removed in China after 1895, women's institutions of formal education began to flourish.

The era covered in this study ends with the rapid transition of Chinese educational institutions into public schools patterned after the Western model. This makes it easy to overlook the fact that the revival of classical academies between 1864 and 1900 generated its own social, political, and intellectual effects that provided the groundwork for all future reforms. A classical academy taught a

---

8 See "Xuexiao kao qi," in *Huangchao xu wenxian tongkao* 100:8591.

9 Mann, *Local Merchants*, 105, 110–111.

10 Zong Yuanhan, *Yiqing guan wenguo ji, juan* 3, p. 13b.

Confucian curriculum with no Western subject matter. At the county level the numbers of academy-educated students from such institutions within the local elite soared by 1900. At the provincial level, the revival of research-oriented academies attained a standard of Confucian learning equal to the best at any time in the late imperial period.

The expansion of Chinese educational institutions from 1864 to 1900 trained a highly educated component of the local elite that had its own needs and interests as a group. Many took jobs managing the continuing expansion of local education. By the turn of the century there existed a local educated elite who expected a degree of autonomy from state supervision corresponding to the actual local managerial power they exercised. Lower degree holders with an academy education comprised the core of this local educated elite. From 1901 to 1911, as the New Policies Reforms designed a vast public school system under central administrative control, this group began to demand legitimate local power. By 1906 the educated elite of the Lower Yangzi organized itself and assumed formal power in administering local and even provincial educational institutions.

A Note on Terminology and Political Geography

The history that follows relies primarily on materials from the economically developed core region of the Lower Yangzi River. Much of the data centers on Jiangsu province, whose two political centers split the administration of the poor northern part of the province from the administration of the economically and culturally rich southern part. Jiangning city near the border of Anhui province (see map, p. 6) housed an assistant to the governor called the financial commissioner (*buzheng shi*), who was in charge of administering the budget of all the northern prefectures of the province. The governor of Jiangsu himself resided in the city of Suzhou, in the heart of the traditional Lower Yangzi core economic zone. Another financial commissioner was in Suzhou to oversee the administration of the remarkable four prefectures, one department (*zhou*), and one subprefecture (*ting*) in Jiangsu south of the Yangzi River.[11]

The Jiangsu *xuezheng* (provincial director of education) had his office in the rural town of Jiangyin, which was nearer the geographic and demographic center of Jiangsu province than either Jiangning

[11] These southeastern Jiangsu prefectures were the heart of the region informally called Jiangnan that was centered in the prefectures around Lake Tai.

city or the expanding commercial center of Shanghai on the coast. The academy founded in that town by the provincial director of education in 1884 will appear in the text as Southern Quintessence Academy so its Chinese name, Nanjing shuyuan (Southern Quintessence Academy), will not be confused with the new name of Jiangning city in 1912, also romanized as Nanjing (or Nanking, meaning southern capital).

PART I

The Post-Taiping Expansion of Formal Education in Jiangsu, 1864–1900

Southern Jiangsu was ravaged in the final suppression campaigns that expelled marauding Taiping troops from the region. Provincial and county officials promoted the reconstruction of education as a part of a much larger effort at recovery. The underemployed lower degree holders were available in each locality to manage and teach at public charitable schools and reconstructed or newly founded academies.

CHAPTER ONE

Post-Taiping Academies and Public Charitable Schools in the Lower Yangzi

Renewal of Confucian scholarship and the revival of educational institutions were basic policies of the imperial restoration in the Tongzhi (1862–1874) reign.[1] In the populous and culturally advanced Lower Yangzi region, these policies fostered a revival of classical academies that lasted from 1862 to 1900. The rationale for the restoration's revival of Confucian education was not the Qing court's blind reassertion of the old order after the defeat of the Taiping Revolutionary Movement. Rather, the revival of Confucian education sought to address critical social demands created by wartime dislocation and to correct certain undesired side effects of other postwar policies.

One policy generating undesired side effects was the sale of offices. After the Taiping suppression and up to 1911, some two-thirds of all officials with titles of appointment in China received their posts without following the regular route of the examinations.[2] Magistrates, in turn, passed along the expense of many of these purchased offices by selling lucrative yamen clerkships under their control.[3]

In the 1860s traditional leadership patterns in Jiangsu province were further affected because the wartime contributions of Jiangsu gentry to the central government caused the court to raise the quota

---

[1] Mary Wright, *The Last Stand of Chinese Conservatism: The T'ung-Chih Restoration, 1862–1974*, 130.

[2] This figure was only about 50 percent before the Taiping Revolutionary Movement. See Marianne Bastid-Bruguière, "Currents of Social Change," in *The Cambridge History of China*, ed. John F. Fairbank and Kwang-ching Liu, vol. 11, pt. 2, p. 538; Chang Chung-li, *The Chinese Gentry*, 116–137; Esherick and Rankin, *Local Elites*, 331–332.

[3] Kwang-ching Liu, "The Ch'ing Restoration," in *The Cambridge History of China*, ed. John K. Fairbank, vol. 10, pt. 1, p. 479.

of students who could pass the prefectural *xiucai* (cultivated talent) examinations and receive *shengyuan* status. Thus the lower gentry with degrees below the provincial *juren* (elevated person) degree increased by an added 360 *shengyuan* twice every three years when the prefectural examinations were held, resulting in a 30 percent increase of Jiangsu *shengyuan* by the end of the Qing.[4] This increasing cohort of lower degree holders needed offices to hold, and they also needed more academies to make it possible for them to prepare for the upper-level *juren* degree examinations.

In addition to policies brought about as a result of the financial exhaustion of the empire, another post-Taiping policy authenticated alternatives to the orthodox route to success through civil service examinations: the introduction of foreign military and industrial technology. This was promoted through the national program of self-strengthening called the Western Affairs Movement (*yangwu yundong*). There is no question Qing officials recognized the efficacy of Western weapons during and after the Taiping war.[5] Arsenals, interpreters' schools, and the introduction of Western transportation and communication technology became a part of dynastic restrengthening in the Tongzhi period. Such controlled Westernization increased the appeal of unorthodox career alternatives for success. Academies, in contrast, provided attractive student stipends and addressed the increasing need to validate Confucian learning and its official civil service route to success even as the state itself looked to other sources of national strength.

The war had yet another effect on civil service candidates from the Lower Yangzi. Since the early Ming dynasty, candidates from this region had excelled in passing upper-level civil service examinations.[6] During the Taiping occupation of Jiangsu, however, examinations in most prefectures and at the provincial capital halted. As a stop-gap measure, native candidates were asked to travel to Zhejiang, if they could, to take the provincial-level examinations. Anhui students were also permitted to take prefectural examinations for first degrees and county-level qualifying examinations in the shifting prefectures of Jiangsu that still managed to offer examinations during wartime. The demands of an increasingly large backlog of Lower

---

4 Chang Chung-li, *Chinese Gentry*, 88, 100. See also Kwang-ching Liu, "Ch'ing Restoration," 479.

5 Kwang-ching Liu, "Ch'ing Restoration," 425–435; Kuo Ting-yee and Liu Kwang-ching, "Self-strengthening: The Pursuit of Western Technology," in *The Cambridge History of China*, ed. John K. Fairbank, vol. 10, pt. 1, pp. 496–500, 519–525.

6 Ho Ping-ti, *The Ladder of Success in Imperial China*, 226–254.

Yangzi candidates unable after 1864 to find ways to take either the prefectural or the provincial examinations contributed to the larger breakdown in the effectiveness of the civil service examination system taking place.[7]

The career pattern of the father of Hu Shi (1891–1962) illustrates the problems of the wartime generation. Hu Chuan (Z. Dunfu, 1841–1895) was coming of age in Huizhou prefecture in Anhui province when the preliminary examinations there were disrupted by the arrival of the Taiping army in 1853. His lineage was active in commerce, and Hu Chuan had already begun carrying family tea down to the mouth of the Yangzi near Shanghai to sell in Chuansha, Jiangsu. In 1859 Hu Chuan passed the county preliminary qualifying examination in Shanghai near his family tea business.[8]

His scores on the Songjiang prefectural examination that followed the qualifying examination in Shanghai, however, were not competitive enough to win him *shengyuan* status; the build-up of talent in the relatively pacified area around Shanghai made passing extremely difficult. Not until six years later in 1865, at age twenty-four, was Hu Chuan able to qualify for the *shengyuan* by succeeding in the reestablished examinations back at his native prefecture in Anhui.[9]

After that he tried unsuccessfully the provincial-level examinations and finally elected to sit for examinations to enter the newly established Longmen shuyuan (Dragon-gate Academy) in Shanghai, where he qualified for admission and did well enough to renew his annual stipend for the next three years. When he left Longmen Academy in 1871 he was still unable to get through the provincial-level examinations. But he had acquired three years of superb higher education, which undoubtedly helped him qualify and succeed in the post of private secretary (*mufu*) to a significant national official whom he served for the next six years.[10]

The Expansion of Academies

Because of the financial exhaustion of post-Taiping China, academies depended more and more on local funding and management. This dependency served to increase local power over academies,

---

7 Benjamin Elman, "The Evolution of Civil Service Examinations," *Newsletter for Modern Chinese History*, no. 11 (1991): 87–88.

8 Hu Chuan, "Dunfu nianpu," 189–191.

9 Ibid., 191; Hu Shi, *Hu Shi koushu zizhuan*, 11–12.

10 Hu Chuan, "Dunfu nianpu," 221–228; Hu Shi, *Koushu*, 12–15.

especially in commercially prosperous regions. Professor Grimm's statistics for Guangdong, a province whose academies were not greatly affected by the Taiping war, suggest a rate of academy construction in Guangdong from 1850 to 1874 averaging twenty-four or twenty-five academies per decade. This high rate was unprecedented in Guangdong during Ming or earlier Qing history. Statistics for Anhui confirm one trend implicit in these Guangdong figures: commercial capital and urbanization correlated with the areas in both provinces where academies expanded most rapidly, and that fact, in turn, implies local demand and sponsorship.[11]

Closer inspection reveals that privately financed academies in the post-Taiping era mushroomed in prosperous regions of some provinces that had experienced long-term increases in commercial capital during the 1700s. In the Qianlong period, the gentry of Zhejiang province—many of whom were involved in producing and trading silk cloth—contributed to academies in unusual numbers.[12] Further, community control over public charitable schools in the 1700s had steadily increased in the Lower Yangzi provinces.[13] By 1800, the role of the local gentry in education had increased enough in the Lower Yangzi to create a precedent for the significantly expanded role of local elites that was to come after 1865.

However, educated local gentry or local officials interested in expanding either charitable schools or academies worked within certain constraints. Both gentry and merchants certainly benefited from any increase in social stability in a locality. But schools were of more interest to the state—in terms of government supervision—than were community charity organizations. Gentry found easy alliance with merchants in establishing charitable institutions, with little intervention from the state. But in the 1700s state officials remained involved in founding about 50 percent of the charitable schools in the important Lower Yangzi region, while leaving about 80 percent of other charitable organizations to be founded by the local elite alone.[14]

---

[11] Tilemann Grimm, "Academies and Urban Systems in Kwangtung," in *The City in Late Imperial China*, ed. G. William Skinner, 481, 484.

[12] Okubo Eiko, "Shindai kosetsu chiho no shoin to shakai," in *Gensei to Ajia kyoiku shi kenkyu*, ed. Taga Akigoro, 246, 384–388.

[13] See Angela Leung, "Elementary Education in the Lower Yangtze Region in the 17th and 18th centuries," paper prepared for Conference on Education and Society in Late Imperial China, Montecito, California, June 8–14, 1989. Public charitable schools are usually called *yixue* in Qing documents, less commonly, *shexue*.

[14] Ibid., 14 and Appendix; and Angela Leung, "Qingdai cishan jigon yu, quanliao ceng pli quanxi" (Charitable institutions and bureaucracy under the Qing), *Zhongyang yanjiu yuan minzu Yanjiu suo qikan* (Bulletin of the Institute of Ethnology, Academia

For the local bureaucrats to tap the prosperity of a county for academy or charitable school donations was, however, not necessarily easy—especially in the difficult times following the suppression of the Taiping movement. This difficulty is illustrated by the work of a Jiangsu native, Zong Yuanhan, who in 1865 was the prefect in Huzhou, an economically developed prefecture in neighboring Zhejiang province. Zong Yuanhan succeeded in soliciting the silk guild of Nanxun town in 1865 to pledge the value of two Mexican dollars of profit from the sale of every roll of silk (and some other items) to build an academy. But seven years later the prefect explained apologetically in a report to the governor that despite such income, higher priority expenditures on bridge construction, temple repair, and internal guild costs in his official budget had left nothing for academy construction. In 1871 the prefect gave up trying to rely on the uncertain donations from guilds. All merchants were required to pay the rest of the needed endowment indirectly, but reliably, through a designated commercial tax, the *lijin*, earmarked for academy construction. He invested equal amounts of his prefectural budget derived from this *lijin* income in five pawnbroker-bank accounts for the five academies he had under way.[15]

An 1863 restoration policy, aimed at those provinces in which the fighting had halted academy education, instructed the governors of each province to recover the landed endowments of academies and to restore student stipends for residential academies as soon as peace was restored.[16] Zhejiang province showed a marked increase in academy construction from 1850 to 1900. Mary Backus Rankin's careful study of the province in this period notes the peculiarity of this increase, when contrasted with the contemporaneous downturn in *jinshi* degrees received by Zhejiangese. Burgeoning commercial towns had more than their share of the new academies, and Rankin demonstrates that post-Taiping academy expansion signified "a weakening rather than a strengthening of ties with the state." As bureaucratic ties of the central government to localities loosened in the post-Taiping era, organizations and institutions managed by the local elite in Zhejiang expanded and continued to develop up to 1911.[17]

Sinica), 66 (August 1989): 85–103.

15 Zong Yuanhan, *Yiqing quan wenguo ji, juan* 3, p. 13b.

16 "Xuexiao kao qi," in *Huangchao xu wenxian tongkao*, comp. Liu Jinzao, 100:8591.

17 Mary Rankin, *Elite Activism and Political Transformation in China: Zhejiang Province, 1865–1911*, 53, 54.

In Zhejiang, Tongzhi period recovery policies often served to pull together a variety of new public institutions into matrices of local elite activism. The new managerial elite working in welfare institutions after 1864, for example, could overlap with persons running new educational institutions.[18] If Zhejiang is representative, the response of local elites to the national crisis of the Taiping suppression and its aftermath gradually generated a new activism in public management within both rural and urban areas. Gentry managers (*shendong* or *dongshi*), who were individuals of varied social background running local institutions, became increasingly prominent. And the determinants of local social status expanded in Zhejiang well beyond scholarly validation allocated by the central government.[19]

The new managerial elite was active in founding new academies.[20] In Zhejiang from 1850 to 1900 newly established or revived academies averaged 16.8 per decade, which was the province's highest rate in the Qing. In Jiangsu province during the same era, new foundings (including renovations) averaged a nearly equally high number of sixteen per decade. In Guangdong the rate of foundings and renovations for the same period was twenty-two per decade. Comparison of these figures with those for the Qianlong era—Zhejiang, 8.8 per decade; Jiangsu, 10.3; Guangdong, 17.2—demonstrates the significant rate of increase after 1850 in all three provinces.[21]

The peculiarity of Jiangsu in terms of academy growth was that the most prosperous core counties south of the Yangzi in Jiangsu were precisely those most affected by the Taiping violence. Of the five southern Jiangsu prefectures, Jiangning prefecture near the Anhui provincial border had been the most affected by destruction and social dislocation. The effects of destruction were gradually

[18] Ibid., 98.

[19] Ibid., 18–21.

[20] Ibid., 97.

[21] For Jiangsu see Okubo Eiko, "Shindai kosetsu," p. 239; for Guangdong see Grimm, *Academies*, 481; for Zhejiang see Rankin, *Elite Activism*, appendix B. These figures provide a gauge of the amount of activity over time in establishing or reestablishing local academies. The gross number of academies at any particular time is particularly hard to discern, as one county's gazetteer reporting them will appear at a time years apart from the gazetteer of the next county. Okubo's statistics give little sense of the total number of academies in Jiangsu. Wang Shuhuai breaks down academies by prefecture and time period. The nearly sixty academies present in northern counties would not have been destroyed in the Taiping violence and are probably underreported in Okubo's record of new foundings and renovations. See Wang Shuhuai, *Zhongguo xiandai hua diqu yanjiu: Jiangsu sheng, 1860–1916*, 57.

reduced eastward through Zhenjiang prefecture to Changzhou prefecture, Suzhou prefecture, and finally to Songjiang prefecture, which included Shanghai county on the seacoast.[22] Rehabilitation of academies occurred after 1865 at a rate proportional to the basic prosperity of the prefectures, reversing the downstream direction of Taiping destruction. It went from rapid development of many post-Taiping academies in eastern Jiangsu near Shanghai to slower development and fewer academies in the war-torn and less affluent western part of the province.[23]

Table 1 shows by administrative division the academy reconstruction that took place south of the Yangzi in Jiangsu from 1862 to the end of such reconstruction in 1900. The totals of post-Taiping academies are compared to the number that existed in the same administrative division according to the national gazetteer of 1820. The 1820 national gazetteer statistics for Jiangsu are themselves reliable when checked against detailed contemporaneous county statistics. These figures make clear certain changes in geographical distribution. In 1820, for example, Songjiang prefecture on the Pacific coast had about the same number of academies as the two western-most prefectures. But in 1900, Songjiang prefecture in the east had twice as many academies as Zhenjiang or Jiangning in the west. The number of academies in the three eastern-most prosperous and populous core prefectures increased dramatically—doubling in Songjiang and tripling in Suzhou and Changzhou.

In Changzhou prefecture, academy foundings increased as reconstruction continued into the Guangxu era. Rebuilding destroyed facilities or building from scratch took more time the further west you were in the province. While only about half the twenty-nine post-Taiping founding dates in Changzhou prefecture (some are restorations) are given in the gazetteer entries, note how many of those given are academies founded after the Tongzhi period ended in 1874:

Daonan Academy (1869)	Changyin Academy (1878)
Gaoshan Academy (1875)	Sanjin Academy (1879)
Liyan Academy (1877)	Jintai Academy (1880)

22 Liu Shiji, *Ming-Qing shidai Jiangnan shizhen yenjiu*, 73–89, 94; Wang Yeh-chien, "The Impact of the Taiping Rebellion on Population in Southern Jiangsu," *Papers on China* (Harvard), 19 (1965): 120–129.

23 Please refer to table 1. See Liu Shiji, *Ming-Qing*, 89–97. Songjiang prefecture on the coast became increasingly urbanized right through the Taiping depredations, as did Suzhou prefecture and Taicang department. Migrations of families from other parts of the Lower Yangzi to avoid the Taiping violence accounted for some of this steadily increasing and largely urban population.

Table 1

Numbers of Academies by Prefecture and Department in Southern Jiangsu Province in 1820 and in 1900

Administrative division	Songjiang[1]	Taicang dept.[2]	Suzhou[3]	Changzhou[4]	Zhenjiang[5]	Jiangning[6]	Totals
1820[7]	8 (17%)	3 (6%)	11 (23%)	10 (21%)	7 (15%)	8 (17%)	47 (100%)
1900[8]	20 (18%)	9 (8%)	32 (29%)	29 (26%)	10 (9%)	10 (9%)	110 (100%)

NOTES:

1. *Songjiang* FZ, 1884, 1656–47; 1673–81; 1703–35; *Huating* XZ, 1878, 406–9; *Lou* XZ, 1879, 285–89; *Fengxian* XZ, 1878, 337–40; *Jinshan* XZ, 1878, 631–32; *Nanhui* XZ, 1927, 647–48, 660, 665; *Qingpu* XZ, 1879, 701–9; *Qingpu* XZ, 1934, 403–423; *Chuansha tingzhi*, 1879, 104–9; *Chuansha tingzhi*, 1937, 283; *Shanghai* XZ, 1882, 686–700; *Shanghai* XZ, 1918, 637–52. The subprefecture Chuansha Ting is added to the seven counties in this prefecture.

2. *Taicang zhouzhi*, 1919, 539–40, 552–58; *Jiading* XZ, 1881, 9:54, 56; 29:30–41; *Jiading* XZ, 1930, 110, 511–13; *Baoshan* XZ, 1881, 5:14–15; *Baoshan* XZ, 1921, 327–28, 449–52; *Chongming* XZ, 1881, 3:22–24.

3. See Wang, 1984, 57; and revised totals from *Suzhou* FZ, 1883; *Wuxian* XZ, 1933, 410–16; *Kunxin* XZ, 1880, 80–82; *Changshao* XZ, 1904, 779–90; *Wujiang* XZ, 1879, 3:4a–5a.

4. *Changzhou* FZ, 1886, 14a–16a; *Wujin, Yanghu* XZ, 1906, 5:5b–7b; *Wuxi, Jingui* XZ, 1881, 114–117; *Yixing, Jingxi* XZ, 1882, 425–30; *Yixing* XZ, 1920, 109–10, 172–183; *Jiangyin* XZ, 1878, 5:19–28; *Jiangyin* XZ, 1921, 361–88.

5. *Jiangning* FZ, 1880, 51–52; *Qiangpu* XZ, 1891, 12:10a–12a; *Lishui* XZ, 1905, 539–40; *Gaohong* XZ, 1881, 5:33a–36a; *Gourong* XZ, 1904, 154–56, 296–97, 307–8; *Liuhe* XZ, 1883, 3:12a; 4:9b.

6. *Dantu* XZ, 1879, 351–53; 3:39ab; *Jintan* XZ, 1885, 5:41b, 7:14ab, 106, 300–2; *Danyang* XZ, 1927, 10:10a–11b; *Danyang* XZ, 1961, 102–6; *Liyang* XZ, 1899, 5:6a–8a.

7. Wang 1984, citing *Yi Tong zhi* (1820), 6:106.

8. All built or renovated since 1862.

Xinan Academy (1878)	Zhuxi Academy (1880)
Xianyang Academy (1881)	Nanjing Academy (1884)
Linjin Academy (1881)	Daoxiang Academy (1885)

The two western-most prefectures of Zhenjiang and Jiangning had to finance more elaborate reconstruction than was necessary in the eastern part of Jiangsu because they suffered more extensive war damage and had a relatively weaker economic base. Furthermore, demobilization of Qing troops drained local resources in western Jiangsu, so that many counties simply had no financial means to reconstruct former academies or finance new ones. In the prefectural capital of Jiangning, for example, Kuiguang Academy was never rebuilt, nor was Yinghua Academy in nearby Jiangpu county. Gaoping Academy in Lishui county had been demolished, and the financially strapped magistrate could not rebuild. He decided instead to set aside the remaining endowment to finance the travel of local candidates to take provincial *juren* or metropolitan *jinshi* examinations.[24]

The largest expense involved rebuilding student dormitories and libraries; then came endowments for monthly stipends. In eastern Jiangsu, magistrates supplemented official funds gathered for these expenses by soliciting contributions from lineages, villages, guilds, and wealthy individuals. But in western Jiangsu, local gentry managers from several related *xiang* (an administrative unit of rural society including villages and towns) might approach a magistrate to found an academy—as happened in Gaochun district in 1863—but then the magistrate of the county had to find the resources, over several years, to slowly endow the institution. In Jiangning prefecture it often took the three-year tenure of two or three magistrates in a locality to accumulate enough endowment to fully reopen an academy. That both Zhenjiang and Jiangning prefectures reconstructed ten academies between 1862 and 1900 was a credit to the persistence of local administrators, who could call upon few resources outside their own budgets.[25]

Despite the financial strain of academy reconstruction, by 1900 the total number of academies in Jiangsu's southern five prefectures and one department was 110, compared to a total of only 47 academies in 1820.[26] Including the northern prefectures, the whole

[24] *Jiangning fuzhi* 1880, p. 51; *Jiangpu beicheng* 1891, pp. 12, 1–2b; *Lishui xianzhi* 1905, pp. 539–541.

[25] *Jiangning fuzhi* 1880, p. 52; *Gaochun xianzhi* 1881, pp. 5, 33–36b; Jonathan Ocko, *Bureaucratic Reform in Provincial China: Ting Jih-ch'ang in Restoration Kiangsu, 1867–1870*, 137; *Jurong xianzhi* 1904, pp. 154–155, 297–298; *Liuhe xianzhi* 1883, pp. 3, 12.

[26] See table 1. Wang Shuhuai cites the national gazetteer *Yi tong zhi* for this figure of 47. Wang Shuhuai, *Zhongguo xiandai*, 57.

province had about 168 academies in 1900, compared to only 70 in 1820.[27] Academy growth in southern Jiangsu after 1862 began by restoring closed institutions, and most closed academies needed to be physically rebuilt after intentional Taiping destruction. Had the academy openings been evenly distributed geographically from 1862 to 1900, each of the forty southern counties and one subprefecture would have contained, on the average, three academies.[28]

Official sponsorship is claimed in gazetteer records for almost all the 110 foundings in the southern Jiangsu prefectures. The insignificant number of private foundings follows a trend true for Jiangsu throughout the Qing. Official sponsorship of academies had been dominant in Jiangsu; but this did not mean the local gentry was not involved. Local gentry, many of whom were involved in commercial activities, often provided the funding.[29] The geographical redistribution of post-Taiping academies makes it clear that the involvement of a concentrated local elite in the highly urbanized core area of eastern Jiangsu determined where academies flourished. The pent-up aspirations of a wartime generation with commercial capital and managerial skills accounts for the mushrooming of academies in southeastern Jiangsu from 1862 to 1900. This expansion of institutions of higher education to meet a pent-up demand in 1865, however, eventually produced new social demands from the cohort of academy-trained students themselves. Localities had many more academy-trained students by 1900 than had been available in the pre-Taiping era. In the inclusive thirty-six-year span from 1865 through 1900, these southern prefectures alone produced between

---

[27] Compiled from figures in table 1 and Wang Shuhuai, *Zhongguo xiandai*, 57.

[28] See Grimm, "Academies," 481. It is instructive to note that the only comparable period of academy growth in Guangdong was 1851 to 1861, when the dynasty was strapped for resources to suppress the Taipings. That is also when private foundings skyrocketed in Guangdong. Pre-Taiping academies had been basically paralyzed or destroyed during the Taiping occupation of Jiangsu, so the starting number in 1862 was effectively zero. This figure of three academies per county was well above the national average in this period. In Zhili province after 1850, one academy per county was a norm achieved that was in conformity with an earlier Qing regulation (Rankin, *Elite Activism*, 49; Richard Orb, "Chihli Academies and Other Schools in the Late Ch'ing: An Institutional Survey," in *Reform in Nineteenth-Century China*, ed. John Schrecker and Paul Cohen, 236. There were thirty-nine counties and one subprefecture in southern Jiangsu in the period. The academies actually built in southern Jiangsu were, in fact, not evenly distributed by county, as an average figure suggests, but were concentrated more heavily in populous and prosperous eastern Jiangsu.

[29] Okubo Eiko, "Shindai kosetsu," 245–247.

25,000 and 35,000 academy-trained students, compared to 22,560 produced in a similar chronological period ending in 1858.[30]

The Expansion of Public Charitable Schools

Ding Richang and the Tongzhi Restoration Expansion of Public Charitable Schools

From 1865 to 1870 the restoration in Jiangsu was increasingly directed by Ding Richang (Z. Yusheng, 1823–1882). In 1867, Ding moved from Shanghai's Daotai (circuit intendant) post to Suzhou city to assume the post of financial commissioner of Jiangsu province.[31] In 1868 he became governor of Jiangsu and ran the province from 1868 to 1870.

Ding aggressively founded public charitable schools.[32] In 1867 he asked each county in Jiangsu to set up at least four public charitable schools (*shexue*) to serve groups of villages and towns in that county.[33] Ding deliberately chose a term for public charitable school indicating official sponsorship and direction. Each city, *xiang*, town, and village could draft proposals to establish a school, which the province would largely finance. Admission preference was to be

---

[30] I assume a rough average of forty students at each academy, just over thirteen of whom finished their studies after the average three years of study. Thirty-six classes finished their studies in the period 1865 through and including 1900. That would yield 25,708 academy-trained students in those forty counties by 1901. But most of the 110 academies had in fact been founded by 1885. Assuming five foundings per year during 1865–1885 to account for 100 of the 110 foundings by 1885 would yield 35,000 academy-trained students by 1901, which is closer to the real number of students produced.

The comparative period is the inclusive thirty-six years between 1823 through and including 1858, for which I assumed a constant rate of forty-seven academies throughout the era. The year 1858 precedes the Eastern Expedition of Taiping troops out of besieged Jiangning city in 1860 who marched into all of eastern Jiangsu.

[31] He was briefly the Lianghuai salt controller in the transition between the Shanghai-based post and the provincewide position. His stint as governor lasted until 1870, when he stepped down to mourn the death of his mother.

[32] More advanced educational goals such as classical literacy were met in clan schools and other private tutorial arrangements. See Sally Borthwick, *Education and Social Change in China*, 10–30; Leung, "Elementary Education," 4–5.

[33] *Shexue*, a term that was fading from use, was Ding's generic term for free public schools. In the Yongzheng and Qianlong periods true charitable institutions—which were open to the public but designed for the poor—were commonly called *yixue* or *yishu*. In the nineteenth-century gazetteers, the latter two terms were normally used for any free community school. See Leung, "Elementary Education," 7–15.

given orphans and the poor, and the education was apparently free for children seven to fourteen years old. Often foundling homes were chosen as locations to build, but Ding recommended using public office space or borrowing empty temple buildings if necessary.[34]

Ding Richang saw his effort in the tradition of the pioneering work of Chen Hongmou (1696–1771), who founded charitable schools in the tribal areas of the Yunnan frontier in the 1730s.[35] Chen, from his post as financial commissioner of Yunnan, succeeded in founding some 650 schools within five years. Non-Han populations were socialized through these institutions—which Chen Hongmou himself funded if local officials were unable to finance them from the variety of local official revenue sources Chen suggested. Like Ding Richang's, the schools in Yunnan were not official institutions, nor were they privately owned by local gentry. The local community supplied a proprietor for each school and for its finances. The whole institution remained public (*gong*), and officials made sure there was public accountability for how funds were used.[36]

Ding Richang's restoration policy in the 1860s was more than relief. In his reinvigoration of public education in Jiangsu, Ding hoped to reassert official authority relative to the gentry. He thought yamen underlings were often compromised by their necessary collaboration with the rural gentry in administering educational or welfare programs at the market-town level. While many of the best minds in the Lower Yangzi were interested at this time in the reform of county administration, Ding's reforms differed significantly from those of literati who were drawing models of gentry prerogatives from Gu Yanwu's early Qing writings on this subject.[37] Ding never conceived of the local scholarly elite, nor certainly the gentry managers in the Yangzi delta, increasing in real power relative to the district magistrate. Perhaps because of aggrandized and abused power from long-term water control initiatives, Ding saw southern Jiangsu gentry managers as too strong already and often as obstructions to good local administration. Nevertheless, the issue of how large a role the local gentry was to take in overseeing the efficient management of schools and welfare organizations in Jiangsu was not resolved in favor of Ding's conservative views in the Tongzhi Restoration.[38]

---

34 Ocko, *Bureaucratic Reform*, 55; *FWGD* 9:1–3b.

35 *FWGD* 9:1a.

36 William Rowe, "Education and Empire in Southwest China: Ch'en Hung-mou in Yunnan, 1733–38," paper presented at the Conference on Education and Society in Late Imperial China, Montecito, California, June 8–14, 1989, pp. 30–31.

37 See Rankin, *Elite Activism*, 124, 185–186.

38 Ocko, *Bureaucratic Reform*, 20, 135–144; Esherick and Rankin, *Local Elites*, 337.

Maintaining constant official supervision required back-breaking vigilance. The opportunities of the educated local elite to manage local institutions were in fact increased as Ding Richang encouraged the founding of hundreds of new public charitable schools.

Two generations later, the Lower Yangzi educated elite who were connected to both academies and public schools had expanded and assumed increased responsibilities. Despite attempts to maintain the kind of official control Ding had in mind in the New Policies era, by 1906 the central government had to hand over management of schools to the local elite.[39]

Foundings

Regardless of county administrative reform goals, the results of Ding's leadership in promoting the construction of schools in Jiangsu from 1864 to 1870 were significant. Evelyn Sakakida Rawski's research demonstrates the dramatically successful expansion of public schools in three important prefectures under his jurisdiction as governor—Zhenjiang, Changzhou, and Suzhou—before the end of the Tongzhi emperor's reign in 1874. This growth in Jiangsu joined the expansion of public schools in provinces throughout China and characterized the fifty years from 1850 to 1900 as uniquely high in the number of public schools open when compared to any similar period in the Qing.[40]

Ding's management style was to provide immediate incentives for implementing policies and to demand follow-up accountability. Teachers' salaries would be paid by the provincial government to the four community schools he requested, but he set a timetable of two months from submission of the proposal to the opening of the new institution. Any city, *xiang*, town, or village could initiate proposals. Reports were required to assess the operation of the schools, including both the progress of students and the ability of teachers. If the office of the inspecting official, the county director of schools (*jiaoyu*), was close to the new school, only a monthly report was expected, as inspections could easily be made. Distant schools were to submit two progress reports each month.[41]

Ding issued an eight-point set of regulations with his proposal to establish schools showing a model of just how localities could

[39] This point will be demonstrated in chapter 5.

[40] Evelyn S. Rawski, *Education and Popular Literacy in Ch'ing China*, 89–92.

[41] *FWGD* 9:1–2a; Ocko, *Bureaucratic Reform*, 56–67.

establish their schools. Details, from teachers' salaries to the role of local gentry managers, were spelled out.[42] He then followed the model himself in 1868 by establishing free schools in several counties of Suzhou prefecture where his governor's office was located. The jurisdiction covered by the schools he established was normally designated to be a *xiang*.[43] He allocated monies to establish three *xiang* schools in the county in which he resided and four more *xiang* schools in two neighboring counties, Yuanhe and Changzhou; then he funded two each in the four *xiang* in nearby Kunshan county, which already had five others—providing a total of thirteen schools in Kunshan county.[44]

Gazetteers from the thirty-nine counties and one subprefecture of southern Jiangsu reveal an unprecedented expansion of community schools after 1867. Most counties responded to Ding's call for foundings within two years, and other schools were founded in the early Guangxu reign. In 1869 Governor Ding Richang memorialized the throne that more than 240 schools, most called *yixue,* had been founded in 1868 alone. That would be an average of six new institutions founded per county, but like academies and the students they produced, the eastern-most counties almost certainly ended up with more than the average.[45]

Such a number of foundings is believable. In Nanhui county on the coast, for example, the Guangxu era gazetteer clearly recorded that in 1868 the county magistrate founded one *yishu* in a town in each *xiang* in the county. In neighboring Qingpu county, a Daotai established one school in the standard four *xiang*. In relatively prosperous Jiangyin county bordering the Yangzi, about midway between Shanghai and Jiangning, all the schools were demolished by the Taipings in 1860. Following Ding Richang's instructions, county officials succeeded in founding seventeen *yixue* in the county by 1874.[46]

The expansion of public schools in the Tongzhi Restoration had one precondition that helped make the expansion succeed. They were built not long after the school and academy foundings that had occurred in the Lower Yangzi during the Daoguang reign (1820–1850). Many gazetteer entries detailing the Taiping destruc-

---

42 *FWGD* 9:2–3a.

43 Hsiao Kung-ch'uan, *Rural China: Imperial Control in the Nineteenth Century,* 11–12.

44 Liu Yizheng, "Jiangsu yixue shexue zhi," *Jiangsu wenxian* (1943), 2:72.

45 Ibid., 1:85–87, 2:70–75; *FWGD* 4:37b.

46 Liu Yizheng, "Jiangsu yixue," 2:74–75; *Nanhui xianzhi* (1879), 7:31b; *Jiangyin xianzhi* (1878), 5:29b–32.

tion of schools noted in passing that several schools initially founded after 1820 were then rebuilt after 1864.[47] In Jiangning prefecture in 1838, for example, Tang Jian (Z. Queshen, 1789–1872), the financial commissioner and later a mentor of Zeng Guofan, began setting up free schools in the nine precincts (*qu*) of the prefectural city, using a Ming dynasty *shexue* model. Following the Taiping control of Jiangning city as their capital from 1853 to 1864, Zeng Guofan appointed Tu Zongying (H. Langxuan, 1810–1894) as prefect in that same prefecture, and Tu, along with the Jiangning county magistrate Mo Xiangzhi (1827–1889), followed up the Tang Jian initiative by vigorously founding more schools there between 1866 and 1874.[48]

Collaboration with the Local Gentry and Its Shenjian *Stratum*

To reestablish local order by providing free education to the disadvantaged made perfect sense in the devastated human landscape of Jiangsu's southern prefectures. The problems Governor Ding Richang faced in establishing such institutions differed little, however, from those facing earlier officials. The views of Huang Liuhong, a former magistrate in Shandong and Zhili and the author of a well-known magistrate's manual in 1699, were reprinted in a 1867 manual for reconstruction officials. Huang put the problem of schools this way:

> In ancient times, well-to-do families had private schools, and communities had public schools for educating youngsters. All talented students were permitted to enter the public schools. . . .
>
> In a department or district today, if we want to establish schools in the urban, suburban, and rural areas to insure all youngsters an opportunity to study, there will be several hundred schools in each district, figuring one school in every village. Even if we exhaust all the resources of the district, there will not be enough to finance such an undertaking. How can schools be universally established?[49]

The author then gave his solution: "I think with the voluntary

---

47 Liu Yizheng, "Jiangsu yixue," pt. 1 and pt. 2.

48 Mo was the younger brother of Mo Youzhi (1811–1871), a significant scholar working at Zeng's Jinling shuju (Jinling Publishing House) in Jiangning.

In the Daoguang era, Tao Zhu (1779–1839) had been governor-general at Jiangning (1830–1839) and a governor of both Anhui and Jiangsu before that. He consistently promoted education and was responsible for founding and supporting many academies in the region. See Wei Xiumei, *Tao Zhu zai Jiangnan*, 226–231, and Liu Yizheng, "Jiangsu yixue," 2:70.

49 See Huang Liuhong, *Complete Book Concerning Happiness and Benevolence: Fuhui ch'uan-shu* (1699), ed. and tr. Djang Chu, 4, 536–537. The reconstruction manual was Dai Zhaochen, ed., *Xue shi lu*.

contributions from the local gentry and the leadership of the authorities, an educational system with features similar to those of the ancient public schools can be established. This is the system of free schools."[50] In short, gentry financial and managerial support was indispensable for a county magistrate in 1699.

In the Jiangsu Restoration two manuals appeared, reprinting the advice of men such as Huang Liuhong and more recent officials. The essays on charitable schools in each gave the same advice: officials should collaborate with local financial benefactors for financing. This position differed slightly from Ding's position that the schools should be officially financed, but it maintained official supervision of the public sphere of educational expansion.

The first manual, *Xue shi lu* (Records of scholars), appeared in 1867; it was edited by a Jiangsu native. In it a magistrate who had served for twenty years in Henan reargued Huang Liuhong's basic position: "A family could endow a school, or several families could endow a school; a village could endow a school or several villages could endow a school."[51] The second manual, *De yi lu* (Charitable deeds), was edited by Wu Yun (1811–1883), a Suzhou friend of the Suzhou literatus Feng Guifen (1809–1874). In this manual, the essay on charitable schools was written by a Zhejiangese who had served with great popularity as a magistrate in Jiangdu county in Jiangsu in the Daoguang period. Chen Wenshu advised local officials to approve the bylaws submitted by native philanthropists willing to set up schools.[52]

In the post-Taiping era, Governor Ding Richang, following the model of Chen Hongmou as well as that of other eighteenth-century officials in the Lower Yangzi who had overseen local elite management of welfare associations, enlisted gentry to manage community schools while keeping the schools under the supervision of local educational officials.[53] The eight-point model for establishing schools

---

[50] Huang Liuhong, *Complete Book*, 537, with minor adjustments in the wording of the translation.

[51] The official was Li Yumei from Shanxi. See "Yixue tiaogui" (Regulations for charitable schools) in Dai Zhaochen, *Xue shi lu* 15:7–8. See also *QDZJ* 157:269–285.

[52] See Leung, "Elementary Education," 12; Wu Yun, ed., *De yi lu*, 685–996; *QDZJ* 105:16–19. Note the proposal for traveling teachers who would teach at a two-month temporary school with the hope students would pass along the basic literary and moral teachings. See Wu Yun, *De yi lu*, 723–742.

[53] See Esherick and Rankin, *Local Elites*, 337, citing Liang Qizi (Angela Leung), "Mingmo Qingchu minjian," 310, 313, 317, 322. See Ding Richang, ed., *Abojia shu jiyao* (Selection from a Baojia handbook), (Taibei: Chengwen, 1968), 214.

Ding promulgated called for regular inspection of public schools by the county director of schools or another educational official. This investigator would oversee the day-to-day management of village-level schools, which was carried out by two appointed gentry directors. The maintenance of these schools in the long run, however, depended on how the gentry directors managed what monies could be invested in small landed endowments or earned as interest from a pawnbroker-bank.[54]

Exactly who were the gentry who were to work with local officials in establishing charitable schools? Ding Richang identified three members of a team needing to be coordinated by the local official: (1) the provincial printing office personnel, who printed texts such as Zhu Xi's *Xiaoxue* (Elementary primer); (2) the gentry manager(s) of the school; and (3) the educational authority at the school.[55] Ogawa Yoshiko has found that the gentry managers who managed the construction and maintained the financing of these charitable schools in the Qing were predominantly local *shengyuan* and *jiansheng* (students of the imperial academy).[56] Ogawa further established that the vast majority of donors and founders (usually the same person) in the sample county in Henan province she studied had *shengyuan* status and were members of the local gentry.[57]

Professor Min Tu-ki has argued that the stratum of the local gentry who had degrees but were not officials should be distinguished as a middling stratum of local leadership. No one with a *juren* provincial degree was in this group of people, as *juren* status was derived from the national examination system. The *shengyuan-jiansheng* stratum, together called *shengjian,* needs independent identification because technically it was local institutions that accorded and periodically revalidated the status of *shengjian.* These institutions were called the prefectural and county schools (*fuxue* and *xianxue*) but were really local administrative offices that kept up-to-date rolls on which *shengyuan* had successfully been reexamined every three years to retain their status.[58]

---

[54] Ocko, *Bureaucratic Reform,* 5–7. Each teacher was in charge of ten students.

[55] *FWGD* 9:2a.

[56] Min Tu-ki, *National Polity and Local Power: The Transformation of Late Imperial China,* 26. Most were purchased, *shengyuan*-level degrees, but there were a few hundred nonpurchased *jiansheng* who studied at the Guozi jian (Imperial College) in Beijing.

[57] Ogawa Yoshiko, "Shindai ni okeru gigaku setsuritsu no kiban," in *Kinsei Chugōku kyōiku shi kenkyu,* ed. Tomoharu Hayashi, 292, 305; Etienne Zi, *Pratique des Examens Littéraires en Chine,* 94.

[58] Min Tu-ki, *National Polity,* 21–28.

It is precisely this stratum of *shengjian* with degrees but no power to be appointed to office who were identified as *shi* (scholars) instead of *shen* (officials). The *shengjian* or *shi* were a much larger group than the traditional *shen* who held office, were retired, or had been accorded an official post because of financial donations to the state. This stratum of local talent was almost identical to Qu Tongzu's "scholar-gentry" but could easily run into conflicts with the official gentry.[59] In this pool we find the founders and gentry managers of charitable schools. Ding Richang in fact required that the teachers at these schools also be from the *shengjian* stratum of scholar-gentry society.[60]

Ding relied upon a variety of incentives to keep the county educational officials vigilant. He used informers to go beyond the monthly reports of educational officials, and he conspicuously rewarded able work.[61] The county subdirectors of schools (*xundao*) and the directors of schools themselves were rated for their diligence, accuracy, and completeness as reflected in their regular reports. Ding regularly published the merits and demerits awarded for the quality of these reports, which became part of the career dossier of the official. Monetary bonuses or awards for meritorious performance were also made public.[62]

Along with the public charitable schools, Ding promoted the older *xiangyue* system of public lectures. Speakers were to lecture from the "Expanded Sacred Edict" of the Yongzheng emperor. Unlike schoolteachers, these lecturers were local men of high standing who were not required to have any civil service degrees. The director and assistant director of schools supervised the public lecturers, and, to maintain a rigorous standard of accountability, Ding asked the magistrates to collect copies of the lectures themselves as well as evaluations by the lecturers of the size of the audience and the percentage of the audience the lecturer felt had been inspired by the talk. Monetary awards for exemplary work were accorded by county officials to supplement the salaries of the lecturers.[63]

---

[59] See Min Tu-ki, *National Polity*, 37–49; and T'ung-tsu Ch'u, *Local Government under the Ch'ing* (Cambridge, Mass.: Harvard Council on East Asian Studies, 1988), 172, 319–326.

[60] Min Tu-ki, *National Polity*, 26–29; Ogawa Yoshiko, "Shindai," 292, 305; Ocko, *Bureaucratic Reform*, 56.

[61] Ocko, *Bureaucratic Reform*, 58.

[62] *FWGD* 32:12–14b; 33:13a–b; 34:6a–6.

[63] *Nanhui xianzhi* (1970), 7:31; *FWGD* 34:6a–b; Ocko, *Bureaucratic Reform*, 60.

This rigorous program to maintain effective supervisors and competent gentry managers responsible for new schools and lectures showed some strains in financing and implementation even by 1869, the second year of Ding's governorship.[64] However, Ding continued to mete out harsh judgments to laggard county officials until he stepped down as governor in 1870.

In neighboring Zhejiang good records remain for a prefect who was almost as proactive an administrator as was Governor Ding Richang in Jiangsu. Zong Yuanhan had used *lijin* funds for academies, as was noted above. In about 1865 he issued orders to the counties composing Huzhou prefecture to follow his model in setting up *yishu* for about ten to sixteen students each. He soon reported to the governor that he had established ten schools servicing more than a hundred students, sixty of whom were fatherless orphans of the postwar era.[65]

Unlike Ding Richang, who assumed officials would take care of the financing one way or another, the Zhejiang prefect details how he got money for the food, lodging, and books of students, plus the salary of the teachers: "The prefecture [i.e., the prefectural official], with officials and gentry (*shen*), will solicit each bank, gentry (*shen*) member, and merchant to donate."[66] According to Ogawa's data, the *shengjian* stratum of the gentry did give this money. Those local elite members who had official status accompanied the local officials and the prefect to solicit the larger group of local elite members who were in the private sector of society, but who here were being asked to sponsor public institutions. When donations were adequate, the prefect established interest-bearing accounts in pawnbroker-banks, and the schools opened under the management of one or two *shengjian* gentry managers per school.[67]

Regardless of how vigilantly later governors fostered county educational officials and gentry managers, the legacy of Ding Richang's and Zong Yuanhan's promotion of public education was a host of new institutions. While some of the many new public charitable schools in each county of the Lower Yangzi region undoubtedly had financial problems, others found reliable local funding. Managerial and instructional *shengjian* from each locality were employed in this charitable enterprise that directly benefited the local community.

---

64 Ocko, *Bureaucratic Reform*, 58–59.
65 Ibid., p. 26.
66 Zong Yuanhan, *Yiqing*, *juan* 4, p. 2b.
67 Ibid., 2–10b.

In 1868 the *shengjian* pool in southern Jiangsu would have had to provide staff for at least Ding Richang's 240 new public charitable schools at a minimum. But the demand was easy to meet as the 30-percent increase in the *shengyuan* quota for Jiangsu raised its level of available first-degree holders from 41,362 before 1850 to 53,754 after the war. These men needed such job opportunities, as their chances to examine into the official gentry were slim. The triennial *juren* quota for Jiangsu—even after it was raised by eighteen persons because of war contributions in 1853—was only eighty-seven persons.[68]

The expansion of charitable schools and even local academies initially employed many of the *shengjian* stratum after 1864. Because the number of first-degree holders continued to increase in the second half of the nineteenth century, however, oversupply remained a problem. The expanding number of local academies generally assumed *shengyuan* status for admission and then trained these scholars for three years. A few could expect introductions to local patrons to become tutors for their families or teachers in lineage schools. Those elite academies with provincewide aspirations could provide enough clout to propel students into provincial and national job markets. But over time, the expanded number of local academies and their graduates would exacerbate the social problem of how to meet the employment needs of a steadily increasing local educated elite.

---

[68] Chang Chung-li, *Chinese Gentry*, 100; Zi, *Pratique*, 118; K. C. Liu, "Ch'ing Restoration," 485.

PART II

Three Classical Academies, 1865–1895

Part 2 examines three major elite academies situated in different parts of Jiangsu province: one in the governor-general's capital at Jiangning in the west, one in Shanghai in the east, and one in the center of southern Jiangsu where the provincial director of education had his office. Accomplished literati were called upon to design a vital curriculum and be the master teachers in each academy. No Western subject matter or pedagogical theory was used. The fate of the Confucian state was known to be in the balance, and scholars rose to the challenge of reviving the best in traditional education to revitalize the Qing dynasty.

CHAPTER TWO

The Governor-general's Academy

Jiangning city was the most important political center in the Lower Yangzi. From here the office of the Liangjiang governor-general oversaw institutions serving Jiangxi province, Anhui province, and Jiangsu province.[1] Zeng Guofan became governor-general with the defeat of the Taipings in July 1864 and by December had restored the *juren* provincial examinations in Jiangning city.[2] Indeed, Zeng's views on how academies fit into the recovery of Jiangsu's devastated countryside and into the restoration of national strength more generally had an important impact on the expansion of education in the Lower Yangzi from 1864 until his death in 1872.

Jiangsu Restoration Officials and Academies

Once on the job in Jiangning Zeng Guofan immediately set about restoring the 1723 official academy in town, as well as other academies throughout the region. In a private letter to Wu Tingdong (H. Zhuru, 1793–1873), a long-time confidant, Zeng worried about what techniques officials could use to make educated and talented persons feel respected in the restoration. Regarding academies, Zeng stated a position more consistent with the administrative needs of recovery than with his personal commitment to the value of Neo-Confucian self-cultivation. He believed average academies were a step along the road to recruitment of government officials, and he wrote his friend that directors of academies must have as their first priority a commitment to teaching the eight-legged essay and poetry.[3]

[1] Each province had had its own governor since Jiangsu separated from Anhui in 1667, ending the Qing political division called Jiangnan province. The governor-general retained some oversight functions for all three. See Arthur W. Hummel, ed., *Eminent Chinese of the Ch'ing Period (1644–1912)*, 920–921.

[2] Ibid., 754.

[3] See Zeng Guofan, "Fu Wu Zhuru shilang," in *ZWZQJ* 33:15900–3.

Zeng repeated this position in another letter to a fellow Hunanese of his generation who had been appointed to an office by Governor Hu Linyi in Hubei. Ding Quzhong (Z. Guozhen; H. Yunwu) sought advice on whether to appoint an older scholar as director of an academy under Ding's jurisdiction. Zeng's careful reply argued that since the academy's purpose was to train people for official positions, the eight-legged essay must be the primary component of the academy curriculum. A director without an established scholarly record in the classics, history, or past scholarly writing might still be appointed, Zeng argued, if his ability to teach the eight-legged essay was unquestioned. Because the candidate under discussion was quite old, Zeng Guofan judged that he had been away too long from the technical skills needed to teach examination-style composition. What was more, because the older gentleman had problems with his eyesight, Zeng judged that protracted work improving student compositions would be too difficult. Zeng advised the writer not to appoint the candidate in question and offered to write the candidate himself and explain the matter.[4]

In contrast to Zeng's definition of academies as a step in official recruitment, Woren (1804–1871), whom Zeng Guofan knew well and whose moral discipline Zeng had emulated from the time they were friends at the Hanlin Academy, firmly maintained that developing the moral talent of a select few was the main purpose of academy education. Woren, who had been named grand secretary in Beijing in 1863,[5] believed that highly select teachers might succeed in inspiring a few students in academies and that such benefits would be enough for the government in the long run. The principle behind so elitist a view was that the virtue of the teacher—the stage of his development of moral perfection—was the element that had to be transferred through disciplined learning and interpersonal modeling in the teacher-student relationship so that ethical and talented students could be prepared to take their places as principled leaders in state and society.[6]

Woren was not a hopeless idealist in considering the realities of education in the Tongzhi Restoration. It was his sense of the existing weaknesses of Qing academies that gave him pause. In contrast to

---

[4] Zeng Guofan, "Fu Ding Guochen," in *ZWZQJ* 28:15526–27.

[5] Kwang-ching Liu, "Ch'ing Restoration," 423.

[6] Lu Baoqian, *Qingdai sixiang shi*, 333, 335.

the scholarly autonomy of private academies in the Ming dynasty, the Manchu state had treated academies as government institutions. Woren saw existing institutions as hobbled by this political and vocational linkage.[7]

Yet Zeng Guofan's priority of reestablishing the functional place of academies in the national bureaucracy mixed uneasily with his personal commitment to self-cultivation as the essential component of Confucian education. This latter objective was clear in his Hanlin Academy writings before the Taiping Revolutionary Movement. The original Hanlin coterie where Zeng applied Cheng-Zhu principles rigorously to his life had been led by Tang Jian, the man who had founded so many public charitable schools in Jiangning prefecture in the late 1830s, and included Woren. Both of these men were given conspicuous posts in the early Tongzhi Restoration. Zeng had been inspired by the Beijing group of friends, and his diary records the standards Tang Jian had exacted within the coterie: Zeng Guofan wrote, "[With regard to self-examination] my teacher [Tang Jian] said, 'In recent years, Woren has been the most dedicated one. Every day he records each word he said, each move he made, and even each meal he ate. He also records his bad behavior, and the lusts that he fails to overcome.' "[8]

In 1864 as governor-general, Zeng invited his friend Wu Tingdong—who was also Tang Jian's student and whom Zeng Guofan once referred to as one of China's three living sages—to lecture in Jiangning at the opening of a *yangxian guan* (hall of worthies). Zeng believed that Jiangning, as the former capital of the Taiping kings, was in desperate need of a figure to provide a moral model (*liu yi ren yangzi*) of how persons should live, as well as how to lead by Confucian values. Zeng's staff of private secretaries and other local restoration officials attended Wu's lectures and treated him as a moral model and visiting consultant on Confucian institutions.[9]

---

7 Ibid., 331–335.

8 Andrew Cheng-kuang Hsieh, "Tseng Kuo-fan, A Nineteenth-century Confucian General," p. 26.

9 Feng Xu, *Haoan suibi*, 68; Liu Yizheng, "Guoxue shuju benmo," *Jiangsu shengli tushuguan disan nian kan* (1930), 1–16. Wu Tingdong returned to live for a while in Jiangning in 1868, when Zeng was appointed governor-general of Zhili. During that visit he lived and worked with other Anhui scholars connected with Zeng, including Fang Zongcheng. See *QDZJ* 4:840.

Yangzi Delta Officials

So, although Zeng Guofan as restoration administrator insisted that the function of academies was to train civil service officials, he encouraged officials themselves to live out the high social norms of Neo-Confucianism once in office. The career of Tu Zongying illustrates the ways Zeng Guofan's very public commitment to the re-establishment of Confucian orthodoxy was carried out by an able, dedicated follower who promoted education after 1864. As governor-general, Zeng selected Tu, who had been Wu Tingdong's student in Anhui, to serve as a magistrate and then prefect in Jiangning under Zeng's authority. Tu served for several years before taking the Daotai promotion in Shanghai in 1870. From there, his advancement was textbook perfect—judicial commissioner of Hunan to finance commissioner of Hunan, then to appointment as governor first of Guangxi, then of Hunan, and finally as governor-general of Hu-Guang in Wuhan. In all these posts Tu Zongying found ways to sponsor editions of Cheng-Zhu scholarship and support institutions of quality training in orthodox Song learning. In Jiangning, for example, Prefect Tu Zongying had worked in concert with Zeng Guofan and his teacher Wu Tingdong, along with a host of other Anhuiese whom Zeng seemed to find particularly able,[10] to set the correct lofty Confucian standards for the reconstruction of Lower Yangzi society.

Tu Zongying's efforts can be documented on two social and intellectual levels. As prefect of Jiangning in the 1860s he established free orphanage-welfare institutions, one of which became renewed as a lasting institution in the 1880s and was still operating as a free orphanage-school in 1927. In 1868 he also acquired buildings to restore a small academy in Jiangning prefecture called Fengchi shuyuan (Phoenix Pool Academy). He also oversaw a sophisticated

[10] In addition to calling three men from Anhui "living sages," Zeng Guofan also labeled seven more Anhui literati the "seven worthies," and with them he used only socially equal forms of address because of their exemplary standards of Confucian learning and conduct. Some of them, such as Yang Deheng (Z. Chungqian, 1806–1876), lived and worked in Jiangning when Tu Zongying was prefect and took part in a kind of Cheng-Zhu salon of friends with Zeng—convinced, as a group, that Neo-Confucian learning was the indispensable point of departure in turning political confusion and disruption into stable government. A list of the Anhuiese can be found in Feng Xu, *Haoan*, 67–69. Chen Ai (Z. Huchen, 1811–1897), one of these men from the same home town as Yang Deheng, was hired directly into Zeng's private bureaucracy; see Li Dingfang, *Zeng Guofan ji qi mufu renwu*, 9. Another, Hong Rukui, succeeded Tu Zongying in overseeing the Jinling Publishing House in 1869; see Liu

scholarly institution, the Jinling Publishing House, packed with scholars from Zeng Guofan's bureaucracy of private secretaries. Further, when he was Daotai in Shanghai, Tu commissioned Wan Huquan (Z. Qingxuan, 1807–1904) to collate a complete edition of the works of Zhu Xi, *Zhu zi da chuan* (Complete works of Master Zhu), and when Tu was governor-general in Hu-Guang in 1882, he again hired Wan Huquan and lauded him for his exemplary work on the Cheng-Zhu school.[11]

From Jiangning's power center down to the thriving customs port of Shanghai, overall official leadership in the Lower Yangzi after 1864 included many committed Neo-Confucians adjusting to the realities of the politically possible. Among other adjustments, the energetic reassertion of Confucian institutions in the last fifty years of the Qing contained an intense combining of the inner-orientation of Cheng-Zhu self-cultivation with the need for strengthening the country, so that China could more capably resist the increasing foreign encroachment. Many resolved this tension by appointing "moral talent" to good academies, while spending the rest of their time on developing arsenals and technology.

The career of Ying Baoshi (Z. Minzhai, b. 1821; *juren,* 1844), the military officer who helped in the final taking of Anhui from the Taipings, illustrates the parallel promotion of material and moral rearmament. Ying succeeded Ding Richang as Daotai in Shanghai in 1865 and passed along that position to Tu Zongying in 1869. Ying Baoshi has been remembered by historians as the director of the newly established Jiangnan arsenal in Shanghai and is often placed with Li Hongzhang and his adviser Feng Guifen as a modernizer who pushed to their institutional limits various proposals on Western affairs.[12]

---

[11] On Tu's welfare institutions see *Jiangning fu chong jian puyu tang zhi,* published by Tu in 1871, and the updated edition republished by Song Yunjing in 1886. See *Shangjiang liangxian zhi* 8:172. See also Andrew Hsieh, "Tongzhi nianjian de Jinling shuju," *Dalu zazhi* 37.1–2 (1968): 46–55; Liu Yizheng, "Jiangsu yixue," 79; and *(Xuzuan) Jiangning FZ,* 51. Wu Dacheng (Z. Qingqing, 1835–1902), the Suzhou literatus and eminent diplomat, had encouraged Wan Huquan to undertake this project. Wu had been a student of Wan Huquan and himself became a director of Longmen Academy in Shanghai in 1898 (*QDZJ* 4:887, 895).

[12] Knight Biggerstaff, *The Earliest Modern Government Schools in China,* 8; Fang Chao-ying, "Ting Jih-ch'ang," in *Eminent Chinese,* ed. Hummel, 722. For another angle on Feng Guifen's career, see James Polachek, "Gentry Hegemony: Soochow in the T'ung-chih Restoration," in *Conflict and Control in Late Imperial China,* ed. Frederic Wakeman and Carolyn Grant, 216–250.

Less obvious, but consistently present in his policies, is Ying Baoshi's commitment to Confucian moral rearmament. In his appointments establishing Longmen Academy in Shanghai, Ying supported the loftiest Neo-Confucian standards as they flowed from Zeng Guofan's headquarters in Jiangning. In 1865 after the sudden death of Longmen Academy's first director in Shanghai, Ying Baoshi appointed Wan Huquan, who had been recommended to Zeng by Wan Huquan's fellow Hubeiese Feng Lifan (Z. Jie'an) as a model Confucian.[13]

Standard biographies of Wan Huquan in Qing compilations repeat a story that gives his scholarly identity an almost sagelike quality. When the Taiping rebels were crossing from Jiangxi into his home province of Hubei, Wan Huquan opted to stay at home in Xingguo county and continue his teaching of the classics in a modest school. As the rampage of destruction reached his hut, the Taiping soldiers were surprised to find Wan sitting erect reciting a passage. The rebels left him untouched and soon left his village as well. His villagers considered such rectitude exceptionally principled living; and it impressed many officials, who thereafter awarded him rank and attempted to appoint him to office. Zeng Guofan and Li Hongzhang both tried to give him jobs during the war because Wan embodied a model of heroic Confucian resistance. But Wan refused all official appointment and remained an academy teacher and a scholar the rest of his life.[14]

In his own reminiscence of Longmen Academy, Daotai Ying Baoshi first carefully outlined the Song tradition of academies dedicated to the best in Confucian values. He then explained the need for a distinctively Confucian academy in Shanghai: "The conditions of this coastal port are such that Chinese and foreign affairs are so mixed together that...there is a special need for orthodox learning....In this way I hope to contribute in a small way to the fulfillment of Ding's [i.e., Daotai Ding Richang's] original intentions."[15]

When the bylaws of Longmen Academy were framed, Daotai Ying consulted one of the most respected scholars of the day, Yu Yue

---

13 For Tu Zongying, Wan Huquan, and Feng Lifan, see *Daoxue yuanyuan lu Qingdai pian*, in *QDZJ* 4:887–888, 897–999. For Ying Baoshi see *Shengqing yuanyuanlu*, in *QDZJ* 4:189–894. Wan was the scholar Tu Zongying was later to patronize.

14 *QDZJ* 019:885–889; *QDZJ*, 007:633–639.

15 Ying Baoshi, "Xundao Ying Baoshi Longmen shuyuan ji," *Shanghai xianzhi* 9 (1870): 34b. Ding Richang had allocated the initial 1,000 taels of silver to spend on the academy when he was Daotai in 1864. See *Shanghai XZ* 1870, 9:34.

(Z. Quyuan, 1821–1907). Yu was then teaching at Suzhou's provincially funded 1733 Ziyang Academy; he was soon thereafter to return to his alma mater, Gujing jingshe (Retreat for the Philological Analysis of the Classics) in Hangzhou, which itself had been founded with a vital commitment to quality scholarship by Ruan Yuan in 1803. Yu praised the bylaws he was asked to review as superior to those at Ziyang Academy, and he noted: "Not only will it [Longmen Academy] be a blessing for the scholars of the southeast, but the benefits of literary and military strengthening will accrue to the restoration (*zhongxing*)."[16]

Following Wan Huquan's appointment to the best classical academy in the region, the Daotai Ying Baoshi continued to patronize scholars and was committed to patronizing publication of new editions of the works of early Qing Cheng-Zhu advocates such as Lu Longqi (1630–1674) and Zhang Lüxiang (1611–1674). He thereby placed his career in the same line of descent as Tu Zongying's—namely, implementing the commitment to Cheng-Zhu moral philosophy that Zeng Guofan and the coterie around Tang Jian in Beijing had been promoting since the 1840s.[17]

The fascination of Tongzhi Restoration officials and scholars with the early Qing is understandable. The seventeenth-century crisis of the Confucian state was the nearest historical parallel to the disunity and near collapse of state authority in the heterodox Taiping Revolutionary Movement. Indeed, the economic collapse of the early seventeenth and early nineteenth centuries may have been parallel for other reasons not so evident to analysts of either time: the constriction in world silver in both periods aggravated considerably the problem of inflation within China and added financial stress to the more obvious population strains in both eras.[18] In any case, Tongzhi literati studied the 1600s to find which Confucian critics of the fall of the Ming dynasty seemed to have relevant answers for the late Qing.[19]

Tang Jian joined several other serious Neo-Confucian scholars in receiving special appointments in the early Tongzhi government. In his writings, Tang Jian had singled out Lu Longqi as the successor of Zhu Xi and the legitimate transmitter of the way (*dao*) to the Qing.

16 Yu Yue, "Yu Ying Minzhai tongnian," in *Chunzai tang quanshu*, ed. Yu Yue, *juan* 414, pp. 502–504.

17 "Ying Baoshi," in *Shengqing yuanyuanlu*, in *QDZJ* 4:893.

18 See Lin Man-houng, "Currency and Society: The Monetary Crisis and Political-Economic Ideology of Early Nineteenth-century China," passim.

19 For the serious interest evinced by Zhejianese scholars see Rankin, *Elite Activism*, 122.

Tang Jian argued that Lu Longqi had been joined by three other major proponents of Cheng-Zhu moral philosophy in the early Qing: Zhang Lüxiang, Lu Shiyi (1611–1672), and Zhang Boxing (1625–1725).[20] It was indeed Zhang Boxing who had argued successfully in 1724 that Lu Longqi should be the first Qing figure enshrined in the national Confucian temple. A similar event occurred in in the Tongzhi Restoration while Tang Jian was still alive. The search for a clear national statement of a unified orthodox direction for scholarship probably lay behind the successful canonization "on the petition of a high official" of Zhang Lüxiang in the year of Woren's death, 1871. A complete edition of Zhang Lüxiang's works appeared in the same year. And Tu Zongying had Jinling shuju—Zeng Guofan's Jinling Publishing House—publish the posthumous works of Woren.[21] In 1878 Zhang Boxing himself was canonized.[22]

Jiangning's Zhongshan Academy

All of Jiangning city's academies were publically financed and supervised before the Taiping conflict, and none was ready to reopen after the Taiping forces left their capital of "Tianjing" in 1864. But within five years, the province had financed the renovation of five pre-Taiping academies that served 384 students.[23]

Straightforward economic evidence in the prefectural gazetteer of 1874 makes clear the hierarchical status of the reconstructed academies. The governor-general's academy, Zhongshan (named for the local Zhong or Zijin mountain) Academy, which was handsomely founded in 1724, admitted fifty top residential students who each

---

[20] See Tang's *Guochao xuean xiaoshi* (Records of dynastic scholarship), in *QDZJ* 2:85–151, and especially the preface, 4.

[21] Andrew Cheng-kuang Hsieh (Xie Zhengguang), "Tongzhi nianjian," 54. One of Woren's final acts before he died in 1871 was to praise Tu Zongying's additions to the endowment of Longmen Academy in Shanghai in that year. See Lu Baoxian, *Qingdai,* 331–334.

[22] William T. DeBary, *Message of the Mind in Neo-Confucianism,* 185–200, 265; Thomas Watters, *A Guide to the Tablets in a Temple of Confucius,* 242; K. C. Liu, "Ch'ing Restoration," 423; see also *QDZJ* 2:76–77; Hummel, *Eminent Chinese,* 52.

It is interesting to note that one of the coterie, Zeng Guofan himself, who died in 1872, was discussed for canonization in 1903. Zhang Zhidong successfully opposed that recommendation, ostensibly because of Zeng's punishment by death of eighteen Chinese for their roles in the Tianjin Massacre of 1870. See Zhang Daxiang and Li Shisun, "Zhang Zhidong shiji shuwen," in *Wen shi ziliao xuanji,* 87.

[23] The following data on Jiangning's post-Taiping academies can be found in (*xu zuan*) *Jiangning FZ* 1874, *juan* 5, "xue xiao" (schools), 7a–8b.

received a monthly living stipend of two silver taels (ounces) and six cash coins (ten make an ounce). The seventy nonresidential students received just 1.3 taels per month.

One hundred students were admitted to the second academy in town, Zunjing (Respect) Academy, which had been endowed in the Jiaqing (1796–1820) era by provincial authorities. The thirty residential students received stipends of 2.2 taels, the seventy nonresidential students, 1.1 taels, for a monthly provincial expenditure of more than 140 taels. The third academy, Xiyin (Be Sparing of Time) Academy, founded in 1837, cost the province only 57 taels a month because this budget subsidized only sixty-four students.

Two smaller academies run by the province had fifty students each and cost the treasury a meager 28 ounces of silver a month—the students receiving a monthly stipend of only 0.8 tael. In addition there was one academy whose enrollment and budget were external to the provincial treasury and whose budget was drawn entirely from the prefectural budget. Only one pre-Taiping academy in Jiangning prefecture was not restored.

A comparison of directors' salaries shows the appeal to a scholar-director of the better-financed institutions. The directors of the two weaker, provincially financed academies received a salary of 300 taels a year. In contrast, the director of Zunjing Academy received 500 taels annual salary, the director of Zhongshan Academy, 800 taels a year. Xiyin Academy was a special case, as it became a kind of graduate school for Zhongshan Academy.

Zhongshan Academy in Mid-Qing History

Ever since its establishment in 1724, Zhongshan Academy had been the most prominent academy in Jiangning. The reputations of its directors reflect the changing emphases within schools of scholarship in the Qing, fostered in part by the direct influence of the Jiangning officials who financed and oversaw the academy. In the eighteenth century, giants of the movement promoting evidential research methodology (*kaoju*), beginning with Lu Wenchao, made Zhongshan a center of academic excellence (table 2). Among these, Qian Daxin and, later, Zhu Jian, eventually transferred that expertise and their directorships to other academic centers in Suzhou and Yangzhou.[24]

---

[24] Elman, *From Philosophy*, 124. Liu Yizheng, "Jiangsu shuyuan zhi chugao," in *Zhongguo gudai jiaoyu shi ziliao*, ed. Meng Xiancheng et al., 279–280.

Table 2
Directors of Zhongshan Academy, 1723–1901

Director	Years at academy
Yang Shengwu	1723–c.1736
Xia Zhirong	not certain
Lu Wenchao (H. Baojing)	1773–78; 1785–89
Qian Daxin (Z. Zhuting)	1778–1781
Yao Nai (Z. Xibao)	1790–1800
[Destruction of buildings occurs at some point in Jiaqing era 1796–1820]	
Sun Xingyan (Z. Yuanru)	1811–1816
Qin Chengye (Z. Buzhi; H. Yitang)	1818–1820(?)
Zhu Jian	1823–24
Cheng Enze	not certain
Hu Peihui (Z. Zhucu)	1832–?
Ren Tai (Z. Jieping)	not certain
Tang Jian (Z. Queshen, H. Jinghai)	1851–1853
[Academy closed, Taiping Rebellion, 1853–1864]	
Li Lianxiu (Z. Xiaohu)	1865–1878
Sun Qiangming (H. Chutian)	1879–1884*
Lin Shoutu (Z. Yingshu)	not certain
Liang Dingfen (Z. Xinghai)	1895
Miao Quansun (Z. Yanshi)	1896–1901

* Sun Qiangming's academic peregrinations can be traced through the following sources: Miao Quansun, "Sun Qiangming muzhi ming," in *QDZJ* 120:547. See also Xue Shiyu, "Xiyin shuyuan xizhai keyi xu," p. 294.

By the 1790s, under Yao Nai's directorship, Zhongshan's reputation changed. Because of Yao's long term as director and his protracted convalescence at Zhongshan Academy preceding his death in 1815, the school became a training ground for a generation of specialists of the Tongcheng Literary School.[25] The Tongcheng movement had resisted the intellectual dominance of the *kaoju* research methods and Han learning in the Qianlong reign. Yao's students at

[25] Named after a county in Anhui province, the school of composition was really a literary branch of orthodox Cheng-Zhu learning. Its interest to Zeng Guofan will be discussed below.

Zhongshan Academy, such as Mei Cengliang, were dedicated advocates of the *guwen* (ancient writing) style and promoted the moral philosophy of the Cheng-Zhu school.[26] The Tongcheng emphasis at Zhongshan Academy did not negate evidential research but allied it with the Song Neo-Confucian emphasis on the search for moral principle (*yili*) in scholarship.[27]

By the Daoguang era emphasis on practical statesmanship or statecraft was discernible on the curriculum at Zhongshan Academy. A major proponent of statecraft priorities in Confucian learning, He Changling (1785–1848, *jinshi* 1808), rebuilt and reendowed Zhongshan Academy in his capacity as Jiangning's financial commissioner in 1828, and a plaque was erected to him on the grounds in 1831. The famous volumes he and Wei Yuan edited on statecraft, *Huangchao jingshi wenbian* (Statecraft writings of the Qing period), thereafter appeared as regular reading in the academy's curriculum.[28]

During the forty years following 1828, three other scholar-officials came from He Changling's native Changsha prefecture in Hunan province and continued to emphasize the importance of practicality in Confucian learning at Zhongshan Academy: Tao Zhu (1779–1839, *jinshi* 1802), Tang Jian (1789–1872, *jinshi* 1809), already referred to as Zeng Guofan's mentor, and Zeng Guofan (1811–1871, *jinshi* 1838). Much of the professional career of each man was spent in the Lower Yangzi. Tao Zhu had been governor of Jiangsu from 1825 to 1830; He Changling served under him as judicial commissioner and then financial commissioner in Suzhou at the time (1824–1827). They collaborated on a variety of economic and transportation projects, such as adopting the sea route for grain transport to the north.[29]

In Jiangning Tao Zhu and He Changling overlapped but briefly, because in 1830 He Changling was released from his duty as financial commissioner to take care of his sick mother. Tao Zhu arrived in Jiangning in that year to begin what extended to a nine-year period as Liangjiang governor-general. Tang Jian, whose home county in Hunan, Shanhua, was the same as He Changling's, replaced him.

---

26 Liu Yizheng, "Jiangsu shuyuan," 46.

27 Zeng Guofan, "Ouyang Sheng wenji xu," in *ZWZQJ* 3:12721–25.

28 One hundred twenty *juan* in eighty volumes, compiler's preface, 1826. See *(Xuzhuan) Jiangning FZ*, 6–7; Xiao Yishan, *Qingdai tongshi*, 4:1961.

29 He Changling and Tang Jian had *jinshi* degrees just a year apart, and Wei Yuan (1794–1856, *jinshi* 1844), He Changling's collaborator on statecraft collections, was from Baoqing prefecture, a prefecture adjacent to Changsha prefecture. *Qingdai zhiguan nianbiao* 3:1895–1908; Hummel, *Eminent Chinese*, 281, 710. See Jane Leonard, *Wei Yuan and China's Rediscovery of the Maritime World*, 24.

Tao Zhu and Tang Jian were particularly energetic in following He Changling's lead in restoring academies and public charitable schools while in Jiangning.[30]

In Beijing in the 1840s Zeng Guofan, studying within the Hanlin coterie of Tang Jian, Woren, and He Guizhen, was also corresponding with He Changling about statecraft ideas.[31] Since Tang Jian subscribed to the same belief as the older He Changling—that moral principles underlying the study of political economy (*jingji*) would be made manifest by looking at history—it is no wonder that near the end of his life, when Zeng Guofan pulled together his advice on the four categories of scholarship literati should pursue, statecraft was prominent.[32]

Tang Jian himself returned to Jiangning when he was in his seventies, well before Zeng Guofan was to arrive and reestablish Zhongshan Academy in 1864. In 1851 Tang Jian accepted the directorship of Zhongshan Academy and in the next few years wrote his encomium to Cheng-Zhu thought in the Qing, *Guochao xuean xiaoshi* (Records of dynastic scholarship). There was no contradiction between promoting orthodox Song Neo-Confucianism and emphasizing practicality (*zhiyong*). For Tang Jian as for Zeng Guofan, the point of departure in advanced learning should be, as Zhang Boxing had earlier advised, reverent seriousness (*jing*). All of these men believed that self-cultivation would lead to practical statesmanship.[33]

Two years after Tao Zhu arrived in Jiangning, the post of director of Zhongshan Academy was vacant. In 1832, Tao Zhu appointed Hu Peihui (Z. Zhucun, 1782–1849), an accomplished scholar of the ritual classics and an advocate of statecraft.[34] As Tao Zhu put his charge to the new director, "If you have practical and substantial knowledge (*shixue*), you have applied knowledge (*shixing*), and you have

[30] Wu Xiumei, *Tao Zhu zai Jiangnan*, 226–231; and Liu Yizheng, "Jiangsu yixue," 2:70. *Qingdai zhiguan nianbiao* 3:1895–1899; Hummel, *Eminent Chinese*, 282.

[31] See Han-yin Ch'en Shen, "Tseng Guo-fan in Peking, 1840–1852: His Ideas in Statecraft and Reform," *Journal of Asian Studies* 27.1 (November 1967): 61–81; Hao Chang, "The Anti-foreignist Role of Wo-jen (1804–1871)," *Papers on China* (Harvard), 14 (1960): 1–29. Xiao Yishan, *Qingdai tongshi*, 4:1961.

[32] K. C. Liu, "Ch'ing Restoration" 439–443, 450, 489. Xiao Yishan, *Qingdai tongshi* 4:1961.

[33] "Xuexiao kao qi," in *Huangchao xu wenxian tongkao* 100:8591; *(Xuzuan) Jiangning FZ* 1874, *juan* 14, section 1, *renwu* (personnel), p. 33a. K. C. Liu, "Ch'ing Restoration," 489; DeBary, *Message of the Mind*, 190–191; Chang Hao, *Chinese Intellectuals in Crisis: Search for Order and Meaning (18890–1911)*, 15–20; Andrew Hsieh, "Tseng Kuo-fan, A Nineteenth-century Confucian General," 27ff.

[34] See Lin Man-houng, "Currency and Society," 587.

practical value (*shiyong*)."[35] Six years later, and after consulting with Hu Peihui, Governor-general Tao also decided Jiangning needed an advanced studies institution that could address the needs of the most advanced students who had already spent a few years at either Zhongshan Academy or Zunjing Academy.[36]

Tao Zhu successfully endowed the new research-oriented academy, Xiyin Academy, just as Tang Jian took office as Jiangning's financial commissioner. The model for organization used was not the official provincial academy but a serious philological research academy that had been set up in Hangzhou in 1801. Governor Ruan Yuan (1764–1849) had established Gujing jingshe (Retreat for the Philological Analysis of the Classics) in Zhejiang and later Xuehai tang (Ocean of Learning Hall) in Guangdong province to revitalize academy education. Ruan Yuan's pedagogical innovations included rigorous philological training and independent study, with accountability for that study visible in a daily journal of ideas and research notes. Further, teachers were tutors, and the library was conceived primarily as a resource at the command of the student for research. The methods those two schools used to foster both practical and substantial learning inspired a select set of fine institutions all over China in the nineteenth century.[37]

Xiyin Academy, one of those institutions, addressed the needs of many *juren* degree holders who were training to become academics.[38] Hu Peihui had emphasized his and Tao Zhu's objective that the institution produce scholarship.[39] Hu Peihui ran it himself for a while as a kind of graduate school of Zhongshan Academy; then in 1848 Feng Guifen took over the directorship. The Taiping movement interrupted Feng's plans to establish a similar institution in his native Suzhou city, but he was able to carry out his plan after the war, using Xiyin Academy's bylaws as one of the guides in establishing Zhengyi (Conform to Requirements) Academy in Suzhou.[40]

---

35 Tao Zhu, "Zhongshan shuyuan keyi xu," in Tao Zhu, *Tao Wenyi gong chuanji, juan* 37, p. 2825.

36 See Hu Peihui, "Xiyin shuyuan," in Hu Peihui, *Jiu liu shi wenchao, buyi,* 1ab. Wei Xiumei, *Tao Zhu,* 228.

37 Zhang Yin, "Gujing jingshe chugao," *Wenlan xuebao* 2.1 (March 1936) 1–47.

38 Gan Xi, *Baixia soyan, juan* 8, p. 14, cited in *Zhongguo jindai jiaoyu shi ziliao huibian,* ed. Zhu Xingui, 291. Feng Guifen, "Xiyin shushe wushen keyi xu," in Feng Guifen, *Xuzhi tang ji,* 204. Adam Lui, "The Academies (*shu-yüan*) under the Ch'ing," *Journal of Asian History* 7.1 (1973): 66.

39 Hu Peihui, "Xiyin shuyuan," in Hu Peihui, *Jiu liu shi wenchao,* 16.

40 Feng Guifen, "Guijian zhengyi shuyuan ji," in Feng Guifen, *Xuzhi tang ji,* 325. See also Wei Xiumei, 269.

After the Taiping suppression, Xiyin Academy itself, however, had difficulty reviving. In 1865 Governor-general Li Hongzhang did provide funding from three sources: lake taxes, pawnbroker-bank investment interest, and salt gabelle revenues.[41] But the director for the next twenty years was simply the same person as the director of Zhongshan Academy. In short, Xiyin Academy became a small humanities graduate school for Zhongshan Academy in Jiangning city.[42]

Zhongshan Academy, 1865–1895

After the Taipings were suppressed, Zeng Guofan solicited the opinion of important literati to select a director for Zhongshan Academy. Feng Guifen, who had directed Suzhou's official provincial academy as well as Xiyin Academy in Jiangning and was busy reconstructing Zhengyi Academy in Suzhou in 1864, recommended the man who was chosen, Li Lianxiu (Z. Xiaohu, 1820–1878). This recommendation was not surprising, as Feng Guifen had a connection to Li Lianxiu through an academy near Suzhou. Li Lianxiu had been a student of Feng's teacher Li Zhaoluo (1769–1841) at Jiyang Academy in Jiangyin county.[43] Three directors after Li Zhaoluo, Li Lianxiu himself had for a while headed their common alma mater and therefore was well qualified to run the governor-general's academy in Jiangning.[44]

Zeng Guofan reviewed Li Lianxiu's collected writings and invited him to serve at Zhongshan Academy. The invitation letter pointed out the critical value of *zhiyong* (practicality) in Confucian learning. Zeng also praised Li Lianxiu's study of a section of the *Book of History* (*Shu jing*) because it avoided the verbosity and frivolity that Zeng felt was the bane of contemporaneous Confucian writing.

Although Li Lianxiu had taught at two academies and worked at a publishing bureau during the Taiping conflagration, he was modest about filling the shoes of an academy directorship whose previous holders had been such eminent scholars. But from the point of view

---

[41] (*Xuzuan*) *Jiangning FZ* 1874, 5:7a–b.

[42] Sun Qiangming, "Xiyin shuyuan dongzhai keyi xu," and Xue Shiyu, "Xiyin shuyuan xizhai keyi xu," both in *Zhongguo jindai jiaoyu shi ziliao huibian*, ed. Zhu Xingui, 293–295.

[43] Elman, *From Philosophy*, 121. Hummel, *Eminent Chinese*, 242, 449. Li Zhaoluo directed Jiyang Academy from 1823 to 1840. See also Feng Guifen, "Gaijian zhengyi shuyuan ji," 301.

[44] *Jiangyin XZ* 1878, 5:21a.

of his previous public service, Li Lianxiu fulfilled well the criteria of an official academy director. Li had in fact already served as the provincial director of education, a post whose status was equal to that of the governor of a province, in both Fujian province (1853–1855) and Jiangsu province (1855–1858). For the thirteen years up to 1878, Li Lianxiu ran Zhongshan Academy, simultaneously serving as director of Xiyin Academy.[45]

His successor as director of Zhongshan Academy in 1879 was to be a scholar-official who also had some official background. Sun Qiangming (H. Chutian, 1817–1901) had supervised the provincial examinations in Guangxi and had been an overseer of the metropolitan examinations. Sun placed a clearly practical emphasis on history as opposed to philosophy in his scholarship and had the same dual function of running two academies at once. Sun Qiangming's scholarship was tied to the Song dynasty Yongjia traditions of his home region, which stressed the value of historical studies. Sun Qiangming, as it happened, had served as an overseer of metropolitan examinations in 1847 when Shen Baozhen (1820–1879) passed his *jinshi* degree. Thirty years later Shen Baozhen, who had become governor-general in Jiangning, appointed Sun Qiangming to the directorship of Zhongshan Academy.[46] Sun Qiangming directed the academy from 1879 to 1884.[47]

Regular essay competitions were a basic method of learning at Zhongshan Academy and at the two other elite academies studied below. But essay competitions were more than a pedagogical tool. At the governor-general's academy the essay examinations since the 1700s had been administered not once but twice a month, a frequency unusual even at better academies. At the first of these examinations a government official such as the Liangjiang governor-general decided the theme for the essay. At the other examination the academy director or his two assistants chose the topic. In addition, Daotais from Anhui and Jiangnan could each fund a special topical exam once a year. All examinations gave the students a chance at significant monetary awards.[48]

---

[45] Wang Shiduo, "Dali siqing Li gong muzhi ming," in *QDZJ* 120:546–547. Miao Quansun, "Qing gu shilang xian Hanlin yuan shidu xueshi Sun Xiansheng muzhi ming," in *QDZJ* 120:547.

[46] Sun Qiangming, "Xiyin shuyuan dongzhai keyi xu," 273–294; Miao Quansun, "Qing gu shilang xian Hanlin yuan shidu xueshi Sun Xiansheng muzhi ming," in *QDZJ* 120:546–547.

[47] Miao Quansun, "Qing gu shilang xian Hanlin yuan shidu xueshi Sun Xiansheng muzhi ming," in *QDZJ* 120:547.

[48] *Shangjiang XZ*, 172; *(Xuzhuan) Jiangning FZ*, 50–51.

After the Taiping war, topics were announced from the governor-general's office on the second day of the month. On the sixteenth day, the second topic was announced from the academy director's office. Students were allowed to work from seven in the morning to seven at night on the essay answers, with a noontime meal—stipulated to include a piece of meat and a bowl of vegetables—provided by the school.[49]

Official controls over these awards were strict. The graded essays were sent to the governor-general's office, where they were inspected before being returned to the office of the Jiangning prefect, who issued the prize money. Careful records on the distribution of the money were required, with copies sent to the governor-general, as well as to the governor of Jiangsu and the governor of Anhui. Such procedures were understandable as the twice-monthly examinations awarded sizable amounts to those who received the highest grades. Everyone who competed got an award, which became a kind of working fellowship pegged to one's grade on the test. The prize money given out annually cost the governor-general a total of 3, 536 taels of silver, three times the amount given out annually as student stipends.[50]

Politically powerful Jiangning city had a cultural life largely dominated by officials. In the post-Taiping era, officials and the scholars they called upon tried to revitalize the strengths in higher education remaining from the reformist Daoguang era. With the best-financed students and the best-financed director, Zhongshan Academy was at the top of the hierarchy of academies in the city. The appointment of Li Lianxiu and Sun Qiangming as directors represented choices of scholars with high-level official experience. Their eminence as scholars allowed them to try to stand on the shoulders of the advances in scholarship for which Zhongshan Academy had been famous earlier in the Qing.

For the students who could get admitted, there was the promise of increased social mobility. The opportunity to enter advanced study at Xiyin Academy once one was a Zhongshan Academy student promised possible access to *jinshi* degrees and advanced academic credentials for scholarly posts and academic patronage positions. Students with three years of training at Zhongshan Academy gained lifelong credentials as a scholarly elite, whether they

49 *(Xuzhuan) Jiangning FZ*, 50–51.

50 *Zhongshan shuyuan zhi*, 9–9b; *Jiangning FZ*, 50–51.

used this training in their native place or elsewhere. Managing local educational or scholarly enterprises was one option, and that included patronized positions as bibliographers for private libraries or editors of family projects. Some might also be awarded appointments to edit or collate official editions of Confucian scholarship, as was the case with the former academy director Wan Huquan from Hubei. Introductions from the well-connected authorities at the academy also opened opportunities to take posts as administrative assistants to officials in the national bureaucracy.

CHAPTER THREE

A Flagship Restoration Academy for Shanghai

Shanghai city in the Yangzi River delta was different from Jiangning city some four hundred miles upriver. Unlike the continuous sustaining influence of official sponsorship of Jiangning academies, Shanghai had long felt the pull away from official direction that was a reality of the commercial activity of the port. While Jiangning's higher education excelled at the elite level after 1864 but county-level academies had more financial difficulties, in the Shanghai area county-level academies mushroomed. Elite higher education came more slowly to Shanghai, with one major exception. In 1864 the Daotai with jurisdiction over Shanghai expressed the need to establish one new first-class classical academy, and by 1865 Longmen Academy was functioning.

Longmen Academy in the Tongzhi Restoration

In the previous century in commercially vibrant Osaka in Japan, a regional academy named Kaitokudo (Cherish Virtue Hall) taught Confucian virtue in a way its merchant-intellectual clientele found relevant.[1] In the Shanghai economic and social environment, a long-term blurring of lines between merchant and gentry had indeed been accelerated by a new interest in Western commerce and technology that arrived as part of the suppression of the Taipings. Would the newly founded regional academy in Shanghai reflect important local merchant interests? Largely because the fourteen-year war of suppression had been fought in the Middle and Lower Yangzi provinces, Shanghai had become a national center of Western knowledge and its propagation. Western arsenals and troops were based there

[1] Tetsuo Najita, *Visions of Virtue in Tokugawa Japan*, 11–15.

and were utilized carefully by the Qing in rooting the Taipings out of Jiangsu. Li Hongzhang began the Shanghai Interpreters' College in 1863 and established the Jiangnan Arsenal in Shanghai in 1865. Translation bureaus and publishing houses in Shanghai then followed.[2] Longmen Academy was founded precisely so that the best in the Confucian tradition would not be overwhelmed by these Western influences found in Shanghai.

Two succeeding Daotais already mentioned allocated the money and appointed the initial directors of Shanghai's Longmen Academy, even though they are more known for fostering the development of Western technical, particularly military, knowledge. In restoration Jiangsu Daotai Ding Richang worked tirelessly for the reestablishment of an effective central government—from the village lecture system up to model standards of provincial judicial and fiscal probity—making sure heterodox Western ideas did not compromise the strengths of the Confucian bureaucratic state.[3] Shen Xianglong (Z. Yuezhai), the top student of the initial 290 select entrance examination candidates for Longmen Academy, later wrote what Ying Baoshi, the new Daotai replacing Ding Richang, told him in an interview about the academy. The student's memoir corroborates Daotai Ying's contemporaneous comments about why Longmen Academy was founded. "[Mr. Ying] thought that from the time Shanghai had begun being active as a commercial port [under the 1842 treaty], its atmosphere had changed too rapidly. In order to stem the tide before it became disastrous, [Ying] founded the [Longmen] Academy."[4] In the thirty years from 1865 to 1895 Longmen Academy flourished as a classical academy, teaching no Western subjects. Confucian humanistic learning was the foundation of the curriculum, and the founders' objectives were realized in that they had endowed one of China's last great classical academies. Merchant influence made no inroads on this traditional curriculum. The academy's success, however, in no way prevented the contemporaneous development of Shanghai as a center propagating publications of the Western Affairs Movement, the 1898 Reform Movement, and finally,

[2] Kuo Ting-yee and Liu Kwang-ching, "Self-strengthening," 499; Biggerstaff, *Modern Government Schools,* 35–36, 157; *SHSTZG* 1:506–525.

[3] A native of Guangdong, Ding had won the patronage of Li Hongzhang as a county magistrate in Jiangxi, and his fortunes rose steadily after the war. In 1868 Ding was made governor of Jiangsu. See Ocko, *Bureaucratic Reform,* 18, 61; *Shanghai XZ* 1870; 9:34; Lu Baoqian, *Qingdai sixiang shi,* 349–361.

[4] Shen Xianglong, "Tandong zashi," *Wenyi zazhi* 9 (1914–1915): 83. For Ying Baoshi's own memoir, see chapter 2, n. 15.

by the first decade of the twentieth century, the movement toward revolution.

Founding Principles

Longmen Academy directors all held *jinshi* degrees and shared many interests with appointed officials of the Lower Yangzi. They could easily agree with the Daotais appointing them on the need for upholding Confucian standards in the midst of rampant Westernization. But they also had their own interests. Their identities as scholars detached from their status in the official class when they insisted that self-cultivation and scholarship supersede any role Longmen Academy might assume in preparing students for vocations in the civil service system. Many academy directors, in fact, were themselves taking refuge from uncomfortable interactions with the centralized government and had not been averse to criticizing officialdom.

Men selected to become directors of Longmen Academy included eminent scholars who had either consistently rejected official appointment and excused themselves from further public service, or, in the case of Sun Qiangming, the former director of Zhongshan Academy, had gravitated to the academic community after censure in the mid-1860s for his inappropriate criticism of a county magistrate.[5] In addition, Yu Yue—perhaps the preeminent academy director of midcentury—might well have been viewed with some apprehension when Daotai Ying Baoshi consulted him on proposed regulations for Longmen Academy: in the 1850s Yu had been permanently prohibited from holding official positions because he posed a provincial examination question judged by a censor to be insulting to the empress.[6]

Longmen's ideals and founding bylaws themselves reveal some tension between scholarly autonomy and state control. When its revised bylaws were printed just before 1870, defiant language regarding the possibility of Longmen Academy teaching the eight-legged essay appeared. These revised bylaws were deposited in the governor-general's office in Jiangning as proof that teaching this vocational technique needed for taking civil service examinations was forbidden at the academy.[7] Scholars at Longmen Academy made sure their new institution protected scholarly prerogatives against

[5] Miao Quansun, "Qing gu shilang xian Hanlin yuan shidu xueshi Sun Xiansheng muzhi ming bei," in *QDZJ* 120:545–546.

[6] Rankin, *Elite Activism*, 134.

[7] Longmen shuyuan, *Xuding Shanghai longmen shuyuan zhangcheng liuze*, 1a.

corrosion from either the political needs of the state or the vocationalism of students:

> In the future the regulations of the academy will be clear to the governor-general and to the governor. If in the future, an official wants to implement the eight-legged essay (*shiwen*), the trustees and enrolled students can refer to the principles [written here]. Or if the trustees and students want to study the eight-legged essay (*shiwen*) or poetry, an official can refer to these precepts and make them public. What is essential is that an academy produce talent. Both substance and function define real learning. Study here is not only aimed at becoming an official. As for the fascination with the eight-legged essay, there are other local academies for that purpose.[8]

From its opening in 1865 to 1895, Longmen Academy sustained a remarkable level of academic excellence. The five directors of this period were eminent scholars, and they enjoyed substantial financial support from sponsoring officials. As earlier in the Qing, Tongzhi Restoration academy directors were not classed as officials; thus all academies, including Longmen, were on the social borderline between state and society.[9] More than a sinecure for retirement, this academy attracted scholarly directors with academic commitment. These directors rejected both the desire of students for vocational education and the urging of the state to make the academy a preparatory school for the civil service examinations. The first director hired by Daotai Ying Baoshi was a Zhejiangese, Gu Guangyu (H. Fangxi 1779–1866), who died within two months of assuming his duties. Nevertheless, Gu Guangyu left a lasting legacy: he wrote the academy bylaws.[10] The second director, Wan Huquan, taught for only half a year because the death of his father required that he return to Hubei for the customary three years of mourning. Then, in 1866, Daotai Ying appointed a Jiangsu native of exceptional renown, Liu Xizai (Z. Rongzhai, 1813–1881), who built the high reputation of Longmen Academy during his fourteen years of leadership.[11]

The first headmaster, Gu Guangyu, stood out in his era as a vocal proponent of adhering to basic Cheng-Zhu school principles in the curriculum.[12] Gu had studied in Jiangsu with Yao Chun (Z.

---

[8] Ibid., 1b–2.

[9] Woodside, "State, Scholars, and Orthodoxy," 166–171.

[10] Qian Mu, *Tongcheng pai wenxue shi*, 5. Longmen shuyuan, *Xuding Shanghai longmen shuyuan kecheng luize*, 4b.

[11] Lu Baoqian, *Qingdai*, 36; Shen Xianglong, "Tandong zashi," *Wenyi zazhi* 9 (1914– 1915): 83, 85.

[12] *QDZJ* 104:332, 17:593, 104:332.

Table 3
Directors of Longmen Academy, 1865–1904

Period in office	Director	Native Place
1865	Gu Guangyu (H. Fangxi)	Zhejiang, Pinghu
1865–1866	Wan Huquan (Z. Qingxuan)	Hubei, Xingguo
1866–1880	Liu Xizai (H. Rongzhai)	Jiangsu, Xinghua
1881–1884	Bao Yuanshen (Z. Huatan)	Anhui, Huzhou
1884–1894	Sun Qiangming (H. Qutian)	Zhejiang, Ruian
1894–1898	Zhu Xiaotang (Z. Xianting)	Jiangxi, Guixi
1898–1900	Wu Dacheng (Z. Qingqing)	Jiangsu, Suzhou
1900–1904	Weng Taofu (Z. Binsun)	Jiangsu, Changshou
1904	Tang Shouqian (Z. Zhen)	Zhejiang, Shanyin

Chunmu), from Songjiang prefecture, who himself was a student of Yao Nai (Z. Xibao, 1730–1815), the composition master of the famous Tongcheng School.[13] Both Gu and the second director of Longmen Academy traced their intellectual lineage explicitly to Zhang Lüxiang, the Cheng-Zhu advocate in the early Qing.[14] Like many Lower Yangzi literati looking for answers to the crisis of the Confucian state, Gu Guangyu found the early Qing an appropriate point of reference.[15]

Gu Guangyu composed the bylaws guiding study at Longmen Academy in conformity with the main ideas Zhang Lüxiang had expressed on academic study. Zhang had insisted particularly upon the place of reflection in mastering classical texts and the essential role of implementing ideas through the student's own behavior.[16] These were ideas explicit in *The Great Learning* and in the writings of Zhu Xi (1130–1200).[17] The opening section of the regulations on study at Longmen Academy, quoted here, were required to be posted at the upper right of each student's desk.

> **Precept one:**
>
> Emphasize implementation. Those studying classical texts should begin with rigorous analysis of the content and then should complete the learning by practicing it.
>
> To know and be able to practice that knowledge is real knowledge.

[13] Shen Xianglong, "Tandong zashi," 85; *QDZJ* 17:593, 94:757.
[14] *QDZJ* 104:332, 7:636.
[15] See Rankin, *Elite Activism*, 121–122.
[16] DeBary, *Message of the Mind*, 145–146.
[17] See Zhu Xi, *Learning to be a Sage*, trans. Daniel Gardner, chap. 7.

According to the *Doctrine of the Mean:* to study broadly, inquire, analyze, and clearly argue an issue should result in earnest practice of what one has learned. Those who want to attain knowledge though learning must reflect to reach that objective. In establishing an academy we ask the students who study the orthodox tradition to better themselves, and thereby not pass along what is bad in one's self. In this way, gradually and through reflection, one can attain sincerity.

If you do not fix your will, you cannot firmly implement what is sought, and practice it. In this case what is analyzed will be of no use. All students should analyze their behavior often to see if it is in conformity with what they study in their books. One must keep what one studies in conformity with one's own behavior or there will be self-recrimination.

Precept two:

Studying should be systematic. First study the *dao* in the *Four Books* and in each classic; then expand your knowledge by studying all the histories, the *Zizhi tongjian* [Comprehensive mirror for aid in government], and Master Zhu's *Gangmu* [Outline]. One can use the following compilations as ladders for assistance: the *Xiaoxue* [Elementary primer]; *Jinsi lu* [Reflections on things at hand]; and various collections on nature and principle.[18] In this way one can use understanding the subtle essence of the principles of morality (*yili*) to direct one's behavior pattern.

Selections from the one hundred philosophers [and from] the classics, histories, and all related practical volumes can be studied according to the ability of the student. After that, remaining energy can be used on composition and on preparation for the civil service exams. One cannot be lazy or inconsistent; and one cannot read carelessly in a variety of books. One progresses according to one's own ability, clarifying the *ti* (substance) and attaining the *yong* (implementation). This will lead to real benefit, and is the right way to approach study.[19]

The Management of Longmen Academy

The Daotai of the Su-Song-Tai region in eastern Jiangsu supervised Longmen Academy throughout the Qing dynasty. After its opening in 1865, Daotai Ying Baoshi moved the institution from

[18] *Xingli zhushu* refers in the text to works in general on *xingli* instead of a single book title.

[19] Longmen shuyuan, *Kecheng liuze,* 1–2a.

borrowed facilities at Ruizhu Academy in Shanghai to its own campus with a dormitory that housed the twenty-six residential stipend students. In 1871 Daotai Tu Zongying was able to add 12,000 treasury taels to Ying's 10,000 and deposit them with a reputable pawnbroker-bank in Shanghai. This investment yielded steady interest for operating expenses.[20] By 1876 thirteen more dormitory rooms were added, and in 1880 the number of residential scholarship students rose to thirty-six.[21] Throughout the history of the academy, operating expenses—excluding monetary awards given as competitive prizes—depended on allocations from monies normally included in the Daotai's budget.[22]

The local board of trustees for Longmen Academy was composed of prominent citizens. The academy regulations reveal some of the functions designated for trustees (*dongshi*). An average county academy would not have had so elaborate a check-and-balance administration of finances as is described below. But the expanding number of county academies probably all employed a gentry manager selected from the local educated elite.

Chief among the functions of Longmen trustees was the administration of the endowment. The business of investing the Daotai's endowment was handled not by underlings in the Daotai's office, but by responsible persons in the office of the Shanghai county government. These county officials selected responsible pawnbrokers and received a formal bankbook for recording all transactions and interest accrued.[23] After these arrangements were made, the county officials were required to report them to the local board of trustees. The trustees, along with one administrator of the academy itself, then requested the withdrawal of funds to run the academy.

Each time there was a withdrawal, the Daotai's office was notified. The four responsible units—the academy administrators, the academy board of trustees, the county official responsible, and the office of the Daotai—served as checks and balances for one

---

[20] *Shanghai XZ* 1871, 9:695; Pan Minde, *Zhongguo jindai diandangye zhi yanjiu 1644–1937*, chap. 2.

[21] *SHSTZG* 1:503; *Songjiang FZ* 1883, 17:1704.

[22] Ying Baoshi, "Xundao Ying Baoshi Longmen shuyuan ji," 9:695.

[23] The system of using pawnbroker houses to provide interest on public funds was called *fashang shengxi*. For a full account, see Pan Minde, *Zhongguo jindai diandangye*, chap. 2, passim. The two pawnbrokers in Shanghai used for Longmen's initial 10,000-tael endowment—Yudingtai and Gongtongchang—produced 1,140 taels in annual interest. Longmen shuyuan, *Kecheng liuze*, 3b–4; T. S. Whelan, *The Pawnshop in China*, 10.

another. Should any trustees resign, for example, the remaining local gentry (*difang shenshi*) on the board would themselves select upstanding and able (*zheng lian ming*) replacements and notify the Daotai and the county officials concerned. The new trustees had to be formally approved by the Daotai's office before they could assume their responsibilities. Similarly, when a change in personnel occurred in either the county or Daotai office, the departing official had to balance the books, write an exit report to the trustees, and then provide an official transcript of the exit report on academy affairs to the incoming official.[24]

Student Selection and Pedagogy

Admission to Longmen was competitive and brought with it substantial stipends of support. In 1865 the Daotai chose the first entering class from candidates who lived within his administrative jurisdiction. Candidates from Suzhou prefecture, Songjiang prefecture, or Taicang department who wanted to compete for residence in the academy and a stipend of four silver taels a month had first to be recommended from the subcounty pools of students. Educational officials at the county level received these names, pruned the list, and forwarded to the Daotai a list of county-recommended candidates. Longmen Academy's first entrance examinations in 1864 elicited 290 student essays. Only twenty students were given stipends. Another twenty-two were allowed to compete for a year in the monthly essay competitions for monetary awards as off-campus Longmen Academy students.[25]

Of the three essays required for the admissions examination in 1864, one had to be written on the crucial Cheng-Zhu principle of abiding in reverent seriousness (*zhu jing*). Zhang Lüxiang regarded this standard orthodox Neo-Confucian concept as the critical point of departure for serious academic study, and Zhang Boxing later insisted upon it to prevent meditation from crossing the line into Chan Buddhist practices.[26] For the second essay, candidates had to write about

---

[24] Longmen shuyuan, *Zhangcheng liuze*, 3b–4a. There is no fixed term for trustee appointments mentioned.

[25] Each month a total of 32.5 taels of silver was awarded as prize money. The top student got a maximum of two taels; the lowest award was half a tael. Forty out of the fifty students were given some monetary award each month (see Longmen shuyuan, *Zhangcheng liuze*, 6).

[26] DeBary, *Message of the Mind*, 145, 190–191. See also K. C. Liu, "Ch'ing Restoration," 489.

the difference between morality and profit; and for the third, on a problem of irrigation.[27]

The number of stipend and off-campus students increased a few per year as facilities and endowment increased. A revised set of academy bylaws written in 1870 stipulated that to renew one's stipend status for a second year required good ranking on the accumulated eight monthly essays one would have taken during the year.[28]

Outside candidates who wanted to become one of the twenty-four off-campus students in 1870 had to submit two former examination papers from another academy (or a civil service examination), then take the sit-down examination on campus. Once accepted as a commuting student, an off-campus applicant who wanted to become one of the elite twenty-six residential students with stipends had to notify the trustees of the institution. All his monthly essays, as well as his marks on his original entrance examination, would then be submitted and reviewed. Such change in status also required a personal recommendation from one of the current residential students attesting to the candidate's scholarship and moral character. Competition among several off-campus students for a residential scholarship would be decided by the academy director in consultation with the Daotai.[29]

The eight monthly essays were a primary pedagogical method at Longmen Academy. Such topical essay examinations were a method of teaching and learning that flourished at good academies in the mid and later Qing dynasty.[30] It was not uncommon to have more than one topic per month, and often two, as we have seen was the case at Zhongshan Academy and at Xiyin Academy in Jiangning. At Longmen Academy the one monthly topic was announced on the thirteenth of each month. Residential students had two days to turn in their answers; more time was allowed for off-campus students, who might live as far away as Suzhou. Decreasing monetary awards were distributed depending upon the rank given one's paper in the monthly grading.[31]

---

[27] Mao Xianglin, "Ji Longmen shuyuan," in *Zhongguo jindai jiaoyu shi ziliao huibian*, ed. Zhu Xingui, 299.

[28] See Longmen shuyuan, *Zhangcheng liuze*, 6.

[29] Ibid., 6b.

[30] Chen Daosheng, "Zhongguo shuyuan jiaoyu xin lun," in *Shida jiaoyu yanjiu suo jikan diyi ji*, 127–129.

[31] Longmen shuyuan, *Zhangcheng liuze*, 66. See also Mao Xianglin, "Ji Longmen shuyuan," 299.

A second pedagogical method accompanied the monthly essay topic. The academy bylaws required students to keep two workbook diaries each day. The first recorded all the day's activities. The other was a notation book of ideas sparked by one's reading. Before the essay topic at midmonth, each student had two tutorial meetings with the academy director to go over these notebooks. On the fifth and tenth of each month the director reacted to how the student used his time, what the student logged as readings covered, and most important, the student's recorded reflections on those readings.[32]

This daily notebook pedagogy was a variation of the daily study timetables used since the Song era to guide individual study in academies.[33] The notation of one's analysis of passages recalls also how Ruan Yuan's pedagogy at Xuehai tang in Guangzhou in 1820 had integrated some evidential research techniques into academy study.[34] Longmen's printed curriculum statement put it this way:

> **Precept three:**
>
> As daily work, all students must record their activities in a diary and keep another diary notebook of daily reading. The activities diary must include early morning, pre-noon, afternoon, and after the lights are lit—four divisions of the day, with appropriate subject entries in each division. Basically, the combined morning hours should be spent on the *Sishu* (Four books); one must go to a second book only when the first is mastered and then do *Xingli* (Nature and principle); every day one should study a few chapters.[35]
>
> In the afternoon the student should study the [standard twenty-four dynastic] *shi* (Histories), and Zhu Xi's *Gangmu*,[36] and [Sima Guang's] *Tongjian*, selecting one book and reading from the beginning, with no skipping. [One] should [also] study the noncanonical Zhou philosophers; the selection of essential points to be studied must be made judiciously. Also one may read current affairs, but

---

32 See the student praise given director Liu Xizai by Shen Xianglong for his care in these tutorials in Shen Xianglong, "Tandong zashi," 83–84. See also Yu Yue on Liu's reading of student work in Yu Yue, "Zuochunfan zuozhongyun Liu jun mu pei," in *Chunzai tang quanshu*, ed. Yu Yue, 2.

33 See Lui, "The Academies," 57–61.

34 See Elman, *From Philosophy*, 174–176; See Liang Qichao, *Intellectual Trends in the Ch'ing Period*, 69–70, 98. See also Man-kam Leung, "Juan Yuan (1764–1849)," appendix 1.

35 See Wing-tsit Chan, "The *Hsing-li ching-i* and the Ch'eng-Chu School of the Seventeenth Century," in *The Unfolding of Neo-Confucianism*, ed. W. T. DeBary, 543; and Zhu Xi, *Sage*, 80–81, on the collections of Song dynasty writings on the school of principle to which this title could refer.

36 This is Zhu Xi's historical textbook, *Tongjian gangmu* (Outline and details of the comprehensive mirror).

> only about actual events. With extra effort one can write compositions—but they must concern principles, and not be careless compositions, or poetry. One can also practice calligraphy—but only the *kaishu* or standard style.
>
> After the lights are on, one might work on civil service career preparation—one must know how former scholars explained the principles of morality (*yili*).
>
> Although there are differences in divisions of the day, one must always be busy. Every subject and activity must be recorded, so that what is learned from study and what one questions must be recorded daily in the notation book. What one records must not be fabricated and must not be written in tedious detail. One must avoid pretexts for not making entries. Every fifth and tenth day one must submit the diaries to the teacher and get advice about the contents. The teacher will direct activity and give reactions to the entries.
>
> Every month there will be a topical essay, and at the end of the year all these essays will be ranked, according to the depth or superficiality of the essay, and the students evaluated accordingly to determine retention or dismissal.[37]

A third and more traditional pedagogical practice at classical academies was combined with the more important monthly essay topics and daily diaries. The lectures of a master teacher had been important in pre-Qing academies, and when Liu Xizai was director at Longmen, he spoke to the students at least every five days on selected topics.[38]

Thus the pedagogy at Longmen Academy, laid out in the bylaws, assumed a curriculum of orthodox Neo-Confucian texts. Reading centered on the canon of Confucian classics, with the central place given to the *Four Books*. Analysis of historical texts was essential, and philosophical texts from Song *xingli xue* (the school of principle) were also singled out. The academicians at Longmen believed that the rigorous study of these materials would prepare scholars and leaders of moral excellence rather than job-seeking bureaucrats.[39]

Confucian Cultivation in the Yangzi Delta

The three Longmen Academy directors during the years from 1865 to 1894 were exemplary academics. Liu Xizai had skyrocketed in his earlier career to a court position tutoring the future Xianfeng

---

[37] Longmen shuyuan, *Kecheng liuze*, 2a.

[38] Hu Chuan, "Dunfu nianpu," 222. See also Chen Daosheng, "Zhongguo shuyuan," 127–128.

[39] Ying Baoshi, "Ying Baoshi Longmen," 9:34b; *SHSTZG* 1:503.

emperor. But when given the chance at age fifty-two to excuse himself from public life, he eagerly devoted himself to teaching and scholarship. His dedication—from diligently correcting student submissions to checking on them at their dormitories at two or three in the morning—was much commented upon by students and colleagues.

Liu Xizai seldom wrote about current affairs and never commented on Westernization. But he once lost his temper and refused further contact with a foreigner whose frustration at not gaining access to an interview with Director Liu led the foreigner to burst unannounced one day into the academy director's office. Director Liu stopped him in his tracks with the statement that he had nothing to discuss with so impolite a person. The anecdote underlines the confidence in Confucian values that this dedicated teacher maintained in a period of national crisis.[40]

The difficulty of living at the interface of tradition and Westernization in Shanghai was perhaps most poignantly illustrated when Liu fell ill in 1880. He had just been recommended for director at Zhongshan Academy in Jiangning when his infirmity became so extreme that he was forced to take leave of his fourteen-year directorship at Longmen Academy to try to return to his native county north of Yangzhou. His close friend who headed the Jiangnan Arsenal in Shanghai offered him the arsenal's steamboat to go up the Yangzi. Liu Xizai, whose illness had no cure, was too frail to resist this symbol of a different kind of learning. He was accompanied as far as Suzhou by the director of the arsenal. Not long after Liu's arrival in his home county north of Yangzhou, the arsenal director had to write a funerary inscription for Liu Xizai.

With Liu Xizai's appointment to Longmen Academy in 1866, officialdom in Shanghai had hired China's best to preserve traditional education against a surging current of commercialism, industrialization, and new political and ethical ideas. Director Liu Xizai sailed his last voyage against that current in 1880, away from the coast and past Jiangnan strongholds of Confucian scholarship earlier in the Qing: Suzhou, Changzhou, and Yangzhou, to find refuge and final rest in the more undisturbed hinterland of northern Jiangsu.[41]

---

[40] Xiao Mu, "Liu Rongzhai zhongyun biezhuan," in *Jingfu leigao*, 25b.

[41] Ibid. For further details on his life, see Wang Qizhong, *Liu Xizai he yigai*, passim. Xinghua county where he died had produced the famous Qing calligrapher Zheng Banqiao (1693–1765).

Longmen Academy's director in 1880 became Bao Yuanshen (Z. Huatan), a *jinshi* from Anhui, who had served as Jiangsu provincial director of education from 1866 to 1867. Bao was known for having addressed the national restoration objectives of reviving learning and fostering talent by re-publication of the classics and histories.[42] The Suzhou publishing house printed these major texts so that scholars in the six major prefectures (the five south of the Yangzi River plus Yangzhou) in Jiangsu would have materials to study.

In 1884 Sun Qiangming, the man who had directed Zhongshan Academy when Li Lianxiu left in 1878, took over in Shanghai from Bao Yuanshen and began a decade-long directorship at Longmen Academy. Like Liu Xizai's, Sun's reputation was preeminent among Lower Yangzi literati. During Sun's tenure, an event occurred that reflected upon his attitude toward the Western presence in Shanghai—a subject he also did not otherwise address. Because admission to Longmen, as well as to another academy Sun served for a period in Shanghai, was so competitive, a candidate for one of these institutions tried an unusual tactic: he had an added letter of recommendation sent to Director Sun from a foreign consul stationed in Shanghai. Sun Qiangming summarily threw the recommendation in the trash can and refused the student admission.[43]

Like Liu Xizai, Sun was confident of the strengths of the Confucian tradition as the West encroached. Yet events of Sun's own career symbolized the larger problem of expecting revitalized Confucian education to correct weaknesses in the Qing dynasty. The problem was not the new impact of Western alternatives as much as the difficulty of reversing the decline of institutions in the Qing polity. Following his *jinshi* degree in 1841 Sun had accepted official posts. But with the midcentury popular uprisings, he returned to his home county of Ruian, Zhejiang, where he led local militia defense efforts from 1853 to 1862.[44] In 1863 Sun began again to supervise examinations as he had in Guangxi before the war. But the Lower Yangzi was plagued with a widespread decline in local government—derived in part from the sale of local administrative posts such as county magistracies that increased after the Taiping War began—and

[42] Bao Yuanshen, "Qing gou kan jing shi shu," in *Huang chao jingshi wen bian xubian*, ed. Sheng Kang, 371–374.

[43] Hu Huaichen, "Xuexiao shenghuo yu shuyuan shenghuo," in *Shanghai yanjiu ziliao*, 162–163.

[44] Sun had led local gentry himself in suppressing the Gold Coin Society rebellion during the Taiping era. See Rankin, *Elite Activism*, 116ff. See also Liu Zhufeng, "Qianfei jilue," in *Oufeng zazhi huikan*, 1–17b.

Sun could not contain his criticism of the poor local administration in his home of Ruian.[45] It was this speaking out of place in criticism of a Ruian magistrate that caused superiors to censure Sun Qiangming, thus preventing him from holding official posts again.[46]

This talented man then dedicated himself to teaching in top Jiangsu academies, which after all aimed to produce the kind of moral and intellectual quality he saw lacking around him. In 1896, when he was seventy-nine, Sun Qiangming's censure was belatedly reversed by the Qing court. He was given high rank and in 1900 was even presented an honorary title on the sixtieth anniversary of his *jinshi* degree. Rehabilitation was apparently welcomed by this man who throughout his career had striven for the most effective possible internal rebuilding of the post-Taiping state. When the court retreated to Xi'an in that same year, this seasoned militia leader from the Taiping era wept openly. He subsequently fell ill, and symbolic of the dream of the revitalized Confucian state itself, Sun Qiangming died in 1901.[47]

---

45 K. C. Liu, "Ch'ing Restoration," 478–479. Frank A. Lowjewski, "Ting Jih-ch'ang in Kiangsu: Traditional Methods of Surmounting Dysfunction in Local Administration during the Late-Ch'ing Period," *Jindai shi yanjiu suo qikan* 8 (1979): 235–253; Ocko, *Bureaucratic Reform*, chap. 6.

46 Rankin, *Elite Activism*, 132.

47 Qian Mu, *Tongcheng pai wenxue shi*, 5; Longmen shuyuan, *Xuding kecheng*, 4b.

CHAPTER FOUR

The Founding of a New Provincewide Academy in 1884

In 1884 the collaboration of Zuo Zongtang (1832–1885) and Huang Tifang (Z. Shulan, 1832–1899) in founding an exceptional classical academy reflected their shared frustration with ineffective reforms and incompetence since the suppression of the Taipings in 1864. Huang had been made the Jiangsu provincial director of education in 1880, after some fifteen years as a leader of critical dissent of national policy and personages from his post in the Hanlin Academy in Beijing. He had helped lead the Qingliu movement, which formed in the 1870s when normal *qingyi* (pure discussion) disagreements within the bureaucracy swelled into a campaign of dissent.[1] It was Huang Tifang who proposed the new academy, and he secured the strong endorsement of Zuo Zongtang, who was the governor-general of the Liangjiang provinces following 1881.[2]

---

[1] Qingliu partisans attacked bureaucratic corruption and were responsible for removing four presidents of boards in Beijing. Huang Tifang himself was indicted in 1878 for denouncing the maladministration of famine relief in North China. He was protected from prosecution by his influential Qingliu, and native Manchu, friend, Baoting. See Hummel, *Eminent Chinese*, 48, 348–349; Mary Rankin, "Public Opinion and Political Power: *Qingyi* in Late Nineteenth-Century China," *Journal of Asian Studies* 41.3 (1982): 453–454, 463; Lloyd Eastman, *Throne and Mandarins: China's Search for a Policy during the Sino-French Controversy, 1880–1885*, 1–29; John E. Schrecker, "The Reform Movement of 1898 and the *Qingyi* Reform as Opposition," in *Reform in Nineteenth-Century China*, ed. John E. Schrecker and Paul Cohen, 289–306; Tang Zhijun, *Wuxu bianfa shi*, 334–344.

[2] Six stone inscriptions remain at the academy site along the Yangzi River. They are cited as steles when they have not been found in published form or vary from a later printed version. See Huang Tifang, "Nanjing shuyuan bei ji," stele inscriptions; Zuo Zongtang, "Jiang tang," stele inscription, rpt. in *Nanjing*, vol. 35 (1935), n.p., and in Yang Shulin, ed., *Zuo Wenxiang gong chuan ji*, as "Nanjing shuyuan ti e bawei" (Inscription for Southern Quintessence Academy) (Taibei: Wenhai, 1979), 6:2633.

In 1883 Zuo noted that Huang, on becoming director of education three years before, had found Jiangsu students poorly prepared for the eight prefectural *shengyuan* examinations he supervised.[3] Other sources confirm that Huang had indeed imposed rigorous new standards for aspiring Jiangsu literati. In previously distinguished Changzhou prefecture, for example, which had eight counties, no one was passed in the first *shengyuan* examinations directed by Huang Tifang. In addition Huang initiated an oral examination to follow the written test, so rote memorization would not get one through the eight-legged essay exercise at the *shengyuan* level.[4] Such rigor undoubtedly impressed Zuo and made him receptive when Huang Tifang proposed building a classical academy within Zuo's jurisdiction.

In his public endorsement of the new academy, Zuo revealed his motivation for supporting it. He was no stranger to promoting the study of modern Western technology and the study of foreign languages. He had launched a school at the Fuzhou Navy Yard with just these objectives in 1866.[5] But, in his commemorative essay at the time of the founding of Southern Quintessence Academy (Nanjing shuyuan),[6] he noted that many Western Affairs advocates had turned abroad even for their accreditation as scholars, neglecting the classical Confucian tradition. The arguments of such young men seemed to Zuo to be directed primarily at popular acceptance and failed altogether to address constructively the critical problems facing China.[7]

Proponents of the *jingshi* (practical studies or statecraft) emphasis in Confucianism had also reemerged in Zuo's lifetime. Men such as Gong Zizhen (1792–1841) and Wei Yuan (1794–1856) had inveighed against the scholastic sterility of some Han learning scholars, and Zuo

---

3 Zuo Zongtang, "Jiang tang."

4 The oral examination demanded the candidate explicate the first couplet of his eight-character essay, to demonstrate that it was not simply memorized. This oral test was called *tifu zhi*. Mr. Yin Baoxian left a personal journal of his life's activities that was privately published by his family about 1930 in Shanghai. I would like to thank Professor Richard Y. C. Yin, his grandson and a professor of economics at George Washington University, for kindly allowing me to read this document. Yin Baoxian, *Zhui yi lu*, 21a.

5 Suzanne Wilson Barnett, "Biographical Notices and Modern Education in Local Gazetteers of Nineteenth-Century Foochow," *Hanxue yanjiu* 3.2 (1985): 771–796.

6 The compound used in the reference naming the academy, *jinghua* (quintessence), requires the pronunciation of *jing* rather than *qing*; see ZWDCD, *Zongwen da cidian* (Taibei, 1973), 12297–98. The origin of the name of Southern Quintessence Academy will be discussed below.

7 Zuo Zongtang, "Jiang tang"; Wright, *Last Stand*, 132.

approved of such critiques.[8] But statecraft proposals had degenerated, Zuo felt, into simplistic panaceas for the ills of the Qing dynasty. Superficial Confucianism, confounded by the same careerism that plagued the Western Affairs reformers, weakened the overall contribution of the *jingshi* proponents. Their efforts resulted only in divisive factionalism.

Zuo's blunt critiques rested upon an unswerving faith in the basic principles of Cheng-Zhu Neo-Confucianism. His advice for the new academy was to avoid reform fads and return to the moral concerns of Cheng-Zhu learning. To make his point, he commented on Jiyang Academy, which after the Taiping destruction had been reorganized into a new institution in the same town where Southern Quintessence Academy was to be built. Director Li Zhaoluo had raised Jiyang shuyuan to prominence before 1840 and trained academic leaders such as Feng Guifen and Li Lianxiu. Zuo praised the wide-ranging teaching of Li Zhaoluo—which had stressed geography, local history, and a synthesis of Song and Han learning—because Li applied theoretical principles to human experience in his teaching. But, Zuo noted with disappointment, Li Zhaoluo's teaching, with its unswerving commitment to the Cheng-Zhu school of Neo-Confucianism, was shared by few of the academy directors of his time.[9]

Zuo Zongtang's own preferences within Confucianism had been formed when he taught in Hunan in 1837 at the same academy as Tao Zhu. Zuo Zongtang favored the liberating, easy style of Tongcheng composition and its implicit revival of Cheng-Zhu thought. In 1866 he had to leave the Fuzhou Navy Yard school he had just established, but he named the Chinese Studies division after the great Qing Cheng-Zhu advocate Zhang Boxing, who had once taught in Fuzhou. In the Southern Quintessence Academy founding documents, Zuo Zongtang advises the students to study Fang Bao's manuals on examination essays, again endorsing Tongcheng and Cheng-Zhu themes in Neo-Confucianism.[10]

---

[8] Zuo Zongtang, "Jiang tang"; Elman, *From Philosophy*, 235–241.

[9] Zuo Zongtang, "Jiang tang"; Huang Tifang, "Nanjing shuyuan"; Elman, *From Philosophy*, 121; Liu Yizheng, "Jiangsu shuyuan zhi chugao," 62. I appreciate the very helpful analysis of Zuo Zongtang's phrasing in this document gained through discussion of it with Dr. Lin Man-houng at the Institute of Modern History in Taiwan.

[10] Hummel, *Eminent Chinese*, 763–764; Barnett, "Biographical Notices," 778. Zuo Zongtang, "Jiang tang," in *Zuo Wenxiang gong quanji*, ed. Yang Shulin, 6:2633. Zuo Zongtang taught Tao Zhu's son at the Hunan academy after Tao Zhu died.

When Provincial Director of Education Huang Tifang wrote to Governor-general Zuo Zongtang to ask for support, he proposed that the projected institution be set up as an elite academy much like Hangzhou's Gujing jingshe had been in 1801 and as Xiyin and Longmen academies currently were. Specialized study of issues in classical scholarship and a curriculum centered on the classics and history, rather than practice of the eight-legged essay, reserved the proposed Southern Quintessence Academy for graduate-level study and research. To make sure that the pool of students was broad and select, Huang Tifang and Zuo Zongtang stipulated that candidates from the entire province could apply for admission.[11]

The clientele within the Jiangsu educated elite who needed opportunities for advanced study had been rising annually. Provincial Director of Education Huang acknowledged this need in Jiangsu when he announced his plans for the new academy in 1881 to a select group of the local elite in Jiangyin town: "Scholars are the teachers of the people. But just as the people need the educated to begin learning, so the educated require study to become scholars. Now if there are aspiring scholars and no facilities in which they can study, it becomes the responsibility of the official of that region to do something."[12]

From their national experience with reform Zuo and Huang brought to the Southern Quintessence Academy project a sense that selfish interest had plagued post-Taiping reform. Although Zuo had been directing troops in Xinjiang when the broad Qingliu critique of Beijing's incompetent leadership formed, he was sympathetic to Huang's views in 1882. The symbolism inherent in the academy's name focused on the pure quality of southern scholarship, and it might, in fact, have even evoked comparisons with southern-faction Qingliu critics who had raised issues regarding the legitimacy of the 1874 Guangxu imperial succession and hence about the moral authority of the court further north in Beijing. Critics tied the ineffective management of floods and foreigners in the recent past to closer signs of poor administration such as the rise in the sale of degrees and new offices. Meanwhile, new officially sponsored schools of translation and technology did not seem to be producing leaders who could correct the overall decline of the state.[13]

---

11 Zuo Zongtang, "Jiangyin chuangjian," 2455.

12 Zhang Wenhu, "Nanjing shuyuan ji," stele inscription.

13 Rankin, "Public Opinion," 463–464; Bastid-Bruguière, "Social Change," 537–538.

What was the explicit southern symbolism of Southern Quintessence Academy? The statement by Zhu Xi from which Huang Tifang had derived the name—"Nanfang zhi xue, de qi jinghua zhe" (Southern scholarship achieves that which is quintessential)—was made when Zhu Xi visited the Changshou town shrine of Yan Zi, one of Confucius's disciples. The visit was after the Northern Song had been forced to move its capital south of the Yangzi.[14] In 1885 Huang Yizhou (Z. Yuantong, 1828–1899), the second director at Southern Quintessence, further noted that in Zhu Xi's essay, written after 1175, Zhu Xi referred to a certain legacy in southern scholarship typified by Yan Zi. That legacy was the ability of many Southern scholars to grasp the essence of an issue without getting bogged down in tedious detail. Yan Zi himself was known to be quick in apprehending the way, and he did not let form obscure its apprehension, noted Huang Yizhou. Then Huang Yizhou recommended that Yan Zi, because he was from nearby Changshou county in Suzhou prefecture, be made a patron sage of Southern Quintessence Academy along with Zhu Xi and Zheng Xuan (127–200).[15]

Huang Tifang's proposal to name the academy from Zhu Xi's quotation was not made to recapture any specific content of southern scholarship at Southern Quintessence Academy, for the mixing of

---

[14] Yan Zi, also called Ziyou, was born in 506 B.C.E. Huang Tifang changed one character, *jing*, in Zhu Xi's phrase that, extracted in a title might have implied southern spirits or ghosts. The character he replaced it with was synonymous with the meaning of quintessence meant by Zhu Xi and became the second character in the academy's name, Nanjing shuyuan. The new character also had a double meaning because of an allusion to a section of the *Shi jing* (Book of poetry) in which the luxuriant growth of the artemisia plant is used metaphorically to mean men who will encourage learning. See Zhang Wenhu, "Nanjing shuyuan ji," stele inscription.

[15] Huang Tifang, "Nanjing shuyuan"; Zhu Xi, "Pingjiang fu Changzhou xianxue Wu gong ciji," in *Zhu wengong wenji,* 1456–1457; Huang Yizhou, "Nanjing shuyuan jiangxue bei ji," stele inscription, rpt. in *JJZZ.* This legacy of southern Confucianism in which the *dao* is directly apprehended had been described before Zhu Xi by Li Yanshou, the Tang dynasty historian. Academy director Huang Yizhou thought that both Zhu Xi and academy founder Huang Tifang knew that Li Yanshou's description of southern scholarship was the *locus classicus* of what was quintessential about southern scholarship. The scholarship of the Southern Dynasties (420–581) differed from scholarship in the north, according to Li Yanshou, precisely because southerners had the distinctive ability to pull together what underlay an issue, come to the point concisely, and thereby grasp the essence of an issue. In contrast, wrote Li Yanshou, Northern Dynasty scholarship delighted in full elaboration and exhaustion of detail. See Huang Yizhou, "Nanjing shuyuan jiangxue bei ji."

strengths from northern and southern schools had long since made these Sui and Tang distinctions inaccurate as descriptions of more modern schools of scholarship.[16] Similarly, Academy Director Huang Yizhou had explained his suggestion to add academy veneration of Yan Zi by saying he liked having some localized progenitor of the southern tradition as a patron sage, because the other academy in town, which succeeded Li Zhaoluo's Jiyang Academy, venerated Wu Jizha, a Warring States prince and exemplar of Confucian virtues buried nearby.[17] Both academies would thus have local figures to venerate.[18]

Still, tying the new academy to southern scholarship was an astute move. The community of scholars in the Lower Yangzi in the nineteenth century identified with a southern tradition that had protected, fostered, and preserved Chinese culture in an era when the influence of foreigners made northern culture suspect. Zhu Xi, after all, had reasserted the importance of a southerner, Yan Zi, in the midst of the political crisis of the 1100s, when foreign influence in the north made the Southern Song dynasty the repository of Chinese culture: they would venerate Yan Zi as well.

With the Confucian bureaucratic state in the balance, Huang Tifang made clear in 1884 that Confucian training was the right antidote for weaknesses in China's leadership. The point applied equally as well to the mismanagement of domestic issues that had long concerned him as to the mishandling of foreign powers: "Those who master only one classic awaken in themselves the inner spark possessed by the sages of antiquity. Those who grasp one of the [six] arts forget their sense of self-interest." As for the relevance of this training to society, Provincial Director of Education Huang stated simply: "How can one compare a sage who has transcended self-interest to someone who, by deviance or conniving, is seeking his own advantage?"[19]

---

16 Liu Shipei, "Nanbei xuepai butong lun," in Liu Shipei, *Liu Shenqi xiansheng yishu*, 1:667.

17 Wu Jizha was the youngest brother of the king of the state of Wu, Zhu Fan. Zhu Fan died in 546 B.C.E., but Jizi zha refused to assume power as his elder brother had arranged. See Sima Qian, *Shiji*, 86, 1016.

18 Huang Yizhou, "Nanjing shuyuan jiangxue bei ji."

19 Huang Tifang, "Nanjing shuyuan." The six arts of the Zhou period were propriety, music, archery, chariot driving, calligraphy, and mathematics.

Southern Quintessence Academy's Financing and Student Recruitment

By 1881, when plans began to establish Southern Quintessence Academy, not only had there been a general recovery of the economy in the Jiangyin town area, but there had been a revitalization of the management of many old local enterprises. As the initial Southern Quintessence director, Zhang Wenhu (1808–1885), described conditions around 1881: "From the destruction by the bandits on, gentry clans were dispersed. Now in addition to restoring organizations and crafts, there is new management of old endeavors."[20] Provincial Director of Education Huang called together four native townsmen to promote the founding of Southern Quintessence Academy in 1881. Two men were specifically identified as local elite figures with scholarly credentials (the Chinese expression had four characters, *xueshi shenshi*). The two other local figures were a man named Cao, who ended up managing the construction, and a gentry figure of high reputation.

Statements regarding who was to provide the financial support for the new institution appear in the founding-stone inscriptions. The steles remained on public display a century later at the academy site, which had been occupied since 1911 by high school–level institutions retaining the name Southern Quintessence. The first statement, made by the founder, asserted that the funds to build the academy, maintain it, and pay student and faculty stipends were to come through his office as provincial director of education from exclusively public and official sources. "I shall write letters to ask governors, and both military and civilian officials, within the province and without, to donate what they can from their budgets," Huang announced in the same statement. At the same time, he explicitly excluded private contributions: "If some people are willing to donate their lands or houses, we cannot accept them."[21] To prove his sincerity, Huang had the solicited contributions cut into another stele. The list was headed by 20,000 taels of silver from Governor-general Zuo Zongtang.[22]

[20] Zhang Wenhu, stele inscription; see *JYXZXZ* 6 (1921): 4b. The redefined version of Li Zhaoluo's Jiyang Academy had managed to reopen in town in 1872. See ibid.

[21] Huang Tifang, "Xuezheng Tifang wei chuanjian Nanjing shuyuan shaoshi bei," stele inscription.

[22] Other contributions were registered from the governor-general's office of Lianghu; the governors' offices of Jiangsu, Anhui, and Hubei; the two lieutenant governors

Director Huang Tifang might be assumed to have promoted some degree of autonomous gentry management of the new institution—which was a trait of some *qingyi* proposals and which had also been promoted by acquaintances in his home county of Ruian, Zhejiang.[23] But such was not the case. Huang founded a formidable institution in a relatively rural county, but one with a rather exclusive alliance with, and commitment to, national direction and financing.

The impressive amount given by Zuo Zongtang had been collected from the northern Jiangsu salt tax. Zuo directed that the 20,000 taels be invested with local pawnbroker banks. The annual interest would go into the annual budget to pay faculty salaries and student stipends at the new institution. The land for building Southern Quintessence Academy was the site of the former Yangzi Admiralty (Changjiang shaishi jingkou yin youji shu), which was donated by Zuo as well. Huang Tifang further asked officials in various provinces to contribute copies of rare books and of standard works available from their woodblocks for the academy's library.[24]

Huang Tifang's definition of the public character of his institution demonstrates an anxiety about the potentially shortsighted, selfish interests of some of the region's expanding local elite. Huang felt it important to exclude gentry contributions and any other special-interest monies. Even within official contributions, he noted that his superordinate status as a national official supervising the founding was essential to assure that there would be equity. County officials who had given funds and who felt they may have given disproportionately after all the gifts had been announced should know that he, as director, had overseen the solicitations to ensure that amounts of donations had been judiciously sought and given. He pointed out that as long as these decisions were the product of his impartial judgment as a national official and the amounts were in no way left to local bartering, everyone could be assured of equity. "If this matter is handled by the people [more locally], there will be conflicts, and the whole program to solicit official funds will become unmanageable."[25]

A second statement in the founding inscriptions of the academy assured the surrounding peasantry that no public funds that otherwise might be used for the ordinary people were to be diverted to

---

23 Rankin, "Public Opinion," 459–462.

24 Zuo Zongtang, "Jiangyin chuangjian," 2455; idem, "Jiang tang," stele inscription; Zhang Wenhu, "Nanjing shuyuan ji," stele inscription; *JYXZXZ* 6:2.

25 Huang Tifang, "Xuezheng Tifang," stele inscription.

build the new academy. Huang Tifang made it clear that even if donations could not support expenses in the future, academy officials should petition his office for additional funds. "No matter what happens," he noted, "the funding to be used for the people cannot be withdrawn" to aid the academy.[26] His forthright argument on this point supports the argument that the Tongzhi Restoration in the near-by Suzhou region may have left the farmers extremely sensitive to the question of at whose expense the restrengthening of the region was to be accomplished.[27] As Huang Tifang put it in 1885, "Not a piece of string nor a grain of millet should be taken from the ordinary people (*min*)."[28]

This issue did not disappear in the Lower Yangzi. Twenty years later, in the final decade of the Qing, poor handling of taxes to finance new public schools led to some 120 antischool riots in China as a whole from 1904 to 1910—sixty-six of which took place in Jiangsu and Zhejiang.[29]

The original donations solicited from public officials by Huang Tifang had totaled some 54,912,516 wen of copper cash. Just over one-third were used in construction costs—including furnishing the academy's facilities. The remaining thirty-nine million pieces of copper cash from official donations provided the initial academy endowment. From this fund, fifty student stipends were given out annually as residential scholarships. These covered room and board, with an added five thousand in cash (about five silver taels) given scholars for personal expenses each of the ten months of the academic year.[30] This was more than a living wage; yet after 1888 when a landed endowment was purchased for the academy, the monthly stipend was increased to seven thousand wen of copper.[31]

Such handsome stipends were a mechanism for recruitment. The response to Huang Tifang's call for applications was described by the first director with the classical allusion to "raining grain," originally applied to the invention of writing in China.[32] The provincial director

---

26 Ibid.

27 See Polachek, "Gentry Hegemony," 213–217.

28 Huang Tifang, "Xuezheng Tifang," stele inscription.

29 Abe Hiroshi, "Shimmatsu no kigaku bodo," in *Kindai Ajia kyoiku kenkyu*, ed. Taga Akigoro, 70, 77. Southern Quintessence later acquired a landed endowment from official sources.

30 Huang Tifang, "Xuezheng Tifang," stele inscription; *JYXZXZ* 6:2b.

31 *JYXZXZ* 6:3a.

32 Zhang interpreted some spring hail figuratively by referring to the passage in the *Huainan zi*, in which Cang Jie's invention of writing is referred to as "raining grain"; see *ZWDCD* 9:15703; Zhang Wenhu, stele inscription.

of education, from his government office in Jiangyin town, acted as the director of admissions for the incoming class. He would decide, upon recommendation of the director or his assistants, who in the previous class should have their stipends renewed and which new students should receive full scholarships.[33]

Of those applicants not qualifying for the benefits of the fifty to eighty residential stipend holders (which expanded as facilities became available), some forty-six more were admitted with no money or housing but with the right to compete for the lucrative monthly essay prizes.[34] These cash prizes began at eight thousand pieces of copper cash for first place. Progressively lower amounts—including wine—were given each month to twenty candidates in classics and another thirty in the broader subject of antiquities (*guxue*). When put with the residential stipend, monthly cash prizes added up to significant material incentives for prospective students.[35]

One group of accomplished students was even automatically admitted. These were the first-place winners in two different public civil service examinations administered by the director of education in the various prefectural capitals of Jiangsu province every two out of three years. These awards were not given to those who had just been awarded their degrees. Rather, one of these awards was allocated to the individual who scored highest on the *kekao* examination, given to *shengyuan* who wanted to qualify for the provincial-level examinations and compete for the *juren* degree. The top candidate in this triennial exam was offered a full residential scholarship at the academy. The other award was given in the *suikao* (periodic examinations), held for all *shengyuan* who wanted to retain their status. The top candidate in this triennial examination was also offered a full residential scholarship. Besides these obviously well-qualified first-place winners, it was also conceivable for holders of the *juren* degree and other select students personally recommended by the director or an assisting teacher to be admitted.[36]

Because of the close ties to sponsorship by the highest educational official in the province, patronage prospects would also attract students to Jiangyin town. This unstated incentive was an added inducement to seek admission to Southern Quintessence Academy.

33 *JYXZXZ* 6:3a.

34 The exact number of nonresident students varied by year. In 1890 the number off-campus was forty-six. See *JYXZXZ* 6:3a.

35 Yin Baoxian, *Zhui yilu*, 37; *JYXZXZ* 6:2b–3a; Wu Xinlei, "Nanjing shuyuan di xueshu yanjiu ji qi dui wenhua jie di gongxian," *Nanjing daxue xuebao* 2 (1985): 18.

36 *JYXZXZ* 6:2b; Wu Xinlei, "Nanjing shuyuan," 17; Zi, *Pratique*, 79–80, 97–99.

The firsthand knowledge of *shengyuan* candidates from throughout the province that the director of education in every province had became an important source of patron-client relationships for many of those who succeeded in the examinations that earned *shengyuan* status. The teacher-disciple relationship emerged from the prefectural-level examinations and established a lasting relationship between the provincial director of education and talented individuals in his province.[37] In the nineteenth century these patron-client responsibilities were sometimes abused by successful candidates who invoked the connection to get favored treatment later.[38]

Large scholarly projects were begun at the academy under Wang Xianqian (1842–1918), the successor to Huang Tifang as Jiangsu provincial director of education. Initiating ambitious scholarly compilations provided ample opportunity for Wang to hire some able academy students who needed extra money. The academic patronage network that existed outside of official posts was common in the Qing. Even Zhang Wenhu, Southern Quintessence Academy's first headmaster, lived for years on such patronage before he was selected to direct the academy.[39] Even without attaining *juren* status, a former student at Southern Quintessence Academy could expect to lean on the reputation and connections of his academic institution in stepping into the late-Qing job market. The relationship between the Jiangyin-based director of education and Southern Quintessence students was particularly close. The director had sometimes selected the topics for monthly essay examinations at the academy and was also known to read some submissions.[40] In fact, when the director of education's office was removed from the town by reform edict in 1906, a crisis ensued at the academy in which the unstated tie of Southern Quintessence Academy to the patronage from the director's office became clearer.[41]

The Academy Endowment

During the three years Wang Xianqian directed education in the province, 1885–1888, Southern Quintessence Academy developed a

37 Man-kam Leung, "Juan Yuan," 37–39.

38 Susan Mann Jones and Philip A. Kuhn, "Dynastic Decline and the Roots of Rebellion," in *The Cambridge History of China*, ed. John K. Fairbank and Kwang-ching Liu, 10.1:115–116.

39 Miao Quansun, "Zhoupan xian houxuan taodao Zhang xiansheng muzhi ming," in *YFTXJ* 1:16a–b.

40 Huang Yizhou, "Nanjing jiangshe wenji xu," lb; Yin Baoxian, *Zhui yilu*, 37b.

41 This crisis will be treated in chapter 6.

stable financial endowment and became nationally prominent as a center of significant academic publications. Wang also acquired a landed endowment by matching the gifts of two benefactors. Thereafter, harvests from the academy *shatian* (polder field) were sold for income that covered annual operations, and profits were plowed into new land purchases and into more interest-bearing investments with local pawnbroker-banks.

The question of whether gentry interests began to subvert the gentry-free founding principles of the academy was, however, raised by the land grant from the two benefactors. In 1881 the lieutenant governor (*buzheng shi*) of Jiangsu commissioned two men to assess the value of a growing sandbar island that had been used only by local brush farmers since its appearance at the mouth of the Yangzi in the Daoguang era. The area was surveyed as containing 40,000 *mu* of land, and the two men recommended it be sold publicly. They set the price at 12,000 taels of silver. Litigation began immediately, however, over which local landlord would get to purchase the property. After negotiating conflicting offers and claims, the two men finally recommended that if the director of education would give half of the capital (6,000 taels), they themselves would donate the rest and make the new public academy in Jiangyin the owner of a permanent landed endowment. Consequently, a total price of 12,000 taels, from these men and the director of education, was paid to the provincial lieutenant governor for the new landed endowment of Southern Quintessence Academy.[42]

The two benefactors had claims to official rank rather than just representing local wealth and status. One, Fei Xuezeng, was a river Daotai (*he dao*) in Zhili province and had received a *jinshi* degree in 1819. Fei Xuezeng was from the same prefecture as Jiangyin (Changzhou), but he had no discernible relationship to Southern Quintessence Academy before his donation.[43] The other benefactor,

[42] Wang Xianqian, "Nanjing shatian ji," stele inscription; Dzung Zung (Zheng Jun), "Two Whites: The Future Policy of Nan-tsin School," *Nanjing* 7 (1924): 5.

[43] He was a native of nearby Yanghu district in Changzhou prefecture, and his sons later took some interest in the academy. One son, Fei Nianci (*jinshi* of 1889), along with Huang Tifang and a large number of prominent late-Qing literati, appears in fictionalized form in the novel *Niehai hua* begun by Southern Quintessence Academy student Jin Songchen (1874–1947) and finished by Zeng Pu (1872–1935) from Changzhou prefecture. See Wei Shaochang, ed., *Niehai hua ziliao*, 331. The brother of Fei Nianci was later discussed by family members as a possible headmaster of the academy, but was not appointed. See Miao Quansun, *Yifeng tang youpeng shuza*, 371; Hong Huanqun, *Zhejiang wenxian congkao*, 271; Zhang Weixiang, *Qingdai Biling mingjen xiaojuan* 9:24; Yan Zhen, "Fei Youting quanche," *Muohua yin guan gan jiu huai ren ji*, in *QDZJ* 29:482.

Yao Wennan (Z. Zirang), was a Zhejiangese from Shaoxing prefecture by native-place origin, also listed as of Daotai rank, but only one "awaiting appointment," when he became a benefactor of Southern Quintessence Academy.[44] As Yao had received only *shengyuan* status, and a Daotai awaiting appointment rank could be purchased, the separation of gentry interests from the public impartiality built into the founding donations to the academy began to erode as the institution accepted this donation.[45]

In 1906 Yao Wennan's status as a Daotai awaiting appointment was to be closely scrutinized by Jiangsu's first commissioner of education under the New Policies reforms. The commissioner questioned Yao's self-interest and raised the specter of gentry malfeasance. The accusations made it clear that by the mid-1880s the swollen ranks of those with *shengjian* status provided an easy target for accusations regarding malfeasance. Yao Wennan was a member of the increasingly large and resourceful group of lower degree holders (often referred to as *shenjin* for the lapel colors permitted in gowns worn by *shengyuan*) following quota increases after 1864. They naturally needed opportunities for the expression of their influence. Some chosen opportunities had undoubtedly been exploitative.

Two men were appointed trustees to manage the construction of dikes and drainage canals on the 40,000-*mu* island endowment of

---

[44] Yao had studied in Shanghai and become known there as a member of the Zhejiangese academic elite. A link to his interest in Huang Tifang's academy may have been Sun Qiangming, under whom Yao had studied when Sun was the director at Longmen Academy from 1884 to 1894. See Miao Quansun, "Qing gu shilang xian Hanlin yuan shidu xueshi Sun Xiansheng muzhi ming bei," *QDZJ* 120:545–548; Rankin, "Public Opinion," 461; and Hummel, *Eminent Chinese*, 348. Yao was not visibly associated with Southern Quintessence Academy later in life, settling in Shanghai as an influential member of the local educated community there. He was a managing editor of the 1936 *Shanghai xian zhi* (Shanghai district gazetteer) before he died. The two men had also, of course, fulfilled their charge to the lieutenant governor by deciding to be benefactors of the academy. See Wang Xianqian, "Nanjing shatian ji," stele inscription.

The charges of malfeasance by private interests mentioned below will be discussed more carefully as they were argued in 1906 when this issue is raised in chapter 6. See Commissioner Mao's letter to the educational association of the province in 1906 in *JSJYZH*, 3d ed., pt. 2, pp. 202–208. See also K. C. Liu, "On Ch'ing Scholarship, Education, and Morality," 1–2.

[45] After 1888 the landed endowment was used for new revenue. It was invested in pawnbroker-banks to earn annual interest. They were the Yuanxiang (Long-range Good Luck) pawnbroker house across the river in Jiangyuan and the Deda (Great Virtue) pawnbroker house in Wuxi city. See *JYXZXZ*, 4:4a, 41.

Southern Quintessence Academy about 1886. Meanwhile, other men were appointed to an endowment committee of financial trustees operating under the supervision of the provincial director of education. Fei Xuezeng continued to serve as a financial trustee; Sheng Kang (Z. Xu Cun), compiler of *Huangchao jingshi wen xubian* (The continuation of empirical essays on statecraft), from nearby Wujin county, also served. Sheng Kang held a *jinshi* degree.[46] In the following two years, trustees managed harvest profits and brought in more sandbar polder land on the Nantong shoreline across the Yangzi and somewhat downstream from Jiangyin. By 1891 profits allowed the purchase of nearly 1,000 more *mu* of sandbar land, and profits thereafter continued to be invested with pawnbroker-banks.[47]

In the 1890s Fei Xuezeng's eminent son Fei Nianci corresponded about academy affairs with the famous bibliographer Miao Quansun (H. Yifeng, 1844–1919), who had taught at the academy in the 1880s. Fei Nianci wrote Miao that there was discussion of instituting eight-legged essay training in the curriculum. Huang Yizhou was aging, and this issue arose as the names of other directors were being discussed. But the trustees finally rejected this suggestion and agreed that Huang Tifang's original intent to keep sophisticated analysis of the classics the mission of the institution should be preserved as policy.[48]

Academic Work at Southern Quintessence Academy

The academy's direct debt to Ruan Yuan's 1801 Hangzhou institution, Gujing jingshe, as a model never appeared explicitly in Huang Tifang's founding documents, inscribed into stone memorials, but did appear in the petition for support he sent to Zuo Zongtang. Academy director Huang Yizhou, who ran the academy during its peak years from 1885 to 1898 and had studied at Gujing jingshe himself, also stated explicitly that his fellow Zhejiangese, Huang Tifang, had

[46] He was the son of a prominent family in Changzhou prefecture and the father of Sheng Xuanhuai (1844–1916). Sheng Kang had been a Daotai in Hubei under Hu Linyi and returned to Jiangsu willing to support academies. See "Sheng Long" in *Qingdai Pilin mingren xiaozhuan*, in *QDZJ* 197:244.

[47] *JYXZXZ* 4:41–44b; *Nanjing shuyuan liushi zhounian jinian*, chronology, p. 2. Because the water near this polder field, and another purchased later, was brackish, cotton and mulberry trees became the source of seasonal capital rather than rice, which required clean, fresh water. Mulberry leaves supported a silk cocoon industry on the sandbars.

[48] Miao Quansun, *Yifeng tang youpeng shuza*, 1:371.

founded Southern Quintessence Academy, "modeling it on Gujing jingshe.... He sought, as Ruan Yuan had in Zhejiang, to produce able scholars by promoting solid and practical learning (*shixue*)."[49] Zhang Wenhu, the academy's initial director, confirmed this by reporting Huang Tifang's founding speeches in Jiangyin town. Those speeches not only mentioned Ruan Yuan's pedagogy as a model but referred to Longmen Academy in Shanghai as an example to demonstrate how well the Gujing jingshe model of Ruan Yuan could work.

> Shanghai was in a similar situation. Then Longmen Academy was opened there [in 1865]. The Zhejiangese Gujing jingshe system of scholars studying in the residential academy was used. Only classics, history, ancient studies, astronomy, and mathematics were studied. Why should we not do likewise?[50]

The founders of Longmen Academy in Shanghai had not referred explicitly to Ruan Yuan's model in their founding documents either. But the founders of Southern Quintessence were correct in identifying this precedent for themselves and Longmen Academy: a revitalized classical pedagogy to master a nonvocational curriculum.

Huang Tifang, as the sponsoring official, and the Southern Quintessence director Huang Yizhou were of one mind in evoking the Ruan Yuan legacy. Academy Director Huang Yizhou spelled it out in the first published edition of student essays in 1889. The scholars of the post-Taiping era who were trying to reform academy education, he wrote, sought clearly to regain the scholarly objectives of a learning environment in which true teaching and solid scholarship took place.[51]

Song academies had attempted such a reform of Tang era education, where the teaching functions of schools had declined. This purpose was lost again in the Ming dynasty when all teaching seemed focused on the *Four Books* and formalistic composition. Ruan Yuan's two Qing academies had begun to recapture the best in Song education by placing the classics, history, composition, and *fu* (rhapsody) writing at the center of study. Coming up with new names for academies such as "lecture halls," as in the initial name used for

49 Huang Yizhou, "Nanjing jiangshe wenji xu," 21a. See also Zuo Zongtang, "Jiangyin chuangjian," 2455.

50 See Zhang Wenhu, "Nanjing shuyuan ji," stele inscription. The founding documents of Longmen Academy nowhere refers to Ruan Yuan's Gujing jingshe model, but the exclusion of eight-legged essays, concentration on the objective of *shixue*, and use of the pedagogy of personal diaries are key similarities.

51 Huang Yizhou, "Nanjing wenji xu," 21a. Zuo Zongtang, "Jiangyin chuangjian," 2455.

Southern Quintessence, *jiangshe,* or even "retreat," as in Gujing jingshe, was a sign of this call for academy reform.[52]

In 1884 Huang Yizhou was disappointed at the post-Taiping quality of academy education in Jiangsu. He noted that Feng Guifen's Zhengyi Academy in Suzhou was one institution committed to the classics—but only recently. Xiyin Academy, he noted, was unfortunately making compromises and becoming more like the official governor-general's academy from which it was to draw advanced students, who themselves should be engaging in research scholarship. An academy in Sichuan, Zunjing (Respect the Classics) Academy, had modeled itself on Gujing jingshe for a time but had recently made the classics a minor subject of study. So Huang Yizhou endorsed the immediate need for Jiangsu to establish a provincewide academy for serious, advanced study as Ruan Yuan had. The purpose was to provide Jiangsu with able scholars by promoting a provincial institution committed to solid and practical learning: "As the Song Confucians founded academies to restore the collapse of schools, today we establish lecture halls to correct the defects of academies, to support serious Confucian scholarship (*puxue*), and eliminate ornamental studies. This is the point."[53]

The Lower Yangzi academic elite were well aware of each other, and networking was as close as it had been in the Qianlong reign. From Wenzhou in Zhejiang—the home prefecture of the mutually friendly clans of Huang Tifang and Sun Qiangming—up to Shanghai, and again along the Grand Canal from Hangzhou to Yangzhou, correspondence about scholarship and its institutions linked a network of academy leaders. In the early 1800s, men like Qian Daxin moved easily from Zhongshan Academy to the official provincial academy in Suzhou; and, as we have seen, in 1884 Sun Qiangming, director of Zhongshan Academy in Jiangning, was appointed director of Longmen Academy in Shanghai. In that same year his acquaintance Zhang Wenhu became the first director of Southern Quintessence Academy. Zhang Wenhu had exchanged scholarly correspondence with the earlier Longmen Academy director, Liu Xizai, and Liu Xizai had seen to the printing of some of

---

52 Huang Yizhou, "Nanjing wenji xu," 20b–21. Partially reprinted in Meng Xiancheng et al., *Zhongguo gudai jiaoyu shih ziliao,* 282–283. Note also Liu Qi, "Ruan Yuan jiaoyu shijian shuping," *Huadong shifan daxue xuebao* 1 (March 1986): 67–76. The *Four Books* refer to Cheng-Zhu interpretations of the Four Books; the eight rhymes refers to the eight-legged essay style required by the examination system.

53 Huang Yizhou, "Nanjing wenji xu," 21b. See also Zhang Yin, "Gujing jingshe," 3.

Zhang Wenhu's collected works in 1879, the year before Liu's death.[54]

However, to seek a traditional model for a new academy was in some ways more unusual in 1884 than it had been twenty years before, when Longmen Academy had been founded. Among the variety of new institutions adopting the respected title of *shuyuan* (academy) in the late nineteenth century was a multitude of missionary schools, which spread up the Yangzi valley. Official translation and technology schools such as the Jiangnan Arsenal in Shanghai were also introducing modern Western disciplines. And then there were reformist new academies sponsored by leaders such as Zhang Zhidong, which were gradually changing the classical curriculum well beyond emphasis on statecraft by introducing modern Western writings. In Zhang Zhidong's innovations from this period, such as Guangya shuyuan (Guangya Academy), founded in 1888 in Guangdong, contemporary issues were emphasized, and Western books were stocked in the library.[55]

The Southern Quintessence curriculum copied from Gujing jingshe the progressive idea of adding selected subjects to the standard curriculum of the Neo-Confucian canon of the *Four Books* and *Five Classics*. The rigorous monthly essay topics included not only classics topics, but antiquities topics as well. Within the rubric of *guxue* a teacher guided students in poetry, especially *fu* composition, and a variety of other subjects. These included the identification of rare books, the collation of editions, evidential research methods, history, mathematics, and astronomy.

By not teaching the eight-legged essay and by demanding a rigorous provincewide admissions examination, Southern Quintessence was able to admit students who were ready for advanced study. In the first class of ninety-four students in 1884, only six had no status accorded from acquisition of previous degrees. All the rest were of *shengyuan* status (eighty-one persons) or had received *juren*

---

[54] XZ 1918, 9:13; Hong Huanqun, *Zhejiang wenxian congkao*, 271; Zhang Wenhu, "Nanjing shuyuan chongji Han Gaomi Zheng shi Song Xin'an Zhu zi," in *Shurang yushu*, frontispiece; idem, "Nanjing shuyuan ji," stele inscription. In 1888 Miao Quansun served with Huang Yizhou as codirector of Southern Quintessence for two years. In 1896 Miao became Zhongshan Academy's final director in Jiangning, serving until 1900. The official provincial academy in Suzhou was Ziyang Academy, and its funding was similar to the funding at Zhongshan Academy at the governor-general's side of the province.

[55] Su Yunfeng, "Guangya shuyuan (1888–1902)," *Jindai shi yanjiu so jikan* 13 (1984): 241.

(five) or even *jinshi* (two) degrees.[56]

In 1888 Miao Quansun was the authority teaching *guxue*, which he modestly called composition.[57] A well-known scholar, he had come home to Jiangyin for the traditional period of mourning for his stepmother. A new Jiangsu provincial director of education at the time, Yang Yi (Z. Rongpu), had just taken office and arranged for Miao to teach a light schedule at Southern Quintessence Academy. Because of his scholarly achievements and his Hanlin status, Miao Quansun was made a codirector, equal in title to the classicist Huang Yizhou, for the two years he was there.[58] These arrangements gave the academy faculty a remarkable national reputation at this time, complementing the enhanced repute Wang Xianqian provided the new academy through his series of publications, described below, from the academy printing house. Miao's teaching included everything but the classics, which were reserved for Huang Yizhou.

Student tenure was never fixed at the academy. With no graduation built in, it was up to the student whether he reapplied and up to the academy whether he could stay. Women did not apply to these institutions, and classical learning remained after 1865 a barrier preventing all women access to power exercised by the educated elite in society. Some enrolled students eventually left to attend other academies; some also left for personal reasons; and some who left later retook the spring entrance examination to return.[59] The rigorous annual selection of stipend students for the coming year was one means of setting the standards the academy desired, and in 1890 only about ten of the previous sixty-two residential stipend scholars were renewed for the next year.[60] Wu Zhihui (1864–1953), in contrast, won renewal of his residence stipends three years in a row and passed his *juren* degree while studying at Southern Quintessence Academy. In his third and last year he tried unsuccessfully to pass the *jinshi* degree in Beijing. Then he left, transferring to the official provincial academy in nearby Suzhou.[61]

---

[56] *Nanjing* (1935), 69–74.

[57] *Yifeng laoren nianpu*, ed. Xia Suntong, 176.

[58] Residents of Jiangyin had been forbidden from holding high office since the loyalist resistance to the Manchu takeover in the 1640s. Scholarship was consequently a common profession. Interview with the Jiangyin artist and calligrapher Huang Boyle (Huang Baoyu), Toronto, Canada, August 15, 1990. Howard Boorman, *Biographical Dictionary of Republican China*, 3:35.

[59] See the case of Ding Fubao, in *Nanjing shuyuan liushi zhounian jinian ce*, 1–8.

[60] Yin Baoxian, *Zhui yilu*, 38.

[61] "Wu Zhihui xiansheng nianpu jianbian," in Lo Jialun et al., eds., *Wu Zhihui xiansheng quanji*, 18:12–13. Wu was from Yanghu county and lived in Wuxi city. He and

Table 4
Directors of Southern Quintessence Academy, 1884–1911

Years at academy	Director
1884	Zhang Wenhu (Z. Mengbiao)
1885–1898	Huang Yizhou (Z. Yuantong)
1888–1890	Miao Quansun (Z. Yanzhi), co-director
1899–1901	Lin Yishan (Z. Jinxia)
Transition to a new school	
1901–0000	Ding Lijun
1902	Ding Liying
1903	Liu Fengzhang (Z. Eshan)
1904	Jin Shi (Z. Hengyi)
1905	Song Yuren
1910	Zhang Jizhi (Z. Qinruo)

The Southern Quintessence Academy's buildings consisted of a lecture hall and places to meet tutorially, but no classrooms. Beyond the bimonthly lectures given by the headmaster of the academy, students consulted with the instructors but were expected to study their subjects largely on their own, making ample use of the excellent library. As at Ruan Yuan's two famous academies, the student at Southern Quintessence was to progress according to his abilities and interests and not limit himself to the teachings of one authority, inside or outside the institution. "Differing editions of works would be collected, and each edition could be critically examined," by those admitted to study.[62]

During the academic year there were ten lucrative essay competitions given monthly (new entrance exams were given during the first month, and there was vacation in the twelfth month of the lunar year). Residential and off-campus students had three days to finish their essays once they received the topics. Off-campus students could write on only one topic. In 1890, to take one example, between 140 and 150 papers were submitted for the twenty possible

his lifelong friend from Southern Quintessence Academy, Niu Yongjian (1870–1965), later worked for the Revolution of 1911 and then became loyal Guomindang members. He studied at Southern Quintessence from 1889 to 1892. See Boorman, *Biographical Dictionary*, 3:44.

[62] Huang Tifang, "Nanjing shuyuan," stele inscription.

classics prizes, and the same number for the thirty possible antiquities prizes.[63]

Just as at Longmen Academy, Southern Quintessence regulations required students to keep two daily diaries, one of personal activities and the other a research journal of ideas. These diaries were to be submitted when requested by a teacher. As the founder had put it in 1885, all students should "record their activities and worknotes in a diary."[64] At Southern Quintessence, as at Ruan Yuan's academies, this journal of work notes or notations on texts was treated as a Han learning evidential research technique. This scholarly technique followed the example of Gu Yanwu's (1613–1683) *Rizhi lu* (Record of knowledge gained day by day). Pearls from years of detailed research and discovery made by a young scholar might be printed later in life by the scholar, his family, or students as the fruits of years of careful labor for others to continue. Other Jiangnan academies used such notation books (*zaji cezi*), and they added a distinct Han learning variation in the Qing to what Benjamin Elman has termed the more conventional "dialogue records" (*yulu*) techniques of Song and Ming *daoxue* pedagogy.[65]

In addition to monthly essays and notation books, oral work was used to verify how well students were studying on their own. Teachers called periodic assemblies of all students in the lecture hall. Students would then be asked to come to the podium and either analyze the content of the books they were currently studying or describe the research they were doing. The academy director would then grade the presentations. This exercise provided accountability for self-directed learning and also fostered skills in the oral presentation of one's ideas.[66]

Publications of the Southern Quintessence Academy Printing House

The Southern Quintessence Academy published sets of student essays to inform the public of the quality of scholarship done there. Recondite analyses of specific passages from the classics were

---

[63] Yin Baoxian, *Zhui yilu*, 37b; *JYXZXZ* 6:2b; Wu Xinlei, "Nanjing shuyuan," 18.

[64] Huang Tifang, "Nanjing shuyuan," stele inscription.

[65] Wu Zhihui saved a portion of the diary that recorded his daily schedule at the academy. He split each day into categories and then distinguished reading materials he simply read through on a single day from those writings he mastered. He noted what personal writing he composed, such as poems, and included the titles of monthly essay assignments for which he competed. His final scheduled category was time for meditation. See *Wu Zhihui xiansheng quanji*, 16:64–65. See also Elman, *From Philosophy*, 174; Huang Tifang, "Nanjing shuyuan," stele inscription.

[66] Wu Xinlei, "Nanjing shuyuan," 18.

combined with a variety of subjects from the antiquities and published in these collections. Three collections of *Nanjing shuyuan wenji* (Collected writings of Southern Quintessence Academy) were printed (in 1889, 1894, and 1901), with the same format as that of parallel collections from director Huang Yizhou's alma mater, Gujing jingshe in Hangzhou.[67]

But another publication from its own press made Southern Quintessence nationally known. When Jiangsu director of education Wang Xianqian memorialized the Guangxu emperor in 1886 to establish a printing house at Southern Quintessence Academy, his aim was to continue the series of scholarly essays on the classics begun by Ruan Yuan himself in 1829.[68] This project was facilitated by a compilation Huang Tifang had carried out in Jiangyin before he left in 1885. Huang had compiled a kind of *yiwen zhi* (bibliographical record) of Jiangsu authors—including biographical data and the titles of their works. Director Huang Tifang sent this list, later printed as *Jiangnan zhengshu wendu* (Documentary evidence on Jiangnan publications), to the state historiographer's office in Beijing, and it was available to Wang Xianqian when he took office as the new director of education.[69] The multivolume collection of authoritative essays on the classics that Wang published under the title *Huangqing jingjie xubian* (Continuation of the Qing exegesis of the classics) included many of Jiangsu's finest nineteenth-century scholars among other national authorities and served to update classical scholarship nationally.

Exceeding Ruan Yuan's 1829 exegesis by some thirty volumes, Wang Xianqian's set had a total of 1,430 separate volumes when the wood-cut plates were finished and the first edition printed in 1888. As the printing house was at the academy, the set was often termed the *Southern Quintessence Exegesis of the Classics* (*Nanjing jingjie*), just as Ruan's 1829 set was often called the *Xuehai tang Exegesis of the Classics* after Ruan's Cantonese academy printing house. Because its selections represented a broad variety of schools and factions of classical studies, one of the major contributions of the study was to serve as a continuing history of classical studies in the Qing dynasty.[70]

---

67 Elman, *From Philosophy*, 125; Huang Yizhou, "Nanjing jiangshe," 2b.

68 Xie Guozhen cites Wang Xianqian, *Ciding nianpu*, n.d., n.p. See also Wu Xinlei, "Nanjing shuyuan," 20; and Wang Xianqian, "Nanjing congshu xu," in *Xushou tang*, 5:245–246; for Ruan Yuan's series, see Elman, *From Philosophy*, 91–93. See also Xie Guozhen, *Jindai shuyuan xuexiao zhiju bianqian kao*, 15.

69 Hummel, *Eminent Chinese*, 349.

70 *Nanjing zaji* (Nanjing miscellany), another collection of materials but including only fourteen selections, was printed in 1894 by Pu Liang, the director of education of

In fact, in 1865 when Zeng Guofan had invited Li Lianxiu to direct Zhongshan Academy, he complimented Li on having proposed just such a continuation of recent valuable scholarship on the classics that would extend Ruan Yuan's 1829 compilation. To Zeng Guofan the idea undoubtedly fit within the revitalization of Confucian scholarship he sensed was so necessary in the Tongzhi Restoration. Southern Quintessence Academy realized this idea some twenty years later.[71]

The Kind of Advanced Learning Achieved at Southern Quintessence Academy

Many of the students who went through Southern Quintessence in the two decades after 1884 have been briefly studied by an alumnus attempting to salvage information after the Japanese bombed the school buildings in World War II. The painfully etched woodblocks for the classical scholarship series produced there in 1888 were burned in the bombing of the former Yangzi Admiralty site, as was the entire library collection. After the destruction, the alumnus recovered a set of school archives that had not been destroyed. They had been assembled earlier, in 1935, for a fiftieth anniversary celebration, and he published them in a wartime memoir in 1941. The archives he edited and printed contained a significant number of student names for the period up to 1900. (There is no comparable student list from Longmen Academy in Shanghai or from Zhongshan Academy in Jiangning.)

The alumnus, Zhao Chunnian (Z. Jianqiu, b. 1868), had received his *shengyuan* degree in Changzhou prefecture at age fifteen. At the *kekao* of 1884 his examination scores qualified him to enter the academy with a full stipend.[72] What Zhao Chunnian assembled was a listing of 119 former Southern Quintessence students, the majority of whom had dedicated their careers to scholarship. He could identify

Jiangsu. The amount of research collected but not included in the exegesis set resulted in a follow-up collection of multivolume publications entitled *Nanjing congshu*. These works were edited by Miao Quansun. See Huang Yizhou, "Nanjing jiangshe," 21. About one-quarter of the forty-one works in this *congshu* were chosen from research done by stipend scholars at the academy. Scholars at Southern Quintessence did independent research apart from their monthly essay exams, and much of it was original. Almost all the works in the forty-one collected essays were previously unpublished, original scholarship. See Wu Xinlei, "Nanjing shuyuan," 19, 21; Xie Guozhen, *Jindai shuyuan*, 15–16; Hummel, *Eminent Chinese*, 349.

71 Zeng Guofan, "Zhi Li Xiaohu dali," 15554.

72 Zhao received his *jinshi* thirteen years later in 1898.

the professional area of academic expertise of almost all. Most had made their mark specializing in the Confucian classics, Chinese literature, and history. A smaller number were philologists, mathematicians, students of poetry, or specialists in a subfield of classical studies. Hu Shi took note of this article in 1958 and singled out twenty-four very prominent intellectual figures from the list, commenting that in his career he had personally crossed paths with thirteen of them. Since Southern Quintessence Academy was perhaps the most eminent academy founded late in the Qing dynasty, the exact academic training given this cadre of twentieth-century scholars deserves analysis.[73]

The first director of Southern Quintessence Academy, although he served only a short term, took a stand on factions within Confucian scholarship that was to be long continued by his successors. Zhang Wenhu condemned the separation of the Confucian tradition into conflicting Han and Song schools of scholarship, a separation he thought defamed each. "Both schools of thought crusted like ice and accumulated much frozen water in each," Zhang Wenhu wrote; "an eyelash of difference was transmitted [by disciples] as a major difference in principle." So it was said that the Han school was concerned only with analyzing the meaning of words and nature, while the school of Song learning was reputed to study only ethical principles. Disciples thereby made the common Confucian tradition into opposing schools that came to look like "handles and sockets that seemed not to match."[74]

The decision of Southern Quintessence to venerate two sages, Zheng Xuan and Zhu Xi, who had been mentors for the two conflicting scholarly factions earlier in the Qing dynasty was intended to establish a united Confucian tradition of substantive study at the academy. This position was in accord with the increasing consensus in the nineteenth century for integrating Han and Song scholarship.[75] The poles that might have separated Ruan Yuan's 1820 academy, Xuehai tang—which stressed Han learning—from Woren's coterie of

---

[73] *Nanjing*, 1935, 1–55; Zhao Chunnian, "Tanyan zhai shiyou xiaoji (bu)," *Zhonghe yuekan* 3 (1941): 7–9. The principal in the years of the 1935 anniversary years was Sun Hanyai (Z. Kuijun), who had been a student in the inaugural class of 1890. *Hu Shi xiansheng nianpu changpian chugao*, ed. Hu Songping, 2751–2754.

[74] Zhang Wenhu, "Nanjing shuyuan ji," 10.

[75] The influential headmaster of Xuehai tang (The Xuehai Hall), Ruan Yuan's 1820 academy in Guangzhou, was Chen Li (1810–1882), who had articulated such a synthesis some years before. See Liu Kwang-ching, "Ch'ing Restoration," 486, 489; Elman, *From Philosophy*, 246–247, 253.

Cheng-Zhu advocates around 1865 were becoming increasingly conceived to be within the same spectrum of opinion. All three elite academies studied in this book—Longmen, Zhongshan, and Southern Quintessence—accepted the importance of self-cultivation (*xiushen*) as a goal for students. Each also kept its curriculum and pedagogy focused on *zhiyong* or true practicality. Southern Quintessence declared it would not only retain the rigor of Han learning as a required standard of study, but also reassert the moral concern of Song learning in order to attain substance and practicality.[76]

The founder of Southern Quintessence Academy, Huang Tifang, noted in his commemorative stele that the teachers appointed to the academy would all be broadly trained and could direct students not only in *lizhi*, the study of the ritual classics, referring to Song learning, but also in the study of *xungu*, philology, referring to Han learning. And in addition, they could teach the study of belles lettres or composition (*cizhang*), referring to the Tongcheng School of literary composition.[77] Such a balanced curriculum included Zuo Zongtang's priority on the importance of Cheng-Zhu Neo-Confucianism and also affirmed founder Huang Tifang's commitment to the obliteration of factional scholarship. Huang Yizhou, the most influential director thereafter, agreed and adopted an intellectual position that sidestepped any conflict between Han learning and Song learning.

Important original ceremonies evoking the ancestral spirits of the two patron sages established the scholarly identity of the academy in the summer of 1883. The ancestral tablets of Zheng Xuan from the Latter Han dynasty and Zhu Xi from the Song dynasty were venerated, and their spirits and writings remained guides for the young Confucians studying there for the life of the institution. The ceremony to venerate Confucian sages as academy patron spirits took the form of a religious invocation of spirits. "The Honorable Mr. Huang chose the propitious time of the seventh month to have us assemble at the Central Building [the library] and perform the sacrificial rites to Zheng Xuan and Zhu Xi," the initial director later recounted.[78] Flowers were then arranged around an altar table that was to remain thereafter the site of the students' daily obeisance to the ancestral tablets of the two sages.

Couplets and poems in memory of the two Confucian thinkers were written on scrolls hung from the rafters in the pavilion

---

76 Huang Yizhou, "Nanjing jiangshe," preface.

77 Huang Tifang, "Nanjing shuyuan," stele inscription.

78 Zhang Wenhu, "Nanjing shuyuan chongji," 9–10.

surrounding the altar. As wine and incense were offered, the academy director was moved by the feeling that the spirits of these two sages actually were infusing the tablets with their presences.[79] Like the ceremonies venerating city gods or other patron deities, this academy ceremony clearly presumed that the ancestral spirits of the sages could be bridged through human ceremonial rites. A spiritual relationship would be thereafter maintained with the ancestral spirits of the two sages through continued observances: "Pure libations fill our cups and notify [the spirits] of our offering. So fragrantly is it presented! The spirit seems as if—its hair disheveled—it will enlighten our region."[80] And why could not each new generation of scholars seek this cosmic connection? "To use words to convey the way is the work of sacred classics," the first director intoned: "From the time the first classic was written, a variety of differing interpretations has emerged. The most distinguished interpretations in the heritage of the *dao* have, however, been from the writings of these two. Their works will remain vital for a hundred thousand years."[81]

The most important intellectual influence at Southern Quintessence Academy was its director from 1885 to 1898, Huang Yizhou. He firmly reasserted the synthesis of Confucian schools propounded by the short-lived first director, Zhang Wenhu, as well as by the founder, Huang Tifang. The son of a fine classical scholar from the coastal county of Dinghai, in Zhejiang, this man ranks first of all with his teacher Yu Yue and with Sun Yirang (1848–1908) as one of the three great Han School masters from Zhejiang, and indeed from the whole country, at the end of the Qing.[82]

The same respect for Han learning that animated Ruan Yuan's earlier new academies is present in Huang Yizhou's writing,[83] as can be seen in the precepts to guide scholarship at the academy that he wrote when he took over in 1885:

> Precept C: It is held that in analyzing the classics, the Han scholars are the closest to antiquity. Among the Han Confucians only one person could both encompass the major classics and encompass as

[79] Ibid.

[80] A small statue of Zhu Xi or Zheng Xuan probably explains the disheveled hair. See ibid., 9. Before 1911 a visitor to White Deer Grotto Academy (Bai lu dong shuyuan) in Jiangxi noted seventeen small statues of Confucius and certain disciples. See Carl Kupfer, *Sacred Places in China*, 80.

[81] Zhang Wenhu, "Nanjing shuyuan congji," 9b.

[82] Hong Huanqun, *Zhejiang wenxian congkao*, 258; see *QSG*, 43:13298.

[83] Elman, *From Philosophy*, 58.

> well the one hundred schools of philosophy. That was Gaomi [Zheng Xuan]. The literary arts can be discussed after that. As for Xu Shen [58–147] as a mentor, one can recognize him, or one does not have to acknowledge him as a master.[84]

As a favored student of Yu Yue while at Gujing jingshe,[85] Huang Yizhou consistently emphasized an idea explicit in Ruan Yuan's original aims for Gujing jingshe.[86] Huang Yizhou insisted that an accurate reading of the classics was fruitless without the foundation of a rigorous philological analysis of language.[87] This belief placed him in the mainstream of much productive research in the tradition of Han learning. His argument regarding how to master the Confucian tradition seems deceptively simple:

> Scholars who want to search out the wisdom in the subtle words of the sacred Confucius must first comprehend the classics. Because the meaning of the classics is hard to clarify, philology and classical phonology are essential for understanding the vocabulary and usage of the classical thinkers. Only if one makes this effort can the meaning of the classics penetrate to the mind's eye.[88]

Yet his own philosophical position asserted the importance of history in understanding the classics to such a degree that he claimed to find no conflict among the strongest points of both Han and Song learning. Huang Yizhou "often told his students," wrote his colleague at Southern Quintessence Academy, Miao Quansun, "that the destructive effects of factionalism among [Confucian] schools of thought in the previous generation were very clear."[89] Miao was confirmed by later student comments stating that Huang Yizhou made a point of not distinguishing between Han and Song learning when he taught.[90]

But Huang Yizhou's personal stand of transcending factions in Confucian scholarship and its contemporary application had roots deeper than the Qing controversy over Han learning versus Song learning. Huang Yizhou argued and taught in the tradition of the

---

[84] See *JJZZ*, 33. Xu Shen was the author of the *Shuowen jieci* (Etymological dictionary) and a founder of Chinese philology. Ruan Yuan had established him as a venerated master at Gujing jingshe, along with Zheng Xuan.

[85] Yu Yue taught there for more than thirty years beginning in 1867. See *QSG*, 43:13298; Wu Xinlei, "Nanjing shuyuan," 2 (1985): 21.

[86] See Man-kam Leung, "Juan Yuan," 88–93.

[87] *JJZZ*, 32b; Man-kam Leung, "Juan Yuan," 9.

[88] Huang Yizhou, "Nanjing shuyuan jiangxue ji," stele inscription.

[89] See *YFTXJ* 1:15.

[90] *QDZJ* 12:345. See also Zhao Chunnian, "Tanyan," 9.

older Eastern Zhejiang Historical School from the southeast. Statecraft was also a subtheme in this tradition.

The Eastern Zhejiang Historical School was not an unbroken transmission of ideas from either its intellectual inheritance in the Southern Song or from its initial Qing inspiration, Huang Zongxi (1601–1694). But because it was a tradition emphasizing the importance of historical studies, different scholars in the Qing referred to it. Zhang Xuecheng (Z. Shizhai, 1738–1801) named it a tradition for the first time in the mid-eighteenth century. In the nineteenth century the Zhejiangese scholar Huang Shisan (Z. Weixiang, 1789–1862) and his son, Huang Yizhou, reasserted several aspects of this tradition. Both argued that the strengths of Han learning should not lead to a neglect of personal values, as tested and applied in personal behavior. Such a danger could be avoided by emphasizing the study of the basic Confucian concept of proper social usage (*li*). Ultimately this idea required broad learning (*boxue*). The classics, critically edited to correct forgery and misstatement by history, were the basis for beginning such broad study.[91]

Scholars visiting Huang Yizhou at Southern Quintessence recognized and commented on the principles from the Eastern Zhejiang Historical School he taught: first, that there should be no exclusive loyalty to any Confucian scholarly faction; second, that study should concentrate on the ritual classics to foster analysis of the past through the actual practice of proper social usage.[92]

As his father had taught, Huang Yizhou developed the concept of proper social usage by emphasizing the in-depth study of the three ritual classics: the *Liji* (Record of rites), *Yili* (Decorum ritual), and *Zhouli* (Rituals of Zhou).[93] The idea that the importance of studying the proper social usage of different eras was compatible with Han learning had been developed in Ruan Yuan's thought and transmitted as a critical scholarly technique at Gujing jingshe.[94] Huang Yizhou summarized its power as follows: "*Li* (proper social usage) must, of necessity, be in accord with past reality, whereas 'principle' [*li*, as in *daoli*, emphasized by Song learning], can be just speculation."[95]

---

[91] Chen Xunci, "Qingdai zhedong zhi shixue," *Shixue zazhi* 2.6 (April 1931): 28–30.

[92] Miao Quansun, *Yifeng tang*, 1:372.

[93] See *QDZJ*, 128:346.

[94] Ruan Yuan contributed to the evolution of the Eastern Zhejiang Historical School, but this formulation may have come to him from Jiang Yong (1681–1762) and Jiang Yong's student, Dai Zhen. See Chen Xunci, "Qingdai zhedong zhi shixue," 5; Man-kam Leung, "Juan Yuan," 92. See also Elman, *From Philosophy*, 31, 116.

[95] See *YFTXJ* 1:14b; Hong Huanqun, *Zhejiang wenxian congkao*, 250.

Huang Yizhou spent nineteen years writing a fifty-part work on the three ritual classics that students used in manuscript form in the Southern Quintessence library. He used charts and diagrams as had Zhang Xuecheng in his histories during the previous generation. The contribution of that magnum opus struck scholars, such as Yu Yue and Zhang Binglin, as exceptional in the way the author extracted the social and political conditions of the ancient period from the classics by analyzing norms and customs of proper social usage assumed in the ritual classics. Yu Yue's preface mentioned that Zeng Guofan had often raised with him the indispensability of reading carefully the 1761 compendium on proper social usage, Qin Huitian's *Wuli tongkao*.[96]

Of the several ideas defining the core of the Eastern Zhejiang Historical School, one that overlapped with the broader Confucian search in the Qing for effectiveness was statecraft. Drawing inspiration from Huang Zongxi's *Mingyi daifang lu* (A plan for the prince), written in 1662, writers of this intellectual lineage demanded that the historical record speak to relevant political issues in the present. Huang Yizhou's father had studied maritime defense and military organization. Huang Yizhou shared this interest with his father, under whom he studied, and he further studied statecraft themes under Yu Yue at Gujing jingshe. He was hired for his first teaching post by Zong Yuanhan, a prefect in maritime Zhejiang who was trying to bolster coastal defenses in Huang Yizhou's home prefecture. This was the same man who earlier had promoted public charitable schools so vigorously when prefect of Huzhou, further to the west in Zhejiang. Prefect Zong Yuanhan had organized an academic institute called the Literary Society to Foster a Discriminating Spirit (Bianzhi wenhui) in Ningpo city and hired Huang Yizhou in 1879 to teach a traditional curriculum of subjects. The objective of the institute was to extract useful knowledge from the materials studied.[97]

---

96 Chen Xunci, "Qingdai zhedong zhi shixue," 29–30. Huang Yizhou's masterwork was entitled *Li shu tonggu* (Understanding antiquity through the ritual classics), 100 *juan* in 2 vols. (Taibei: Huashi chubanshe, 1976). It was originally published in 1893. See Yu Yue's preface, 1–2.

97 Chen Xunci, "Qingdai zhedong zhi shixue," 33; Rankin, *Elite Activism*, 121. See also William T. DeBary, "Chinese Despotism and the Confucian Ideal: A Seventeenth-Century View," in *Chinese Thought and Institutions*, ed. John K. Fairbank, 163–204. Zong Yuanhan was a native of Jiangning prefecture in Jiangsu. He worked successfully with Daotai Xue Fucheng in resisting the French on the Zhejiang coast at Zhenhai in 1885. See *QSG*, 12, 578.

Such aims fit the regional historical school of Eastern Zhejiang perfectly. All the scholars studying at the institute already had their first civil service degree, so instruction was at an advanced level. Huang Yizhou wrote an essay on the concept of discriminating spirit in the institute's title (*bianzhi*) and often repeated it: "In all personal conduct and thought, rely on critically examined (*bian*) experience, and in all your work rely upon determination (*zhi*)."[98] In his scholarship Huang Yizhou spent years on a practical study of military conduct and administration (*junli si ma fa*), which he eventually published in two volumes. In it he praised the equal-field system of the Northern Dynasties period. He believed this model of agricultural organization was still viable, but he insisted on combining it with properly performed social usage, which, he said, must accompany such a plan if the agrarian reorganization was to work.[99]

In the decade after 1885, Director Huang Yizhou frequently summarized his own teachings using the *Analects* passage "Junzi boxue yu wen, yue zhi yi li."[100] The passage sets as a standard for the student the idea that a person of superior moral attainment must be broadly erudite in knowledge of written texts and, furthermore, understand the knowledge in those texts in the light of proper social usage. Sticking to the hard evidence of a socially grounded history provided a compass for the present.

The moral health of a state could even be discerned from analyzing social practice and rhetoric. Huang Yizhou documented this point in his book *Jingxun biyi* (The comparative study of glosses on the classics) in which Huang Yizhou argued that discussions of proper social usage became popular when the Zhou state (1027–256 B.C.E.) declined, and proper social usage again reemerged as a major issue of debate just when the Jin dynasty (265–419) proved incapable of reunifying post-Han China. In other words, basic honesty and how people lived up to their word (*li qi wei wo bei she*) were eroded by the immorality of the times. Then the formalities of propriety became much discussed, because they were needed just to break the ice between parties who had to communicate despite the decline in

[98] Chen Xunci, "Qingdai zhedong zhi shixue," 34, citing Huang Yizhou "Lijing bianzhi shuo" (parsing "bian" and "zhi") in his *JJZZ*, n.p., n.d.

[99] See *QDZJ*, 12:346.

[100] Huang Yizhou, "Nanjing shuyuan jiangxue bei ji," stele inscription. The passage is from the *Analects*, bk. 11, chap. 25; see James Legge, *Confucius* (New York: Dover, 1971), 193. An alternative translation of the second clause, favored by James Legge, is that proper social usage is essential to restrain one's behavior. Whether applied to scholarship or personal ethics the effect is the same.

mutual trust. Huang concluded that "proper social usage appears when faithfulness and trust get too thin" (*li wei zhong xin zhi bo*).[101]

The antidote for such a decline in the state of affairs was to establish orthodox values. As Huang Yizhou put it: "If scholarship is not clear, the affairs of a country will be faulty" (*xueshu bu ming erh zhishu bi*). In his era, academic scholarship could make a difference. Huang Yizhou taught the most critical tools of textual analysis from Han learning and added historical insights from the traditions of the Eastern Zhejiang Historical School. But, in transmitting the Way to his era, his advice for Southern Quintessence students was to go to the works of Master Zhu:

> Precept D: It is held that essayists and minor Confucian genres do not reveal the Way. When Zhongni [Confucius] passed away, the subtle and profound language [of the Way] was interrupted. The masters of the Northern Song were again able to transmit it. The most accomplished single person to do this was Xinan [Zhu Xi].[102]

Southern Quintessence students used these guidelines to become scholars. The provincial director of education's institution in Jiangyin town achieved the graduate-school pedagogical objectives Hu Peihui and Feng Guifen had in mind earlier for Xiyin Academy and Zhengyi Academy. And the students who studied the average of three years at any of the elite regional or provincial-level academies entered the upper layer of the educated elite of the Lower Yangzi. Most of these academy students did not get degrees higher than *shengyuan* and never entered the ranks of officialdom. Many, however, did research. Rigorous scholarship analyzing the present as informed development from the past allowed realistic assessment of the present. Life in the academies also demanded behavioral implementation of the ethical values studied. Research scholarship in these academies similarly eschewed speculative learning. Scholarship at Zhongshan Academy, Longmen Academy, and Southern Quintessence Academy sought profound practicality. Whether the issue be material or moral, analysis was designed to be grounded in the realm of actual lived experience that could generate practical knowledge for the present.

---

[101] "Dinghai Huang shi fuzi juan, Shisan, Yizhou," in *Qingdai puxue dashi liejuan*, in *QDZJ* 12:346.

[102] *JJZZ*, 33.

PART III

The Lower Yangzi Educated Elite, 1896–1911

During the fifteen years from 1896 to 1911 the Lower Yangzi educated elite began acting as a group. A sense of national crisis in these years, following the defeat by Japan, posed issues of restoration and rehabilitation similar to national needs in the 1864–1874 decade. In both periods the power of the Lower Yangzi educated elite expanded unnaturally fast because of state recovery policies. The difference in the 1896–1911 period was that the Lower Yangzi educated elite also organized.

The suspension of much national supervision and many services in the war years after 1894 fostered the early stages of this organization. Implementation of a nationwide public school system reached below the county level after 1904 and stretched bureaucratic resources to their limit. Official institutional means could no longer meet the expanded educational objectives of the New Policy reforms. By 1906 management rights over local education had been assumed by local elites and acknowledged by national policy regulations.

The demand for public institutions of learning after 1905 stimulated the dynasty's already awakened gentry initiative in the public sphere of local extrabureaucratic initiative, and it became the engine generating the region's massive new system of public schools. Community-funded schools were public in the sense Chen Hongmou in the 1670s and Ding Richang in 1868 understood that term. In each of these cases, institutions promoted by the state called forth expanded state-sanctioned activities by the local elite. In the first decade of the twentieth century, locally financed and locally managed public schools in Jiangsu dwarfed in number those remaining under more direct official management.

In the final five years of the dynasty, 1906–1911, Lower Yangzi associations of educators coordinated their efforts and even dared to extend their claim to management rights beyond local education, to include control over provincial-level educational institutions.

CHAPTER FIVE

Lower Yangzi Education Transformed, 1896–1906

The trauma of national defeat by Japan in 1894–1895 had an important effect on the educated local elite in the Lower Yangzi. For nearly two generations, the revival of academies and public charitable schools in Jiangsu had expanded the opportunities and initiative of the educated elite in localities throughout the province. The Japanese military blow in 1895 stunned the centralized government and forced it to release its control over many national institutions.[1] Inspired, in part, by the need for radical change after the Japanese defeat, decentralizing reform initiatives were begun in 1896 but were viciously repressed after the Hundred Days of Reform in 1898. Despite national-level repression, however, regional officials and local elites were impelled of necessity to expand their range of activities as the crisis caused the discontinuation of many central government functions—until the New Policies attempted to reimpose them in 1901.

The birth of the first municipal government in Shanghai, for example, resulted from the inability of Qing officials, after the war with Japan began in 1894, to carry out long-standing projects already under way, such as widening narrow streets to increase public safety. The 1894–1895 war diverted the time and resources of national officials in charge, with the result that by default and for the first time local figures organized and ran the new city council.[2]

---

[1] See Philippe Aries, "Introduction," in *A History of Private Life*, vol. 3: *Passions of the Renaissance*, ed. Roger Chartier, 9–9, for developments in early modern Europe in which the relationship of state power to localities posed similar problems. See also William Rowe, "The Public Sphere in Modern China," *Modern China* 16.3 (July 1990): 323–323.

[2] *SHSTZG* 2:4, 1213–1215. Mark Elvin points out that the organization of the new city council owed a debt to the foreign-run municipal council of the International Settlement. See Elvin, "The Administration of Shanghai, 1905–1915," in *The Chinese City between Two Walls*, ed. G. William Skinner, 246.

The political crisis itself also stimulated changes in education. In 1896 there existed in Shanghai a branch of the strident self-strengthening organization Qiangxue hui (Society for the Study of Self-strengthening). In the next few years several early revolutionary organizations also formed—fueled by students returning from Japan and by Shanghai students at the new Nanyang gongxue (Nanyang public school). Sheng Xuanhuai set up this school in 1896, and a former Longmen Academy student, Zhang Huanlun, later became its director.[3]

Many educational institutions, societies, and clubs were founded in Shanghai and throughout the country after 1895; after the repression of the reformers of 1898 most continued to exist inconspicuously, and with no national support. Then, after 1900, local educators formed new organizations in Shanghai at a surprising rate. While most of these organizations were without explicit political platform, the fact that they were set up at all indicated the increased role of local elites in education.[4]

In 1902, for example, a Shanghai Education Society (Hu xuehui) formed, with monthly contributions required of its members. The society established a charitable elementary school, a physical education society, and a night school that taught a wide spectrum of subjects. In 1905 the society was joined by the Education Research Society (Jiaoyu yanjiu hui)—cofounded by Yuan Xitao (b. 1865), a Longmen student who had been important in Longmen's own transformation into a teacher-training school the preceding year—and staffed primarily by former Longmen Academy students. The two organizations combined in 1908 to form the Shanghai County Educational Society (Shanghai xian jiaoyu hui).[5] The extraordinary proliferation from 1906 to 1911 of these associations, so many of which had connections to 1890s *xuehui* (study societies), reveal an all but irrepressible organization taking place among Jiangsu's local educated elite.[6]

---

3 The revolutionary activity centered in the Chinese Education Society (Zhongguo jiaoyu hui) and in the Patriotism Society (Aiguo xueshe) until both were quieted in the suppression of the *Su bao* newspaper in 1903; see *SHSTZG* 2:3, 832–840. Zhang Huanlun ran another school in Shanghai in 1904 called Meixi xuetang whose curriculum was simple but progressive. Hu Shi attended that school because of the Longmen Academy friendship between his father and Zhang Huanlun. See Hu Shi, *Sishi zishu*, 47–50; *SHSTZG* 2:3, 832–840; 1:2, 628–629; *Shanghai xian xuzhi*, 18, 42a–43b.

4 Rankin, *Elite Activism*, 197–201; *SHSTZG* 2:2, 531; Frederic Wakeman, "The Price of Autonomy of Intellectuals in Ming and Ch'ing Politics," *Daedalus* 102.2 (1972): 61.

5 *SHSTZG* 2:3, 842–846.

6 Bastid, *Educational Reform*, 62–64; Wakeman, "Autonomy," 55–60.

Critical Reassessment of Classical Education, 1896–1901

After 1895 Zhang Zhidong was a dominant force in educational reform in the Middle and Lower Yangzi provinces. He promoted a central path of reform between the hard-line preservation of classical education and the Kang-Liang proposals to introduce compulsory public education. Zhang Zhidong had been a Qingliu comrade-in-arms of his *tongnian* (classmate) *jinshi* degree holder Huang Tifang. But after China's defeat in the 1884–1885 Sino-French War, Zhang Zhidong began believing in the necessity of large-scale institutional change. Zhang Zhidong served as acting governor-general of Jiangning twice in the decade after 1895, first on the heels of the Treaty of Shimonoseki in 1896 and again for half a year in late 1902 when Liu Kunyi died in office.[7] But even when he was in Wuhan as governor-general of Hunan and Hubei, Zhang's intellectual influence seemed to flow like a current down the Yangzi—as Zeng Guofan's influence had after 1864 from Jiangning—influencing the whole Lower Yangzi region after 1895.

In 1895 Zhang Zhidong brought Liang Dingfen (Z. Xinhai, 1859–1919) to Zhongshan Academy as director. Liang Dingfen had been the founding director of Zhang Zhidong's progressive Guangya Academy in Guangzhou in 1888. But when Zhang returned to Hubei in 1896, Liang went with him to manage the systematic establishment of new schools in Hubei province.[8] In his place was appointed Jiangsu native Miao Quansun, a follower of Zhang Zhidong's from the 1870s in Sichuan who had taught at Southern Quintessence and who ran Zhongshan Academy until its demise in 1901. What stands out in Miao's chronological biography during the decade after 1895 is the regularity of his trips up the Yangzi to Wuhan to consult with the man he called his teacher, Zhang Zhidong.[9]

The influence of Zhang Zhidong's yamen in Wuhan was felt down river in Jiangyin town as well. At Southern Quintessence Academy Wu Zhihui's lifelong friend, the prodigy Niu Yongjian (1870–1965), who had entered the classical academy at age nineteen, chose to leave Southern Quintessence Academy to go to Wuhan and enroll in a military school.

---

7 William Ayers, *Chang Chih-tung and Educational Reform in China*, 130, 229.

8 Su Yunfeng, "Guangya shuyuan," 256–57; Ayers, *Educational Reform*, 218, 248; Daniel Bays, *China Enters the Twentieth Century: Chang Chih-tung and the Issues of a New Age, 1895–1909*, 25.

9 *Yifeng laoren nianpu*, 21–39.

The change in political thought after 1895 pervaded new and old educational institutions. In Wuhan, Huang Shaoji (1854–1901), the son of Huang Tifang, ran another modified classical academy that Zhang Zhidong had also sponsored called the Lianghu shuyuan (Academy of Hubei and Hunan). It, however, soon produced revolutionary leaders such as Huang Xing.[10]

Looking at the Lower Yangzi academic community from Shanghai rather than from upstream Wuhan, the loosening social ties of the post-1895 era are easily as visible. The attraction in Shanghai of alternative paths to success and alternative educational patterns had, in fact, been gradually affecting even former Longmen Academy students—despite the original intentions of the 1865 Daotai to curb the effects of Western influence in the city.

Of the many able students at Longmen Academy, Zhang Huanlun is a good example of how the Shanghai local elite gradually expanded their energies and the range of their occupations after 1865. He was a favored student of Liu Xizai, and when the local Daotai decided in 1876 to found another classical academy in Shanghai modeled after Longmen, Zhang Huanlun was appointed director. Other officials attempted to appoint him to bureaucratic office—a bit like the second director of Longmen, who had stood up to the Taiping rebels. Zeng Guofan's son, Zeng Jize, and Zhang Zhidong both tried unsuccessfully to appoint Zhang Huanlun to office.[11]

What Zhang Huanlun preferred to do was not actually to lead the classical academy or become an official but to found a progressive academy of his own in Shanghai. In 1878 he began a school whose objectives stretched to the breaking point the premises upon which classical academies such as Longmen Academy were founded. His new school, Zhengmeng (Correcting Youthful Ignorance) Academy, taught moral principles that students tied directly to contemporary political issues.[12] No subject matter relating to the examination system was taught. But further, foreigners were hired to head academic departments, and military training was part of the curriculum, as were English and French. [13]

Two other Longmen students went with Zhang Huanlun to set up the more progressive academy, and at least one other Longmen

---

10 Wu Jingheng, "Hanyai shiji xu," *Wu Zhihui xiansheng wencui*, 4:302–306; Ayers, *Educational Reform*, 218, 222.

11 *SHSTZG* 1:2, 504.

12 The academy's name was taken from the most important work of Zhang Zai (1020–1077). See Zhu Xi, *Reflections*, 27.

13 *SHSTZG* 1:2, 504.

student was hired to teach there. Local gazetteers reveal that soon one of these cofounders of Zhengmeng Academy went on to teach at the Jiangnan Arsenal in Shanghai, an institution devoted explicitly to self-strengthening, where eventually even more former Longmen Academy students were attracted.[14]

A final example of the internal transformation of classical education is the work of Yuan Chang (H. Shuangqiu, 1846–1900), a fellow student at Longmen Academy of Hu Shi's father. Yuan Chang had an extraordinary career that ended in tragedy. After an 1876 *jinshi* degree, he spent eleven years in the Zongli yamen (Bureau of Foreign Affairs). His expertise on international law and experience as lieutenant governor of Zhili province led him to denounce the government's reliance upon the Boxers. He was executed by the court's pro-Boxer faction in 1900. What deserves analysis here is his educational innovation when serving as Daotai in southern Anhui province in 1894. He handsomely reendowed the local Wuhu town academy in 1895 and wrote a curriculum based on the best in nineteenth-century academies. This curriculum implemented some Longmen Academy practices he knew firsthand, including personal diaries and competitive monthly essays. But he also included in the curriculum a serious set of modern Western courses.[15]

His preface to this curricular document states the case for adapting academy pedagogy to a modern curriculum. Yuan Chang stated that the major difficulty for all schools—whether traditional academies, innovative local schools, public community schools, or private family schools—was getting good classics teachers who were also committed to applied fields of study. Either such good teachers were not on campus, or if they were there, they were swamped with duties and could not give enough time to teaching to stimulate students. He then listed recent teachers who demonstrated that these limitations could be overcome and whom he thought of as models for his new institution: Li Zhaoluo at Jiyang Academy in Jiangyin; Qian Yanshi at Daliang Academy in Zhili; Tang Queshen (Jian) at Zhongshan Academy in Jiangning; Chen Lanfu at Jupo Academy in Guangzhou; his own teacher Liu Xizai at Longmen Academy; Zhu Dingfu at Guangya Academy in Guangzhou; and Huang Yuantong (Yizhou) at Southern Quintessence Academy. These scholars

---

14 *Shanghai xianzhi*, 42–44; *Shanghai xian xuzhi*, 50.

15 Hummel, *Eminent Chinese*, 945–948; Yuan Chang, "Zhongjiang jiangyuan jianli jingyi zhishi liangzhai zhangcheng," 1–13b; Yin Baoxian, *Zhui yilu*, 44b.

stood out because they were personal models of self-cultivation, and their learning was both solid and practical.[16]

Following what Yuan Chang called the Ruan Yuan / Xuehai tang (Ocean of Learning Hall) model and the Jupo Academy model in Guangzhou, he broke the major part of the curriculum into two divisions under the guidance of two directors of study with a total of ten students each. The first division was to study the meaning of the classics (*jingyi*) and encompassed the Song school of principle, the Tongcheng school of composition, Han learning evidential criticism, and phonology. The second division was committed to applied social sciences (*zhishi*) and covered history, especially Sima Guang's *Mirror*, the dynastic administrative studies called *San tong* (Three comprehensive) and *Zhanggu xue* (Administrative history),[17] and current policy studies.[18]

Yuan Chang's reforms were carried out at Zhongjiang (Middle Yangzi) Academy in Wuhu, Anhui. He required two daily diaries, as at Longmen Academy, from students in either the first or second division of study. In addition, he required a third diary be kept at the end of each day assessing the merits and demerits of how one carried out the activities described in the other two diaries—in other words, a self-evaluation of accomplishments. A student's director of studies reviewed and critically evaluated these diaries every five days; the diaries were then submitted to the director of the academy for a final assessment.

In addition to the traditional pedagogy involved in these humanities and applied social science subjects, a series of subjects drawn more directly from foreign higher education was required. All students studied introductory-level mathematics, foreign languages, natural sciences, law, engineering, commerce, military science, and map making. These curricular reforms were published in 1896, making this curriculum surely one of the last classically based pedagogies—with the complementary Western subjects added—implemented in China. It was shortly after this date that all academies became transformed in the rush to establish China's first universal, compulsory system of public education.[19]

---

16 Yuan Chang, "Zhongjiang jiangyuan," 12.

17 See Ssu-yu Teng and Knight Biggerstaff, *An Annotated Bibliography of Selected Chinese Reference Works*, 147, 167.

19 Yuan Chang, "Zhongjiang jiangyuan," 1–2b, 5–13b.

The Passing of a Generation and Redefinition of Southern Quintessence Academy

Zhang Jian was the top metropolitan exam graduate, *zhuangyuan* (optimus), in 1894. His sympathies with the Later Qingliu proponents of that war year made him a vigorous opponent of court weakness and lack of resistance. His decision to go back to his home city in the Lower Yangzi was repeated by other literati after the suppression of the Hundred Days Reform movement in 1898 and again after the Boxer uprising. In 1895 Zhang Jian traveled to Jiangning, where Governor-general Zhang Zhidong immediately found a military assignment for him.[20]

The governor-general, fearing a diversionary Japanese attack on the Lower Yangzi—in the manner of the British during the Opium War—asked the new *zhuangyuan* to head the north bank militia. Zhang Jian agreed and had just begun militia training from a headquarters in his home in Nantong department when, in his eyes, Li Hongzhang unnecessarily conceded the war. As the treaty was signed, Zhang Zhidong, looking ahead rather than back, suggested that Zhang Jian take on an equally important task. The Treaty of Shimonoseki gave the Japanese the right to build factories in China. Zhang Jian agreed to beat them to it and to develop cotton mills in his home town of Nantong in advance of Japanese construction.[21]

In the next two decades Zhang Jian expanded his activities beyond economic development issues, becoming also the unofficial doyen of educational reform in Jiangsu. In general, he followed Zhang Zhidong's commitment to the promotion of teacher training. Zhang Jian described this commitment as an imperative of the times:

> From the time of China's utter defeat in 1894 and the lowering of her national prestige at the signing of the Treaty of Shimonoseki in 1895, the Chinese intelligentsia have come to realize the necessity of universal education. Yet universal education must rely on the training of teachers; therefore, I began to see the necessity for establishing normal schools.[22]

In 1903 Zhang Jian went to Japan to study Meiji success in popularizing education. His personal commitment in 1903 to the founding of a normal school in his native Nantong included the adoption of

---

[20] See Rankin, "Public Opinion," 471.

[21] Samuel Chu, *Reformer in Modern China: Chang Chien, 1853–1926*, 21, 88, 106.

[22] Zhu Youxian, *Zhongguo jindai xuezhi shiliao*, 88, citing *Zhang Jizi jiulu*, "Jiaoyu lu," 3:15b.

Japanese models and the hiring of Japanese visiting professors. Zhang Zhidong's Sanjiang shifan (Three River Provinces Normal School) had done the same in 1902 when it opened in Jiangning city.[23]

In 1896 Li Duanfen (Z. Xinchen, 1833–1907), then a vice-president of the Board of Punishment, memorialized that schools be established in every district and that academies be converted to *xuetang* (schools) and take their place as part of a national system of public education.[24] In the Hundred Days of Reform in 1898 when Li Duanfen was made president of the Board of Rites, he mandated his earlier proposal and called for governors to enlist the help of the local elite to manage county-level schools.[25] Even though these reforms were temporarily suspended by the suppression of the 1898 reformers, in 1901 all academies in the country were instructed by edict to convert into public schools to comprise a three-tiered public school system.[26]

The first formula for national conversion of academies required that the public academy in each provincial capital become a university-level institution called a school of higher learning (*da xuetang*). Prefectural academies were to become middle schools, and county-level academies were to become lower elementary schools. By the early months of 1902, provincial officials in Jiangsu responded to the national directives by issuing regulations implementing the 1901 edict.[27]

In the case of Southern Quintessence Academy the change registered quickly. On August 27, 1898, the Jiangsu provincial director of education memorialized the throne that the academy should be converted into a new school. The unusual quality of Southern Quintessence suggested, he argued, that it be considered to have the status not of a county-level academy, but of an institution officially sponsored in the provincial capital. In 1902 the newly appointed provincial director of education accepted this argument for special status by recommending that Southern Quintessence become a higher

[23] Zhu Youxian, *Zhongguo jindai*, chap. 5; Nanjing daxue, *Nanjing daxue xiao shi ziliao xiuanji*, 1–19.

[24] Cyrus Peake, *Nationalism and Education in Modern China*, 25; Zhu Youxian, *Zhongguo jindai*, 155, 484.

[25] Ayers, *Educational Reform*, 175, 178.

[26] Several edicts spelling out how to do this and how to ensure implementation were promulgated from the eighth month of 1901 to early 1902. See Zhu Youxian, *Zhongguo jindai*, 785.

[27] Zhu Youxian, *Zhongguo jindai*, 453–455, 785–787.

school (*gaodeng xuetang*), the highest educational level. The status accorded it acknowledged Southern Quintessence as equal to Zhongshan Academy in Jiangning city, which itself was dissolved in favor of creating a fully new institution. Southern Quintessence and the new school that succeeded Zhongshan Academy in Jiangning became Jiangsu's first two university-level institutions in the twentieth century.[28]

Although the director of education himself had allocated status to the transformed academy, the transition was anything but smooth at Southern Quintessence. The violent repression of 1898 deeply affected some scholars connected with Southern Quintessence. In 1898 the emperor's faction, or Later Qingliu faction in national politics, included, for example, lineal descendants of an original Qingliu proponent who had founded Southern Quintessence in 1884: Huang Tifang's son and nephew were both Later Qingliu proponents after 1895. The director of Southern Quintessence in 1901 just after the Boxer repression was Ding Lijun (1854–1902), who was also a Later Qingliu supporter of the Hundred Days of Reform movement.[29]

Ding's militant patriotism after 1895 was similar to Huang Tifang's at the time of the Sino-French War. Ding had long been a vigorous organizer of opposition to Li Hongzhang's negotiations with Japanese power. Ding angrily withdrew from national politics, somewhat as Zhang Jian had withdrawn in 1895—as upset with the repressions of the Hundred Days of Reform in 1898 as with the intolerable foreign pressure on the court. His final year of life (1901–1902) was spent running Southern Quintessence Academy in Jiangyin. His feelings were expressed in his preface to the third and final set of student essays published by Southern Quintessence Academy in 1901. The essays themselves were radically different from the scholia in the 1889 and 1894 editions of student essays. Ding claimed in the preface, perhaps to protect the careers of the writers, that the essays written from 1894 to 1898 had disappeared; and he strongly endorsed the current-affairs dimension found in the majority of topics collected from 1899 to 1901. The following citation reveals his spleen and his thinly veiled sympathy for the action of the Boxers' open resistance to China's weakness in 1900, as many of the scholar-officials in office, whom he felt should have taken action, sat

---

[28] Zhu Youxian, *Zhongguo jindai*, 413–421; *Nanjing shuyuan liushi zhounian* chronology, 2.

[29] Rankin, "Public Opinion," 479. Continued crisis in the transition of Southern Quintessence to a modern school will be treated in chapter 6.

on their hands:

> The unorthodox character of these essays is due to the abrupt seizure of arms by the Boxers. Influential people, both in power and out of power, were startled, but not really scared. They preferred to stay in Confucian schools and play music as before. They are indifferent to right and wrong. Morality is in chaos, and ceases. This situation cannot continue without problems....
>
> When parents are ill, there is not a son living who would neglect to find curative medicine. But if a highly qualified doctor from a family of three generations in medicine cannot be found to consult, and even if it is known that the right medicine will provide a cure, prolonging any decision may mean no cure is ever tried.... Extreme sickness then may have no effective cure. So, while the chatter of country bumpkins is vulgar and insulting, it is better to take note of it than reject it. By the time the disease becomes too extreme, the filial son may finally have to turn to what the bumpkin advised, but it will then be too late.[30]

The year 1901, when Ding Lijun wrote such anticourt sentiments in a Southern Quintessence publication, was the last year Southern Quintessence was a classical academy. In fact, 1901 marked a point in time when the generation who staffed the revival of classical academies passed from the scene. Sun Qiangming died that year after lamenting the disgrace of the court's post-Boxer move to Xi'an. His militia comrade-in-arms from the Taiping war, Huang Tifang, had passed away in 1899, and the great classicist Huang Tifang had hired from Zhejiang, Huang Yizhou, had passed away in 1898.

It was ironic that in 1898 Southern Quintessence printing house had printed copy after copy of Zhang Zhidong's manifesto smuggling Western technology into Cheng-Zhu thought. Zhang Zhidong's deputy, Miao Quansun (already appointed to preside over the final conversion of Zhongshan Academy into a modern school), was probably instrumental in having Southern Quintessence chosen to cut the woodblocks for that book, *Quan xue pian* (Exhortation to learning).[31]

Huang Tifang had never relented in his aim to correct poor leadership through good Confucian training. In 1890 he had been

---

[30] Ding Lijun, "Nanjing wenchao sanji xu," in *Nanjing jiangshe wenji: disan ji*, 1–3; Tang Zhijun, *Wuhu bianfa shi*, 334–339.

[31] On substance and function, see Zhu Xi, *Reflections*, 8, 368. When those woodblocks were burned in the Japanese bombing of the academy in World War II, some 222 sets of the two-volume work were still stored at the school. See *Nanjing*, 1935, 140, 144. See also Joseph Levenson, "T'i and Yung—'Substance and Function,'" in *Confucian China and Its Modern Fate: The Problem of Intellectual Continuity*, ed. Joseph Levenson, 59–79.

appointed to head what was probably the last newly founded classical academy in the Lower Yangzi. The institution was given Zeng Guofan's posthumous title, Wenzheng, and called Wenzheng shuyuan. Huang Tifang worked in Jiangning as its director from 1890 to 1895. It must have seemed to him eerie that his former Qingliu partner, Zhang Zhidong, arrived in Jiangning that same year to oversee the Yangzi River defenses. Twenty years before, Zhang Peilun, their Hanlin collaborator in attacking poor leadership in high places, had tried to hold off the French in the defeat at the Fuzhou Naval Yard. This foreign pressure had brought out Huang Tifang's militant Confucianism in 1884 as he founded Southern Quintessence Academy in Jiangyin. One assumes Huang Tifang was as vocal in 1895 regarding resistance to the Japanese as his Qingliu group had been in 1884 against the French, and indeed as he had been in the 1860s, back in Zhejiang, when, with his gentry-led militia, he fought against the Taiping challenge to the Confucian state.[32]

The times continued to change quickly, and Huang Tifang was probably surprised by revisions in the curriculum of Wenzheng Academy after Zhang Jian took over from him in 1895. In 1898 Western subject matter began to be introduced into the Wenzheng Academy curriculum in response to a national edict. In 1899, the year Huang Tifang died, Wenzheng Academy established a course of study introducing the study of English, translation, and mathematics—along with Chinese. When the final implementation of the 1901 edicts converted Jiangning's academies into schools in 1902, the namesake academy of Zeng Guofan was itself converted into an elementary school (*xiaoxue tang*). A respected Jiangning literatus, Chen Zuolin, was then appointed director of the new school and its eighty beginning students.[33]

The Transition to the New Educated Elite in the Lower Yangzi, 1901–1906

National educational reform policy after 1900 attempted to maintain central control over the new public schools. In 1901 there was a national edict to create schools. In 1904 the standardization of public schools, on a Japanese model, was implemented. Then followed the rapid establishment of the national Board of Education (Xue bu) in

[32] Liu Yizheng, "Jiangsu shuyuan zhi," 49.

[33] Ibid.; Chen was the chief editor of *(Xuantong) Shangyuan Jiangning xiangtu hezhi* in 1910.

1905 to manage the new system and the appointment of educational commissioners in each province the next year to oversee an educational administration reaching down to the subcounty level.[34]

An important issue implicit in the establishment of this modern public school system was how local elite initiative expressed itself in the years from 1901 to 1906. In Jiangsu, local organizations of the educated elite preceded the national edicts of 1906 that formally sanctioned their existence as offices of local administration. These new organizations, in fact, may well have pressured the central government to issue the edicts establishing local management. Shanghai can be used as a case study of specific steps taken by the local elite in one locality to organize after 1900. Following the 1901 national edict to create schools, the Shanghai county magistrate called a meeting of the trustees of academies. He then proposed, without opposition, that the boards of trustees of former academies simply shift over and become trustees of the new schools as each academy itself became a new school.[35] Old gentry leadership was continued, but myriad brand-new schools were also founded.

In 1903 there were four kinds of schools in Shanghai. First were those few public schools run under the aegis of officials with the assistance of trustees appointed by those officials, such as the interpreter's school at the Jiangnan Arsenal and the successor to Jingye Academy. Then there were at least three new public schools, including the radical Nanyang public school, that were run jointly by officials and private educators. Third, there were at least eight schools run as open enrollment public community schools but managed only by the private citizens who founded them. Finally, there were private schools managed by the citizens who founded them. These latter ran the gamut from the radical Patriotic Study Society (Aiguo xueshe) to the Catholic predecessor of Fudan University, Aurora School (Zhendan xueyuan).[36]

---

[34] Ichiko Chuzo, "Political and Institutional Reform, 1901–1911," in *The Cambridge History of China*, ed. John K. Fairbank and Kwang-ching Liu, vol. 11, pt. 2, pp. 376–383.

[35] *(Minguo) Shanghai xian xuzhi*, 633.

[36] *SHSTZG* 1.2, 504–505; "Shanghai xuetang yiban," *Jiangsu*, 3 (1903): 159–165. Within the third group was an academy set up in 1872 through the leadership of the Niu family. Niu Yongjian, the Southern Quintessence student who later went to a Hubei military school and then became a staunch revolutionary against the Qing, was a descendant of that family. In 1900 he oversaw the transformation of the original 1872 academy into the Strength and Reciprocity School (Qiang shu xuetang).

In 1905, following the abolition of the examination system, a respected local educator, Yao Wennan, a *shengyuan* who had been one of the two benefactors of Southern Quintessence Academy in 1888, formed an organization open to all teachers. Shanghai area urban and rural teachers alike were urged to join this association to organize the needed new schools, which the government seemed inadequately prepared to establish. This Society for Educational Affairs (Xuewu gonghui) agreed upon a six-provision set of bylaws in November 1905 and selected officers for a formal Bureau of Education (Xuewu gongsuo). The bylaws called for dividing Shanghai county into school districts, finding funding, and opening elementary schools as soon as possible.[37]

Shanghai's Bureau of Education was not the first in China. Each county in Guangdong had received provincial-level instructions to begin such organizations before 1905, and at least one had been formed near Canton in 1904. Also in the Lower Yangzi, Zhang Jian had applied in January 1905 to the Jiangsu provincial government in Jiangning to set one up in his home department of Tongzhou on the northern bank of the Yangzi; it opened in June 1905.[38]

The next year, the national government caught up with these developments in provincial and local educational administration. The national edict of May 1906 set up Offices to Encourage Education (Quanxue suo), which nominally claimed the right to exert administrative control over all counties. The same document, however, empowered the local educated elite to manage the new school districts.[39]

In Shanghai the full reaction to this edict came in just over a year, by November 1907. Administratively, the magistrate responded by transforming the existing Bureaus of Education into the new Offices to Encourage Education, as the national edict suggested. The leadership, however, was precisely the same as it had been in the 1905 organizations initiated by the local educated elite. The three officers in the local Bureau of Education in Shanghai—Xiang Wenrui, Gu Yan, and most prominently Yao Wennan—were named by the Suzhou commissioner of education to lead the Shanghai Office to Encourage Education. A limit on the number of years one local

---

[37] *(Minguo) Shanghai xian xuzhi*, 633–634; *SHSTZG* 2:2, 532–533. They took up housing initially at the former campus of Ruizhu Academy (Ruizhu shuyuan).

[38] On Guangdong, see Edward Rhoads, *China's Republican Revolution: The Case of Kwangtung, 1895–1913*, 53–54. See also Bastid, *Educational Reform*, 42–43, 209n44.

[39] *SHSTZG* 2:2, 532–533.

figure could serve as director of the Shanghai Office to Encourage Education was stipulated, and the office began full steam in 1907. Shanghai was neatly divided into twenty-four school districts, which the office supervised from then until the beginning of Republican government in 1912.[40]

Educational Associations

Most of the many educational societies that emerged in the first five years of the twentieth century in Shanghai were legitimately committed to improving education rather than acting as fronts for political mobilization. The era, however, was so politicized that it was all but impossible to be politically neutral. In 1903, well before the government legitimized the formation of educational associations in 1906, the revolutionary journal of Jiangsu students in Tokyo carried an article pointing out that the formation of a resist-Russia movement army in Tokyo was announced at a meeting of the Shanghai Educational Association (Shanghai jiaoyu hui). The organization referred to was probably, in fact, the Chinese Educational Association (Zhongguo jiaoyu hui), established by reformers in 1902 in Shanghai and not originally a front for revolutionaries. At the meeting some eight or nine hundred persons heard of the sacrifice these students in Tokyo were willing to make for their country. The advice of the author in Japan was that educational associations were a natural base for group organization and mobilization.[41]

As the educators of Shanghai organized, the Daotai in Shanghai followed Zhang Zhidong's guidelines and promoted teachers' education. He converted Longmen Academy, which was under his jurisdiction, into a teachers' college in 1904, although there was resistance, as shall be seen later. Also in 1904 he chose several former students at Longmen Academy to go to Japan on a special trip to study teacher training. When they returned in 1905 they formed the Educational Research Society (Jiaoyu yanjiu hui), chaired by Yao Wennan, who himself had been a student of Sun Qiangming at Longmen Academy before the Sino-Japanese War.[42]

---

[40] *Shanghai xian xuzhi*, p. 533; *SHSTZG* 2.2, 533–534.

[41] See *Xinhai geming shiqi qikan jieshao*, 1:329. "Jiaoyu hui wei mintuan zhi jichu," *Jiangsu* 3 (1903): 3–4. See Wang Ermin, *Wanqing zhengzhi sixiang shi lun*, 134–165; Wakeman, "Autonomy," 61; *SHSTZG* 2.3, 832–842. See Mary Rankin, *Early Chinese Revolutionaries*, 50–61.

[42] *Shanghai xian xuzhi*, 730–731; Shen Enfu, "Shen Enfu zizhuan," *Renwen fukan* 1.2 (1947): 1.

In 1905 the predecessor of the Jiangsu Provincial Educational Association, called the Jiangsu xuewu zonghui, was formed, using a Japanese model of appointing representatives from different localities and listing detailed subdivisions for specialized departments. One hundred ninety educators attended the October opening meeting in Shanghai, which was chaired by Zhang Jian. While most members were professionally committed to education, their initial draft of regulations noted the purpose of preparing the province for local autonomy and included plans for special courses to train judges and police officers. Indeed, soon after full incorporation, the association gradually shaped a law program and spawned a law school. After the association's formation, these self-starting educators notified the governor-general and the Ministry of Education of the society's existence and asked for support and recognition. They received both and became an officially sanctioned organization without the participation of officialdom.[43]

Several counties in Jiangsu province, in addition to Shanghai county, spontaneously formed local educational associations. Well before the national edict of July 1906 sanctioning such organizations, these counties in Jiangsu had set up self-initiated educational associations (table 5). The local educated elite in Jiangsu were willing to rapidly express their common interests in a given locality by organizing. Seventeen such county associations formed before a national sanction for them was promulgated. These data demonstrate the existence of a vigorous local educated elite. They were not alone. With chambers of commerce nationally authorized in 1904, by the end of 1906 at least forty-one local business associations formed in Jiangsu.[44] The seventeen educational associations still stand out for their spontaneous formation, as the earlier business organizations did not precede their national authorization.

In July 1906, when the national edict defining the legitimate organization of educational associations was promulgated, these associations and the provincewide educational association were converted into legal national entities conforming to that edict. In the case of the Jiangsu Provincial Educational Association (Jiangsu sheng jiaoyu hui), that final title was accorded after July 1906 to conform to

---

[43] Bastid, *Educational Reform*, 127–128; JSJYZH, 3d ed., pt. 3, pp. 1–12; *Ten Years of the Kiangsu Educational Association*, 5. See also Zhu Ying, *Xinhai geming shiqi xinshi shangren shetuan yanjiu*, passim.

[44] Zhang Yufa, *Qingji di lixian tuanti*, pp. 112–116. The number of educational associations established by the end of 1906 (an extra six months after governmental authorization) was twenty-nine. See *JSJYZH*, 3d ed., pt. 3, pp. 91–108.

Table 5
The Founding of Local Educational Associations in Jiangsu before July 1906

Place	Prefecture/ department	Founding date (lunar month)	Members
Dongtai county	Yangzhou	1904, winter	78
Ganchuan county	Yangzhou	1906, 4th month	57
Jiangdu county	Yangzhou	1906, 3rd month	55
Yizheng county	Yangzhou	1906, 3rd month	n.l.
Gaoyou county	Yangzhou	1905, 10th month	n.l.
Jiangyin county	Changzhou	1905	n.l.
Yixing/Jingxi counties	Changzhou	1905, 8th month	n.l.
Wujin/Yanghu counties	Changzhou	1905, 10th month	131
Wujiang/Zhenze counties	Suzhou	1905, 9th month	over 120
Changshou/Shaowen counties	Suzhou	1905, 9th month	276
Kunshan/Xinyang counties	Suzhou	1905, 7th month	136
Dangshan county	Xuzhou	1905, 9th month	180
Xiao county	Xuzhou	1906, 1st month	139
Tongshan county	Xuzhou	1906, 1st month	141
Liuhe county	Jiangning	1905, 11th month	n.l.
Jiangning prefecture	Jiangning	1905, 6th month	over 80
Tongzhou	Tongzhou	1905, 5th month	141

SOURCE: See *JSJYZH*, 3d ed., pt. 3, pp. 91–108. *(Minguo) Jiangyin xianzhi xuzhi*, 1921, p. 224.

national standards, but there was no alteration in the composition of the provincial association; it functioned almost as a provincial office of education, taking over the coordinating and statistic-gathering functions of a government office. Headquartered in Shanghai, the administrative organization required that representatives from both the Suzhou (southern) region of the province and the Jiangning (northern Jiangsu jurisdiction) be in the top leadership. The association aimed to establish provincewide standards and thereby maintain professional standards of quality for the explosion of modern public schools then taking place in the Yangzi Valley.[45]

[45] Bastid, *Educational Reform*, 127–128; *JSJYZH*, 3d ed., pt. 3, pp. 1–12.

Assumption of Power by the Local Educated Elite

The year 1906 was the year of no return for the rising power of the Lower Yangzi educated elite. The increased public responsibilities required by expanded educational institutions energized the swollen ranks of public sphere, local elite activism after 1895—partly by default of official obligation and partly by the national policy shifts requiring unusual initiatives from local educators. Two policies in 1906 worked together to acknowledge and legitimate a larger role for the local educated elite. In May 1906 the county Offices to Encourage Education were set up under the general supervision of county magistrates. Under this national regulation, the actual schools in each school district were to be founded, financed, and managed not by officials, but by members of the local educated elite. The second national change was the formal recognition in July 1906 of the local educational associations that were cropping up throughout China, which have just been analyzed as they formed in Jiangsu.

Analysis of the May 1906 document establishing the Offices to Encourage Education clarifies the significant evolution that had occurred between 1864 and 1906 in the managerial power of the local educated elite. This regulation accorded nonofficial appointees a seven-button bureaucratic rank without accompanying salary, to oversee county-level educational administration.[46] The position was called county inspector of education (*xian shixue*), and the inspector was to supervise the county-level Office to Encourage Education. He was to be chosen from the pool of local *shenjin*—that is, be someone of *shengyuan* status without any official appointments. Other qualifications such as study at a normal school were also noted, to be sure the *shenjin* chosen had some background in modern education. This county inspector of education then appointed a native of each school district to manage the financing, construction, and administration of new schools in the district. These school district directors (*quanxue yuan*) were also of *shenjin* status within local society, "concerned about education, competent, and of high moral character."[47] The effect of this document's definition of the management of China's new public school system in 1906 was to formalize and authorize the nonofficial local educated elite to run public education.

---

46 Seven buttons was equivalent to the rank of a county magistrate.

47 Taga Akigoro, comp., *Kindai Chugōku kyōiku shi shiryō,* 1:423. Both the document dated GX 32/4/20 and its attached regulations for the Office to Encourage Education are relevant. See also H. S. Brunnert and V. V. Hagelstrom, *Present Day Political Organization in China,* 409.

This officially endorsed emergence of gentry management, it should be noted, had been foreseen in the preceding ten years of reform proposals. As noted earlier, the earliest decentralization of modern public schools, implemented temporarily by Li Duanfen in 1898, called for enlisting the local elite to manage county-level schools. After suspension because of the repression of the Hundred Days of Reform, this idea again accompanied the national initiation of public schools in 1904: "Local officials may select gentry members . . . and charge them with responsibility for the management of educational affairs."[48]

The effects of the spread of gentry-managed and gentry-staffed county and district Boards of Education are clear over the next three years. In 1907, forty-seven of Jiangsu's sixty counties had county Offices to Encourage Education; by 1909, fifty-seven counties had complied.[49] As for the new schools actually founded, the first 564 existing in 1905 doubled to 1,182 in 1906 and continued to rise to 5,982 in 1915.[50]

Perhaps most important, local elite initiative led these foundings in Jiangsu as in Guangdong.[51] Between 1902 and 1909 community-funded public schools represented 64 percent of all foundings in the southern prefectures and 53 percent in the less affluent northern prefectures. Fully private schools split the remaining foundings with the small number of officially funded schools. Officially funded schools never reached one-third of all the new schools founded in Jiangsu.[52]

THE TRANSITION TO THE NEW ELITE IN JIANGNING CITY. The leadership of the new schools and their local administrators comprised at least three kinds of backgrounds: old established gentry, the rising generation of returnees from study abroad, and increasingly, graduates of new schools. In politically central Jiangning city, most of the prominent educated elite leadership were active in institutions with provincewide influence. One day in 1908 seventeen such prominent members of Jiangning's educated elite gathered to hear war stories. Their friendly exchange took place in the Cockcrow Temple (Jiming si) on a bluff overlooking the Yangzi on the northern exposure of Jiangning's city wall. Younger men among them such as Liu Yizheng

---

48 See Borthwick, *Education*, 93n25 citing Taga, 288.

49 Wang Shuhuai, *Zhongguo xiandai*, 232.

50 See Bastid, *Educational Reform*, 44, citing *Jiaoyu tongji tubiao* (Charts on education statistics), 1907, 27; see also *Zhonghua minguo disan ci jiaoyu tubiao*, ed. Jiaoyu bu, 98.10 (1915): 203.

51 Rhoads, *Republican Revolution*, 75.

52 Wang Shuhuai, *Zhongguo xiandai*, 244.

(Z. Yimou, 1880–1959) and Liu Shipei (1884–1919) listened carefully to the tales of men who had worked closely with Zeng Guofan. The stories were of retaking cities from the Taiping "bandit" kings some forty-five years before.

Zhu Kongzhang (Z. Zhonguo, 1842–1919) from Suzhou was the oldest storyteller that day. He had been part of the publishing house Zeng Guofan had set up in the 1860s after taking Anqing city in Zeng's move toward the Taiping capital. To reprint works appropriate to the restoration of the authority of the Confucian state, Zeng Guofan had, in fact, appointed a number of reputable southern scholars hailing from Yangzhou prefecture in Jiangsu down to Wenzhou prefecture in Zhejiang. More than one member of that 1908 group of intellectuals was then working for the lineal descendant of that Jinling publishing house, which had been under the direction of Miao Quansun since 1902.

Its new mission by 1908—which reflected the influence of Zhang Zhidong rather than Zeng Guofan—was to help publish works that established standards for the new national reform policies in education being implemented. The academies that had been reconstructed so vigorously in the 1860s were now being rapidly transformed into a public school system; and the renovated publishing house was charged to fill the need for modern textbooks for the multitude of new institutions, ranging from elementary schools to teacher-training colleges.[53] The men who headed the new publishing house were of one mind with the heads of new college-level institutions, educational officials, and the directors of China's first public libraries. Unlike the educational leadership provided by scholar-officials such as Zeng Guofan and scholars such as Liu Xizai in the period 1864 to 1884, the new leaders conceived of public instruction as increasingly separated from national politics.

Increasing regionalization of educational power after 1901 accompanied this redefinition of the role of education in the state. This began when the men Zhang Zhidong deputized as educational leaders in Jiangsu were explicitly natives of the province—men such as Zhang Jian from Nantong department and Miao Quansun from Jiangyin. After 1901, from the powerful political center of Jiangning

[53] Liu Yizheng, "You guan Taiping Tianguo de liangze shiliao," *Jianghai xuekan* 2 (1983): 73–74; Liu Dingsheng, "Liu Yizheng zhuan lue," in *Zhongguo dangdai shehui kexue jia*, 274; Liu Yizheng, "Guoxue shuju benmo," *Jiangsu shengli tushuguan disan nian kan*, 10–16; Andrew Cheng-kuang Hsieh, "Tongzhi nianjian de Jinling shuju," *Dalu zazhi* 37.1–2 (1968): 46–55.

city downriver to Shanghai, native sons began to lead educational institutions and related organizations.

In the case of Jiangning city, the early-twentieth-century redefinition of higher education felt the lasting imprint of Miao Quansun. It was his fate to preside over the dismantling of classical education in Jiangsu's political power center. In 1901 he oversaw the transition of Zhongshan Academy, which he had directed in its final five years, into a new middle-level school. Then he became the director of the one true university-level institution established in the city. In 1901, Miao also became the founding chief editor of the Jiangsu-Hubei Compilation and Translation Bureau (Jiang-Chu bianyi ju), succeeding Jinling Publishing House, set up to publish new textbooks. Finally, in 1907, he resigned from the directorship of Jiangnan Higher School (Jiangnan sheng gaodeng xuetang) to set up the first major public library for scholars in Jiangning.[54]

While he was the most prominent academic leader in Jiangning Miao made an appointment that began an intellectual lineage that lasted in the city beyond his own death and through World War II. Miao worked closely on most of his Jiangning academy projects with a self-professed disciple of Huang Yizhou from Southern Quintessence Academy—Chen Qingnian (Z. Shanyu, 1863–1929), from Zhenjiang city just downriver, who had been at Southern Quintessence Academy from its entering class of 1884 until about 1890. Chen Qingnian had been Miao's student then and had been selected for his excellence to serve as a salaried academic adviser in one of the specialized dormitories of the academy.[55]

Chen Qingnian was a late-Qing scholar whose external accomplishments were modest, but about whom everyone could not seem to say enough good things. Tang Wenzhi's (Z. Rujing, 1865–1954) funerary inscription brings out the sublime quality of Chen's standards and the personal affection of those with whom he worked or studied.[56] Although he never attained the *juren* degree, Chen Qingnian became the county director of schools in Jiangpu county, near

[54] *Yifeng laoren nianpu*, 28–29; Liu Yizheng, "Guoxue shuju," 10–16.

[55] *Nanjing*, 1935, 69–74; Liu Dingsheng, "Liu Yizheng," 269–275; Nanjing daxue, *Nanjing daxue*, 15–16; Liu Yizheng, "Guoxue shuju," 10–16. See also Chen Xunci, "Qingdai zhedong zhi shixue," 31n154; Liu Yizheng, "Jiangsu shuyuan," 69.

[56] Chen was the son of the older sister of Liu Xingen (Z. Binshu, 1795–1880), a renowned scholar from Zhenjiang city who was of the same *juren* class as Guangzhou's Chen Li (Z. Lanfu) and whose scholarship the latter greatly admired. See *Qing shi gao lie zhuan*, in *QDZJ* 94:620. See also Tang Wenzhi, "Chen jun Shanyu muzhiming," 415–421.

Jiangning, and then entered Zhang Zhidong's private secretariat in Wuhan before returning to Jiangning at the turn of the century.[57]

Once affiliated with his old Southern Quintessence teacher, Miao Quansun, in Jiangning, Chen administered two academic enterprises as Miao's second-in-command. The first was the Jiangsu-Hubei Compilation and Translation Bureau, begun in 1901. After Governor-general Liu Kunyi died in 1902 and Duan Fang (1861–1911) became acting governor-general in Jiangning, Chen joined Duan's private secretariat and continued to operate the publishing house.[58]

Then, in 1907, Chen Qingnian helped Miao purchase the extraordinary Zhejiangese book collection that became the basis of the new Jiangnan library (Jiangnan tushuguan). Chen was considered by some the founder of the library, but his superior Miao, who was a famous bibliographer, was the senior scholar overseeing the collection. Not long afterward, Miao Quansun was called to Beijing to set up the National Beijing Library, where he ended his career. As at the publishing house, Chen took over the daily administrative work of the library. In 1909 the Jiangnan library and the Compilation and Translation Bureau were combined into just the library when the Jiangsu provincial assembly disbanded the publishing house and transferred its stock of books to the new library for storage. Many classics and histories printed by Zeng Guofan's Jinling shuju (Jinling Publishing House) since the 1860s were included.[59]

Miao Quansun's 1902 appointment to Jiangnan Higher School, just reviewed, had been announced in a major school reform document written by Governor-general Liu Kunyi. Following the 1901 national policy to convert all academies into new schools, the governor-general along with the Jiangsu governor and the provincial

---

[57] See Chen Dongyuan, "Qingdai shuyuan fengqi zhi bianqian," *Xuefeng* 3.5 (1933): 19. Tang Wenzhi, "Chen jun Shanyu muzhiming," 415–421.

[58] See Hummel, *Eminent Chinese*, 781.

[59] *Yifeng laoren nianpu*, 28–29; Liu Yizheng, "Guoxue shuju," 10–16; Liu Dingsheng, "Liu Yizheng," 275. See Tang Wenzhi, "Chen jun Shanyu muzhiming," 417. In 1927, Liu Yizheng, a man Chen had brought from Zhenjiang to Jiangning, became the librarian of the expanded library. Liu Yizheng, who became a major professor of history and Sinology and a promoter of the national essence movement in newly named Nanjing city until 1949, reestablished a National Studies Publishing House (Guoxue shuju) in that year at the library and saw to it that the stored materials were made available for purchase by other scholarly collections. *Nanjing*, 1935, pp. 69–74; Liu Dingsheng, "Liu Yizheng," 269–275; Nanjing daxue, *Nanjing daxue*, 15–16; Liu Yizheng, "Guoxue shuju," 10–16. See also Chen Xunci, "Qingdai zhedong zhi shixue," 31n154; Liu Yizheng, "Jiangsu shuyuan," 69.

director of education of Jiangsu wrote up this conversion document, using Jiangning city as an example. Each of the four academies then in town was designated to be converted into a specific institution in a three-tiered school system that was itself different both from the elementary, secondary, and higher education system in the United States and from the lower primary and higher primary school division adopted in Japan in 1904.[60]

Wenzheng Academy became a lower school, admitting only students from the two counties comprising Jiangning city. Zhongshan Academy became a middle school for anyone resident in Jiangning prefecture's seven counties. Two other academies in town, Zunjing (Respect the Classics) Academy and Fengchi Academy—the latter established by Tu Zongying in 1868—both had their endowments allocated to support further study by those scholars in the prefecture who had *shengyuan* status and who were preparing for the *juren* examination. At the same time, a weaker school, Kuiguang (Glorious Stride) Academy, was dissolved.[61]

Miao's Jiangnan Higher School opened on the old Zhongshan Academy campus in 1902 with 150 students, amid continued construction to expand dormitory capacity so the school could eventually house 300 students. The best middle school students from prefectures throughout both Anhui and Jiangsu provinces were to be admitted. Once graduated from Miao's institution, they were allowed to apply to Beijing's Imperial University (Jingshi da xuetang). After a single examination in Beijing, admitted students would qualify for either an Imperial Student (*gongsheng*) degree or an Elevated Person (*juren*) degree. After graduation from the Imperial University, the Board of Rites (Li bu) then administered a final examination. Students who attained a certain rank in that examination could then receive a Presented Scholar (*jinshi*) degree.[62]

Whether these students went beyond their study in Jiangning city or not, their curriculum was quite Westernized during their study at Miao's Jiangnan Higher School. On the faculty by 1910 were specialists in several sciences, English, German, and French, and professors teaching chemistry, political science, mathematics, and Western history, using Western-language reading materials. For traditional

---

[60] "Liangjiang zongdu Liu Kunyi zouchen chouban Jiangnan ge xuetang zhe," in Zhu Youxian, ed., *Zhongguo jindai xuezhi shiliao*, 785–787.

[61] Ibid.

[62] "Jiangnan sheng gaodeng ji fuxue xianxue tang," in *Jiaoyu xiao ce huiji* 34.4 (1902): 26–28; Ayers, *Educational Reform*, 239.

subject matter, there were professors of classics, a geography specialist, and a history specialist who also was responsible for classical Chinese composition and ethics. By 1910 the Jiangnan Higher School had expanded to enroll 221 students.[63]

After academy conversion the training of teachers was the next obvious priority in educational reform. From 1902 to 1903 regional administrators saw to it that a major normal school was built in politically strategic Jiangning. Liu Kunyi began the establishment of San Jiang Normal School, and Zhang Zhidong finished it, hiring Japanese instructors for several positions in 1903. This major institution was to become more important than Jiangnan Higher School. In 1915 it became Nanjing Higher Normal School (Nanjing gaodeng shifan xuexiao), and in 1920 was upgraded to National Southeastern University (Guoli dongnan daxue). As the most important official institution in the Lower Yangzi, it later took new names and even shifted facilities to become National Central University (Guoli zhongyang daxue) in the post-1927 period and then Nanjing University (Nanjing daxue) immediately after 1949.[64]

Even before 1910 the crushing need for teachers in the proliferating new elementary schools in Jiangning led to the creation of another teacher-training institution. Zunjing Academy had been restricted to residents of the prefecture before 1900. Its old endowment included monies supporting the continuing education of *shengyuan* in the prefecture; that endowment was subsequently allocated for the construction of a new normal school serving residents from the immediate vicinity of Jiangning.[65]

By 1910 the total number of lower elementary schools created in the prefectural city of Jiangning numbered ninety-four. Thirty of these were community funded (*gongli*) and had been created from scratch since 1901. They enrolled 1,156 students, compared to the 2,516 students enrolled by the other sixty-four schools that were either officially funded or fully private schools.[66] Having one-third of

[63] *JSJYZH*, 6th ed., 82, 87–89.

[64] See Nanjing daxue, *Nanjing daxue*, passim. As Nanjing University after 1949, the university moved across town to the former campus of the missionary college Jinling daxue (University of Nanking).

[65] See *JSJYZH*, 6th ed., 84.

[66] Ibid., 40. The number of students in school in 1910 represented 11.4 percent of all school-age children. The steady growth in the number of schools, elementary and secondary, and the total number of students attending for the years 1921–1923 is shown by the following figures: 1921—122 schools, 9,487 students; 1922—130 schools, 10,112 students; 1923—145 schools, 11,065 students. See JSJYZB, *Jiangsu jiaoyu gongbao*, 1918–1926, 4.7 (July 1921): 1; 5.6 (June 1922): 17; 6.4 (April 1923): 9.

all these new schools community funded can be considered high in the traditionally government-dominated culture of Jiangning city, but it was still low compared to the rash of community-funded schools in the rest of the province.[67]

The legacy of the appointments made by Miao Quansun and Chen Qingnian is almost as important as the academic institutions they fostered in Jiangning. Miao had inspection responsibilities at the teacher's college Zhang Zhidong opened in Jiangning in 1903. Chen Qingnian recommended some of the faculty approved by Miao, including Liu Shipei, a precocious native of Ruan Yuan's home county in Jiangsu. Liu was a descendant of two scholars who had been on Zeng Guofan's staff at Jinling Publishing House.[68] After 1909 it was Liu Yizheng who took over Liu Shipei's history courses when Liu Shipei went to Beijing, and Liu Yizheng became an important figure in the intellectual lineage emanating from Miao and Chen Qingnian.[69]

Liu Yizheng was a fifteen-year-old prodigy when in 1896 he won a residential stipend from the prefectural examinations to attend Southern Quintessence Academy in Jiangyin. This was the officially sponsored system of gleaning top students for the new academy set up by Huang Tifang in 1884. Liu became an intellectual disciple of Huang Yizhou's Eastern Zhejiang historical scholarship, although whether he was even in residence in Jiangyin is not certain. He also studied with Miao Quansun, apparently after Miao took over Zhongshan Academy in Jiangning. In the flux of reassessing scholarly institutions after 1895, it was probably good fortune that Chen Qingnian had once been the student of Liu Yizheng's father in Zhenjiang.[70] Chen befriended the young Liu Yizheng and brought him to the Jiangning publishing house he was managing. Thus began Liu Yizheng's distinguished intellectual career in Jiangning, which lasted with a few breaks from 1901 to 1949.[71]

Compare Borthwick, *Education*, 94.

[67] See Wang Shuhuai, *Zhongguo xiandai*, 244.

[68] The two scholars were Liu Shouzeng (Z. Zhiyun, 1838–1882), his father's older brother, and Liu Yusong (Z. Boshan, 1818–1867), his paternal grandfather. But until he returned from Japan to work with Duan Fang in 1909, Liu Shipei had not been a prominent presence in the city and had never stayed there long.

[69] See Liu Shipei, *Liu Shenqi xiansheng yishu*, 1:22–23; Xie Guozhen, *Jindai shuyuan*, 49. On Liu Yizheng, see note 59, above.

[70] Liu Yizheng's own father was named Liu Quan (Z. Fengyuan). He died when Liu Yizheng was seven, and the young boy's education was put in the hands of his learned mother, Bao Huanzhu (Z. Puqing), who was from another well-educated family in Zhenjiang.

[71] Liu Yizheng, "Liu Yizheng zizhuan ji zishu," *Wenxian* 7 (1981): 122–124.

In the next few years Liu Yizheng was in demand to teach at many institutions. He accompanied Miao on a trip to Japan, sponsored by Zhang Zhidong, to survey schools and in 1903 published at Southern Quintessence printing press the record of the trip. Then he accepted for a while Chen Zuolin's invitation to teach at the successor of Wenzheng Academy. In 1905 Liu Yizheng turned down Zhang Jian's invitation to go to Nantong department to teach at Zhang's newly opened and private Nantong Normal School (Nantong shifan xuetang). Miao had asked him to teach at the prestigious Jiangnan Higher School, which Miao still directed, and Liu Yizheng accepted to teach history, composition, and ethics.[72]

Liu Yizheng finally took up a post as a professor of history at Nanjing Higher Normal School from 1916 to 1926. His accomplishments there, and then as director of Jiangsu Sinological Library from 1927 to 1949, made him a leader of the movement in Nanjing city (newly named after 1912, and formerly Jiangning city), promoting National Essence (*guocui*) scholarship. His scholarly writing after 1915 often counterattacked the New Culture Movement centered in Beijing. He seemed, like a latter-day Huang Yizhou, to take inspiration from the culturally preservationist role of the south, as had the founders of Southern Quintessence Academy in 1884. His debt in many areas to Huang Yizhou's intellectual heritage is clear.

Liu Yizheng was tied explicitly to the flexible academic traits of the Eastern Zhejiang Historical School because of Huang Yizhou's inspiration. Liu Yizheng shared this legacy with his senior colleague Chen Qingnian, whose own scholarly work centered on historical scholarship and whose prolific writing on local history included compiling new source materials on military history, frontier history, and the history of commodity prices. Chen Qingnian explicitly promoted the study of the ritual classics and taught Huang Yizhou's favored maxim from the *Analects*, which can be assumed to have also inspired Liu Yizheng: *boxue yueli* (liberal learning grounded in the realism of social practice).[73]

Liu Yizheng's own major scholarly contribution was to a modernized historical scholarship on traditional China. His three-volume

[72] Ibid., 125; Liu Dingsheng, "Liu Yizheng," 270; Liu Yizheng, *Ri you huibian*, (Jiangyin, 1903), preface, 1–2.

[73] Zhang Qiyun, "Wu shi Liu Yimou xiansheng," *Zhuanji wenxue* 12.2 (1968): 40; Tang Wenzhi, "Chen jun Shanyu muzhiming," 415–419. Zhang Qiyun was Liu Yizheng's student at Nanjing Higher Normal School and promoted some of these ideals later in his work at Taiwan's Institute of Chinese Culture on Yang Ming Mountain.

Zhongguo wenhua shi (History of Chinese culture) was broad, consciously inclusive of many schools of thought, and placed China carefully in the broader context of South Asian history and world history. Liu Yizheng lived out the Eastern Zhejiang Historical School's scholarly legacy by vigorously promoting the use of local gazetteers and the study of geography and by reinterpreting traditional sources to yield economic and political insights relevant to the present. He appeared to some defensive in resisting the sweeping effects of the vernacular literature movement in the north, but his own scholarship was anything but conventional. In 1905 he published a three-*juan* study of the history of commercial enterprises in China, and among his more than one hundred scholarly articles are studies of the historical records of Jiangsu's legal tender and fiscal administration. An undying advocate of the realistic and relevant insights that could be drawn from the study of history, Liu Yizheng persistently argued that China's modern historical scholarship had to develop organically from the ground of its own tradition.[74]

THE TRANSITION TO THE NEW ELITE IN EASTERN JIANGSU. Within three months of Governor-general Liu Kunyi's memorial reporting Jiangning's transition to new schools in 1902, the governor of Jiangsu's second political power center, Suzhou, also reported to the court that all former academies in Suzhou city had modernized their curricula. The governor's office in Suzhou was responsible for implementing all reform edicts in these four rich prefectures, one department, and one subprefecture south of the Yangzi River. All former academies in these political subdivisions had introduced the required study of current policy issues, and most had also introduced the study of Western subjects.

The provincial-level Ziyang Academy in Suzhou was to retain its campus and funding after 1902, although a new name had yet to be chosen. Two other former academies would serve as its feeders. Feng Guifen's graduate-level Zhengyi Academy was to be the first feeder, once it had been converted to a middle school with Western subjects introduced and a sixty-student enrollment. The former Pingjiang Academy, now converted into a lower school admitting forty students and introducing new Western subjects, was the second

74 Liu Yizheng, "Liu Yizheng zizhuan," 126; Liu Dingsheng, "Liu Yizheng," 275, 278–290; Laurence Schneider, "National Essence and the New Intelligentsia," in *The Limits of Change: Essays on Conservative Alternatives in Republican China*, ed. Charlotte Furth, 73, 75, 80, 86; Zhang Qiyun, "Wu shi Liu Yimou xiansheng," *Zhuanji wenxue* 12.2 (1968): 40; Shen Songqiao, *Xueheng pai yu wusi shiqi de fan xin wenhua yundong* (Taibei, 1984), 72–86; Liu Yizheng, *Zhongguo wenhua shi* (Taibei, 1985).

feeder. Finally, a second fancy provincially funded institution, which had been under construction since 1898 as a Chinese-Western school, was to open with a hundred students.[75] At the end of the memorial report, the governor looked east and west from his provincial capital in Suzhou and notified the court that five other institutions in the three easternmost prefectures of Jiangsu had already introduced not only courses on current policy, but also courses on Western subjects. These included, in Changzhou prefecture, the late-Ming center of political dissent, Donglin Academy, as well as Practicality Retreat (Zhiyong jingshe); in Suzhou prefecture, Wenyou Academy; and in Songjiang prefecture Young Talent School (Yucai xuetang).[76]

Shanghai. Probably the first study conducted by the Shanghai county Office for the Encouragement of Education (Quanxue suo) after its formation in 1906 was a survey of Shanghai's existing schools. It revealed that the authorities had sponsored one normal college and six lower primary schools, while the new office took credit for sponsoring two teacher-training institutions. But even in 1906 what stood out as distinctive in Shanghai were the new schools sponsored by the professions. In inner-city Shanghai these sponsorships were particularly prominent, providing funding for lower primary school foundings right up to 1911.

In 1907 new schools had been sponsored by the bean and rice guild, the cotton guild, textile guilds, the small fruit and pear orchard guilds, silver artisans, shipping organizations, the chicken and duck producers, and tea sellers. In addition the Buddhists founded schools. By 1911 these schools were joined by others sponsored by the dyer's guild and the fresh meat guild and several founded by the local autonomy association. A smaller number of schools was sponsored by Zhejiangese or Jiangsu native-place organizations from trading-port areas, including those from Nanhui county on the Pacific coast and Zhenjiang at the mouth of the Grand Canal on the Yangzi River.[77]

Traditional educational institutions had not admitted women, who were, therefore, excluded from classical literacy. Once the monopoly on education and learning was broken, however, women were no longer excluded from access to roles in society presuming higher

---

75 "Qian Jiangsu xunfu Nie Jigui zouchen gaishe xuetang zhe," in Zhu Youxian ed., *Zhongguo jindai xuezhi shiliao*, 454–455.

76 See ibid., 455.

77 *Shanghai xian quanxue suo diaocha ge xuetang yilan biao*, ed. Shanghai quanxue suo (n.p., n.d.), passim; *Shanghai xian xuzhi*, 661–665.

learning. One of the greatest social changes brought about by the expansion of education in the first decade of the twentieth century was the beginning of the formal education of women. In 1907 there were twenty women's schools in Shanghai, all founded privately by local gentry figures—many of whom ran the schools.[78]

Three of the new Shanghai women's institutions were founded by women—one by five female descendants of the Su family. Four schools had women as their directors. Students attending varied enormously in numbers, from about two dozen at some schools to 210 at the most populous. The Patriotic Women's School (Aiguo nü xuexiao) had 96 students in 1907.[79]

Many of these initial attempts at women's education failed within three years of operation, apparently for financial reasons. In 1911 fourteen out of the twenty earlier institutions were still operating. Among these fourteen, several reflected a vocational dimension. Specialization in the following areas was indicated either in the titles of institutions or in courses offered: handicrafts, physical education, Chinese medicine, the silk industry, and teacher training.[80]

The explosive expansion of modern public schools as a whole in Shanghai county occurred primarily in 1906 and 1907. The rural schools in Shanghai county—still by far the majority despite a growing urban population—were founded almost entirely by local residents or individual wealthy patrons. Because almost no professions or endowments, official or private, contributed to village schools, this dominance of community-funded schools was more typical of rural schools throughout the province. The expansion of lower primary schools at the population centers of Jiangning in western Jiangsu and Shanghai in eastern Jiangsu continued up to the 1911 revolution. While some 94 such schools existed in Jiangning county on the other side of Jiangsu by 1910, in Shanghai by 1911 there were 133 lower primary schools. Foundings sponsored by officials in Jiangning, however, contrasted with the guilds, native-place associations, and religious organizations that sponsored public schools in Shanghai.[81]

The conversion of Longmen Academy in Shanghai to a Daotai-sponsored normal school was completed in the fall of 1904. Daotai

---

78 *Shanghai xian quanxue suo,* 9b.

79 *Shanghai xian xuzhi,* 119–723.

80 Ibid.

81 In 1907 the total of all public schools in Shanghai county through senior high school was 74 schools in the metropolitan area and 107 more in rural villages in the county. *Shanghai xian quanxue suo,* conclusion. *Shanghai xian xuzhi,* 661–694.

Yuan Shuxun (Z. Xiangting) had planned the transition and sent four Shanghai-area scholars to Japan to survey normal schools there. Two former Longmen Academy students from this mission, Shen Enfu and Yuan Xitao, became the first and second presidents respectively of the new Longmen Normal School.[82] An affiliated elementary school was also quickly established. But the transition from academy to normal school was far from smooth.

In early 1904 the established Zhejiangese scholar Tang Shouqian (Z. Zhen, 1857–1917) had accepted appointment as the new director of Longmen Academy.[83] When rumors of the conversion of the academy to a normal school spread on the campus in 1904, Tang requested that the Daotai report Tang's dissenting views to higher authorities. He resisted the move to declare the academy a teacher-training school because such a move would place the school under close government control.[84] But instead of setting up a timetable for negotiations, official response was to simply begin renovations to expand the dormitory and classroom capacity of the academy for its new functions as a normal school. Longmen Academy's last director resigned in open dissent.

The student in Longmen Academy's initial class in 1865 who reported Daotai Ying Baoshi's intentions when founding the academy sympathized with Tang Shouqian's resignation in 1904. He also lamented the lost era of Neo-Confucian education, as he reviewed the distinctive education this elite academy had offered:

> All the directors were pure Confucians—basing their work on the Cheng-Zhu school. All the disciples stressed high character and studied moral principles. The traditions studied required the students to live their learning while in residence. Later, when modern schools (*xuetang*) were begun and Western studies introduced, the study of *xingli* (Song school of principle) was considered outmoded and impractical. So such academies were changed to teacher-training schools. But can the new schools equal the quality of the teaching of

---

[82] Shen served as the first president from 1905 to 1907, when he resigned to become the manager of Shanghai's Zhongguo tushu gongsi (China Book Company), which later published school textbooks. Shen remained a trustee until 1911. Yuan ran the school from 1907 to 1909, when a third member of the mission, Xia Riao (Z. Langyun), took over. See *Jiangsu shengli dier shifan xuexiao*, 1.

[83] Tang, a *jinshi* of 1895, was a reformer with strong ties to his native Zhejiang who had published extensively on philology (Rankin, *Elite Activism*, 261–262; *QDZJ* 016–509). See Shen Xianlong, "Tandong zashi," 84, for the account of Tang's connection with Longmen, which follows. His later sobriquet was "Zhen" in honor of a dissenting Ming official whose full name was homophonous with Tang Zhen.

[84] Bastid, *Educational Reform*, 121.

> the previous era? Can they produce followers of open heart and sincere feelings like those who followed the teachings of [directors] Liu or Bao?[85]

Shen Xianglong further commented that critical essays appeared at the turn of the century attacking Longmen Academy. Collections of essays exploring how to reform China's national institutions had been published about 1898, particularly in Shanghai. In one essay from 1900 the curriculum of Longmen Academy was indeed attacked because its focus on *xingli* was too speculative. The argument centered on Japan's strength and on the need to introduce current affairs into classical academies for the country's survival. The essay concluded that becoming a teacher-training institution would be a good decision for Longmen Academy.[86]

For two generations after 1865, directors, trustees, and students enjoyed the relative autonomy of establishing and running schools and academies in the Lower Yangzi. The national crisis after 1895 had fostered the organization of this local educated elite, and in the first decade of the twentieth century, the local educated elite found ample opportunity to lay claim to management rights over educational institutions. New Policies officials, however, did not envisage local control over regional institutions. Tang Shouqian resigned from Longmen Academy in 1904 for a principle that had important precedent by that time within the educated elite of the Lower Yangzi. The relative intellectual autonomy of Longmen Academy was defended by affirming its right not to teach the eight-legged essay in its revised 1870 regulations. As Qing society came unstuck after 1896, Longmen Academy leaders expected the kind of supervisory authority that bordered on management rights. It was not surprising that Tang Shouqian took a stand on these principles and soon after 1905 openly supported constitutionalism and later Sun Yat-sen's republican government. When the proposal to convert Southern Quintessence to a normal school arose in 1906, the reaction of a variety of Jiangsu educators was to be even more severe.[87]

---

[85] Shen Xianglong, "Tandong zashi," 84.

[86] "Lun Shanghai Longmen shuyuan Jingye ge shuyuan yi gai-shi shiwu," in *Zhongwai wenxian celun huihai*, vol. 22, "Xuexiao" (schools), 33b–34a.

[87] Rankin, *Elite Activism*, chap. 7; Elman, "Imperial Politics," 392–402; Min Tu-ki, *National Polity*, 182–218. The Southern Quintessence crisis will be treated in the next chapter.

CHAPTER SIX

Power and Conflict: Jiangsu's Local Educated Elite, 1906–1911

The unprecedented formation of community and privately funded public schools from 1901 to 1906 in Jiangsu province was managed by the swollen local educated elite generated largely by the expansion of local education in Jiangsu after 1864. But local conflicts and abuses abounded in the five years after 1906. The lack of firm centralized controls over proliferating local institutions generated confusion and increased local dissatisfaction. The extraction of the provincial directors of education from each province in 1906, in particular, invited conflicts among sections of provinces and between different social status groups, while setting up competition for inadequate resources that had previously been resolved according to the ground rules set by the office of the provincial director of education.

The Local Power of Jiangsu's Educated Elite

As in Guangdong province, the expansion of gentry-financed schools after 1904 served the immediate needs of families for whom education promised success.[1] But the poor in Jiangsu had also gradually to be served by new public schools, the funding for which had to be found locally. New and often unwanted forms of local taxation, affecting farmers as well as merchants, were tried. Confiscation of religious property for school use further pitted directors of local Offices to Encourage Education against local interest groups.[2]

---

1 Rhoads, *Republican Revolution*, 76.

2 See Borthwick, *Education*, 103; Philip Kuhn, "The Development of Local Government," in *The Cambridge History of China*, ed. John Fairbank and Albert Feuerwerker, 13:340; Wang Shuhuai, *Qingmo Minchu Jiangsu sheng de xinshi jiaoyu*, in *Zhongyang yanjiu yuan guoji Hanxue huiyi lunwen ji*, 263ff.

The edict of 1906 replacing provincial directors of education with commissioners of education in each province left the details of implementation imprecise. Yet the new provincial commissioners of education were to direct all administrative systems down to the appointed gentry directors of school districts. Posts in the expanded subcounty administration were all appointed, raising questions of favoritism and accountability. Natives of each school district provided the pool from which local gentry directors of school districts were selected.

But by 1909, newspapers were full of charges of personal favoritism and suspicion about the quality of many of the heads of the new public schools, who were all by definition nonofficial gentry members appointed by the new local gentry directors of school districts. Even above the county level, the administrators in the provincial capital's Bureau of Education who oversaw all the component county offices were primarily appointees from the local gentry.[3]

According to the 1906 edicts setting up the administration of local education after the abolition of the civil service examinations, the qualifying criteria for a director of a school district were simply that the person be from the locality, have some background in education, and have *shengyuan* status.[4] Academy educations certainly qualified. But the conflicts that soon emerged revealed the underside of *shengyuan* abuses in the Qing. Such abuses after 1906 seemed all but out of control.

From 1907 on, conflicts erupted in localities up and down the Yangzi, from Jiangning to Shanghai.[5] Often factions controlling the local education association even had conflicts with local elite figures staffing the local Office to Encourage Education, and the appointed leader of a specific new school might come under attack from another local faction. Occasionally, underworld influence or scholars of bad reputation in the community (*lieji*) would capture control of the educational association or illicitly expand the activities of the Office to Encourage Education.[6]

Within a year of setting up the provincial educational system, the national Board of Education (Xue bu) in Beijing began to promulgate regulations to avoid the imposition of inappropriate school levies by local educational leaders. In March 1907 the directors appointed to

---

[3] Wang Shuhuai, *Jiangsu sheng*, 232–233.

[4] Taga, *Kindai Chugōku*, 1:423.

[5] Wang Shuhuai, *Jiangsu sheng*, 266–267.

[6] See *JSXW*, 55, and Wang Shuhuai, *Jiangsu sheng*, 266.

set up schools in each school district were reprimanded:

> Recently we have heard that some gentry directors of education in various provinces had used their office to detain the common people. Some of these gentry members have had local officials prosecute them. Other gentry members have also imposed harsh fines of large amounts [on the people]. Of course they were motivated by the hope of raising large sums early, and daily increasing the number of schools, not knowing that this is just what former sages called "More haste, less speed."[7]

A year and a half after this regulation, the Board of Education in Beijing, citing two abuses from the Lower Yangzi, issued a regulation to the Commissioners of Education of all provinces to discipline both the Office to Encourage Education and education associations. These organizations had exceeded their authority in the two counties in Zhejiang and Jiangsu cited by engaging in activities not related to education. Malfeasance concerning public funds by bad gentry (*lie shen*) was the problem in Zhejiang; in Liyang county, near Jiangning city in Jiangsu, the local education association had used the authority of its seal of office to settle conflicts between native residents and outsiders. All provincial commissioners of education were instructed to watch for such abuses of statutory authority.[8]

After 1908 local self-government attracted many promoters of new schools. But right up to 1911, New Policy officials at the national level treated the coming of local self-government in education as only adjunct assistance to the appointed directors of education.[9] Yet the gradual assumption of local power over taxation and appropriation of public facilities for schools became common in self-government experiments.[10] The exercise of those powers—aggravated by crop failures—accounted for at least twenty antischool riots in local Jiangsu communities from 1908 to 1911.[11] On January 26, 1911,

[7] See Borthwick, *Education*, 99, citing text in Taga 1:472. This original regulation was dated March 23, 1907, and I have used Borthwick's translation, with slight variations.

[8] Wang Shuhuai, *Jiangsu sheng*, 266–267.

[9] "Xuebu da ge sheng...," in Taga, *Kindai Chugōku*, 1:674. This regulation was issued September 9, 1908. Kuhn, "Development," 335–338; Borthwick, *Education*, 103.

[10] Borthwick, *Education*, 103.

[11] Door-to-door census taking and resistance to Christian evangelism and other Western ideas added to these eruptions, which centered on the year 1910. From 1904 to 1911, there were about 120 antischool riots in all provinces in China, and 66 of them occurred in Zhejiang (38) and Jiangsu (28) combined. See also Abe Hiroshi, "Shimmatsu no Kigaku bodo," in *Kindai Ajia kyoiku kenkyu*, ed. Taga Akigoro, 77, 129.

one of the last Qing regulations on local education clarified how the county Office to Encourage Education should function when within local self-government auspices. Abuse of power by whoever was controlling local education remained a manifest problem amid the rather chaotic grasping for power that was taking place. The national regulations clearly repeated the prohibition on any activities exceeding the stipulated educational purview of the new county-level educational organizations.[12]

The Provincial Power of Jiangsu's Educated Elite

In the first decade of the twentieth century, locally financed and locally managed public schools in Jiangsu dwarfed in number those remaining under more direct official management. In 1906 government authorities went further and allocated management rights to the local educated elite. Thereafter, official authority slapped hands as best it could in its effort to assert continued authority over a level of institutionalized community management unprecedented in the Qing.

In 1906, in the midst of these difficulties maintaining governmental authority, the single educational authority representing access to national rank and civil service degrees in each province—the provincial director of education—was eliminated. In Jiangsu the extraction of this vertical pole of status-giving power forced ambitious Jiangsu natives to rely largely upon horizontal networks within the province to provide status. Beyond the eruption of conflicts over local power already occurring, the political stability of Jiangsu province itself experienced seismic tremors. Sectional interests opened along a fault line between the poor north and the prosperous south.

Jiangyin town was one epicenter of the social earthquake. On April 25, 1906, the Suzhou commissioner of education, administering the southern prefectures, and a Jiangning commissioner administering the north both took office, severing educational authority into sectionally defined units. At the same time, the personal sponsorship and patronage of the resident national official suddenly disappeared with the elimination of the office of the provincial director of education. The new commissioner of education with jurisdiction over Southern Quintessence as an institution would no longer live in Jiangyin, but be resident in Suzhou city. The story of how Southern Quintessence survived over the next few years reveals a host of new strategies for processing claims to patronage, brokering negotiations

[12] See Taga, *Kindai Chugōku*, 1:674.

with the new Suzhou power structure, and mediating student demands at the school and the interests of the new local officials.

The interest of the Jiangyin example is not just its rural and politically important location in the province. Rather, a larger issue emerged in negotiating the school's interests with the government. The new provincial organization of educators became the advocate and broker for the school. In arguing and resolving the future status of Southern Quintessence school after 1906, Jiangsu's provincial educated elite united to face off against the policy priorities of New Policy educational reformers in the central government.

The 1906 Crisis at Southern Quintessence Higher School

Classes had begun at the converted Southern Quintessence Higher School (Gaodeng xuetang) in 1902. The curriculum was radically revised from the one emphasizing traditional classics and history, studied since 1884. In the morning, required courses included foreign languages, such as Japanese; in the afternoon, drafting and mathematics were mandatory. Only half the curriculum was still focused upon the humanities, which before 1898 had been the entire curriculum. Final examinations were to be administered by the Jiangsu provincial director of education,[13] and the first class of 49 students finished its four years of study in April 1906.

But that would be the only graduation attended by the provincial director of education, as his post was soon after abolished. By the fall of 1906 student discontent at Southern Quintessence Higher School had exploded. There was no longer a provincial director of education to oversee and support the institution. Students paid high tuition fees that fall to attend. But many dropped out, while others wrote petitions and letters of protest. In the December 1906 winter examinations, representatives from both the office of the new commissioner of education in Jiangning and the office of the newly appointed commissioner of education in nearby Suzhou ended up attending the examinations in Jiangyin. Patronage needs for graduates and those promoted to higher grades were thereby met, but larger issues of reform of the institution were not resolved.[14]

---

13 Zhu Youxian, *Zhongguo jindai*, 1413–1419; *Nanjing shuyuan*, chronology, pp. 4–5; *Nanjing* 1935, pp. 140, 144.

14 Bastid, *Educational Reform*, 117–119, 242n8; Yin Baoxian, *Zhui yilu*, 60a–61b; *Nanjing* 1935, pp. 140, 144.

When the Southern Quintessence students went on strike, the institution ground to a halt. Petitions from students went to the educational association of the province, named the Central Educational Association of Jiangsu (Jiangsu jiaoyu zonghui) which, after reflection, wrote provincial educational officials recommending a reversion of the entire curriculum to those humanities subjects that had typified excellence in the history of the institution. The creation of a higher literary school (*wenke gaodeng xuetang*) was finally promoted by the leaders of the Central Educational Association as a solution, and, in March 1907, accepted by the Board of Education in Beijing.[15]

Zhang Jian, in his capacity as head of the Central Educational Association—renamed in 1912 the Jiangsu Provincial Educational Association—pointed out to the provincial government officials that a base in Chinese studies was being neglected in the rapid introduction of modern schools. He referred to Zhang Zhidong's 1898 notion of the danger of not providing students with a foundation of knowledge in the Chinese language before having to master that of another civilization.[16] At this same time, indeed, Zhang Zhidong himself was developing just such a school for the preservation of antiquity (*cungu xuetang*) in Wuhan to prepare teaching talent in China's traditional literature.[17] In Jiangsu at the end of 1906, Zhang Jian wrote that "since it is feared that Chinese culture is approaching oblivion, it would be best to convert Southern Quintessence into a higher literary school. Its departments of industry, agriculture, medicine, law, and the sciences can be transferred to Nanjing, Suzhou, and Shanghai."[18]

Within a year of this statement, Zhang Zhidong himself had left Wuhan to accept appointment in Beijing as head of the Board of Education; a small movement in China subsequently developed to found institutions preserving traditional humanities. Indeed, another impressive classical institution founded in Suzhou prefecture in 1888 and halted in 1905 was revived in 1908 to become another *cungu xuetang*.[19]

---

15 See Bastid's superb analysis of this development in *Educational Reform*, 117–122, 246n13. The assocation had initially been named Jiangsu xuewu zonghui in 1905.

16 See Bastid, *Educational Reform*, 117; Zhang Zhidong, *China's Only Hope: An Appeal*, 66. Zhang Jian could easily have known about this plan, since Zhang Zhidong had promoted it since 1904.

17 Ayers, *Educational Reform*, 249. See also Su Yunfeng, "Guangya shuyuan," 239–304.

18 Bastid, *Educational Reform*, 117–118.

19 Ayers, *Educational Reform*, 251; for the Jiangsu school for the preservation of antiquity, which later became a library, see Dian Yuan, "Keyuan cangshu jishi," *Jiangsu*

But in the case of Southern Quintessence, the real reasons for the proposed reversion to Chinese humanities were not cultural or pedagogical. Although Zhang Jian used the cover of asserting preservation of traditional humanities to resolve the real conflicts behind the 1906 crisis, the underlying issues involved the interests of new social groups and focused upon the autonomy and status of the local educated elite and the possible removal of a prized, status-giving regional educational institution.[20]

The student petitions of 1906 took up the idea initiated by the provincial educational association and requested conversion of Southern Quintessence into a higher literary school. They proposed that Miao Quansun, an illustrious alumnus, become the school's director and that the curriculum center on philosophy and literature, in accord with the institution's excellent intellectual legacy. But even this request had its hidden agenda. Students—as well as faculty—were trying to head off the arriving commissioner's orders from the Board of Education to try to convert Southern Quintessence into a normal school. From its central location, the training of teachers in all the northern and southern counties of Jiangsu province could be coordinated from Jiangyin, but Southern Quintessence students would then just become high school teachers.[21]

Zhang Jian's support introduced the idea of concentration in literary studies as part of a larger proposal to create a university of the south. At the time a higher school graduate, but not a normal school graduate, could apply for admission to Peking University for graduate work and consequent national placement. Instead of reducing the mobility of elite students from Jiangnan, Zhang Jian's

---

wenxian 1.3–4 (May 1944):53–67. See also Li Xibi and Zhang Shuhua, *Zhongguo gudai cangshu yu jindai tushuguan shiliao,* 315–318. See Su Yunfeng, "Guangya shuyuan," 239–304.

[20] A comparison might be made briefly here with a historical situation quite different in time and place but otherwise parallel. In Salem, Massachusetts, in 1692, townswomen and townsmen were hanged as witches and wizards for what has been analyzed for years as religious fanaticism. The faction doing the hanging in that small community was the defensive old order of farmers threatened by incoming commercial capital flooding the Massachusetts coastline and buying up the delimited resources of the farm community. The farmers combined with the clergy in using the devil to attack the new threat. Accentuating this tragedy was the temporarily inoperable administrative structure of colonial administration in the colony of Massachusetts. In China the expanded local educated elite assumed powers threatening the official prerogatives of the old order. Paul Boyer and Stephen Nissenbaum, *Salem Possessed: The Social Origins of Witchcraft,* chap. 3.

[21] See *JSXW,* 1:200; see also Bastid, *Educational Reform,* 117–118, 121, 245n8.

counterproposal would have made Southern Quintessence the Faculty of Letters of another university still to be built. Final authorization from the Suzhou commissioner of education in the fall of 1908 did not set up a university, but it did establish the evolution of Southern Quintessence into China's first higher literary school. The two-year back-and-forth exchange between Jiangsu's educated elite and the commissioner resulted, therefore, in the defeat of the normal school proposal, a defeat that revealed the strength of new social and political forces in the province.[22] The Jiangsu educated elite—students first, and then a provincewide, newly organized voice of established educators, the Jiangsu Provincial Educational Association—had faced down the central government to maintain the former status of a local institution.[23]

The poverty of Southern Quintessence was one dimension of the crisis of 1906 that was resolved by skillful brokering. When the examination system terminated in 1905, there was some corruption reported at both Suzhou and Jiangyin in connection with the establishment of the two new higher schools.[24] With the needed expansion of facilities and faculty for the increase in students, finances were severely taxed. Profits from the Southern Quintessence endowment of land were also decreasing year-by-year as Japanese silk increasingly dominated the world market.[25] Further, top prefectural candidates for *xiucai* degrees could no longer be given stipends at Southern Quintessence because of the elimination of the civil service examinations and its provincial monitor, the provincial director of education. By 1906 the private wealth of new applicants was important for the first time in decisions regarding who got admitted.[26]

---

[22] See *JSXW*, vol. 1, document by commissioner Mao dated GX/34/X/5. See also Bastid, *Educational Reform*, 117–118.

[23] It is interesting that resistance to reform policies reasserting the power of the central government over local institutions focused on the town of Jiangyin, the same town that had resisted the wearing of queues and submission to Manchu authority to the point of massacre in the 1640s. In the 1906 reaction in Jiangyin, as before, local loyalties and their bonds were the trusted base of resistance. But in the 1906 Southern Quintessence dispute, the interests of a newly organized educated elite from Jiangning to Shanghai jelled to come to the aid of more localized interests. Frederic Wakeman, "Location and Loyalism during the Ch'ing Conquest of Kiangnan," in *Conflict and Control in Late Imperial China,* ed. Frederic Wakeman and Carolyn Grant, 73. See also Min Tu-ki, *National Polity,* 207, 216.

[24] *JSJYZH*, 3d ed., pt. 3, p. 6. See also the *North China Herald and Supreme Court and Consular Gazette,* April 17, 1905, p. 12, cited in Bastid, *Educational Reform,* 245n6.

[25] Dzung Zung (Zheng Jun), "Two Whites," 4.

[26] Bastid, *Educational Reform,* 118.

The financial crisis of 1906 revealed a few of the financial strategies available to a rural academy with many elite connections. Jiangyin was a prosperous county; its gazetteer mentioned it maintained an office building in Jiangning for examination candidates and another in Shanghai for trade. When the academy director could not control the students in the fall of 1906, he wrote to the governor of Jiangsu asking that a certain lower official from Jiangning be sent to mediate so that the second graduation examinations scheduled for December 1906 would be conducted smoothly.[27]

This assignment was not simple, for when Yin Baoxian, the official—who was also a former Southern Quintessence student—got to Jiangyin he found the institution "without a penny in the coffers, and thousands in debt."[28] His task gradually changed from mediating between groups of students or between all students and the administration to brokering the interests of his alma mater with officials from the county and the province:

> A visit to the kitchen revealed the crisis—no coal or rice. The kitchen had a debt of 300 taels.
>
> Teachers resisted writing examinations, as they were not being paid. The cook could make no more meals, as he owed debts. Hungry, the students would no longer take examinations. All difficulties came from A Du [the god of mammon].

Yin estimated a minimum of a thousand taels was needed just to get through the December examinations.[29]

The tact of the outside broker now had to be exhibited. Yin Baoxian had to turn to the Jiangyin county magistrate, as no one within the academy had other financial resources. What was more, the new Suzhou commissioner of education, Zhou Shumo, was soon to arrive from Jiangning to oversee the December graduation examinations along with Yin himself. Zhang Jian had argued that such an official visit was essential to end the student protest. The magistrate

---

[27] Yin Baoxian, *Zhui yilu*, 60.

[28] As a resident of Jiangyin himself, Yin knew well the point of view of struggling students. He had himself failed Huang Tifang's toughened prefectural examinations after 1885 but was admitted to the less impressive Liyan Academy in town, where the stipends were quite modest (but better than at the Western Suburb Academy [Xijiao shuyuan] on the edge of Jiangyin). As a result Yin took on a heavy schedule of tutoring local children until his teacher at Liyan Academy recommended he try the admission exam at Southern Quintessence in 1890. He was admitted at age twenty-nine, resided on campus with a stipend of 7,000 cash per month, and began working with Huang Yizhou when the school year opened in the second month of 1890. Yin Baoxian, *Zhui yilu*, 216, 37b.

[29] Ibid., 60b.

knew that but immediately made it clear he did not want to be asked to defray the costs of the commissioner's trip.

Yin Baoxian nevertheless borrowed two thousand taels on the condition he would pay it back quickly. He promised he had other sources of revenue that would soon be made available. The kitchen stoked up for the commissioner's visit:

> Commissioner Zhou arrived with three followers. They looked well dressed, and spoke beautifully. Mr. Jin [the school's director] and I served them tea in the reception room of the school. They then said they had brought six thousand taels of silver for the school, and that it was in their boat. The whole campus was so happy.[30]

The broker's intercession with the county was not over: "All admired my ability. Mr. Wang [who may have been connected to the academy] thinks I can still get two thousand more taels from the county because I am so tactful." Since academy director Jin had established almost no contact with the county since taking office, Yin agreed to try to see the magistrate again. On this return visit, Yin first made clear he had received not only the two thousand taels, but more than enough to repay the magistrate. Further, Yin assured the magistrate that he would not ask him for further funds. Because the commissioners underwrote him, Yin commented in his diary, he himself suddenly seemed to be the host of this meeting, rather than a visitor from Jiangning.[31]

The final financial pressure was applied on yet another visit from Yin to the magistrate. This time, with his connections to the commissioner of education who was the magistrate's superior a given fact, Yin asked for some financial support for the school. After all, he explained, with the commissioner willing to underwrite the finances this time, it would be terribly awkward if in the near future classes were again interrupted: "We are all officials, I said, and cannot do embarrassing things. Mr. Wang smiled; we said nothing."[32] Monies were allocated. After the examinations went smoothly and the commissioner departed, the successful broker Yin Baoxian then continued on to Shanghai himself.

The Lower Yangzi Educated Elite and Southern Quintessence

While the 1906 Southern Quintessence crisis was calmed temporarily by the funding provided by the commissioner of education

---

30 Ibid.

31 Ibid., 61.

32 Ibid.

from Suzhou, it was really the arrival of a new administrative system and the new commissioner that was behind the destabilization of local society and the local institutions with it. Without a single national representative to overrule sectional authorities in the province, factionalism quickly festered over issues such as equity of access to good public education. External officials had run Jiangsu's higher education throughout the Qing. In the case of Southern Quintessence itself, the director of the academy in 1906 was from Sichuan, but had just resigned. And the man then newly appointed as director, Jin Shi, was from Jiangsu just north of the Yangzi River.[33] He represented northern sentiment at an institution that was under consideration to become a teacher's training college for the northern and the southern sections of the province, and this set the scene for the crisis of 1906.

When Southern Quintessence students first understood the threat of the government-ordered conversion to a lower-status institution, they had no official channels of protest. Zhang Jian received their petition because a Southern Quintessence alumnus passed it along to the Jiangsu provincial education association, which became an important advocate for the school's high status. But the two new commissioners of education in Jiangsu had just been appointed as the student petition was received by the Jiangsu provincial education association, and they had not yet taken charge of their offices.[34] Zhang Jian's counterproposal was on their desks when they did get there, and its content revealed that national reforms had already intensified sectional rivalries in the province:

> As a result of the two commissioners of education being moved to these two capitals, growing disturbances have taken place at the Southern Quintessence school in Jiangyin.... Among the [Southern Quintessence] students from prefectures run from Suzhou, more than forty have taken leaves of absence. The province is split between northerners and southerners.[35]

A background fact of importance is that just two years before, Zhang Jian had proposed that a separate province be created from all of northern Jiangsu. The idea was originally argued in terms of strategic nationalistic resistance to railroad imperialism. The underlying issue, however, was the fault line separating the prosperous rice-producing and culturally advanced southern prefectures from the

---

33 *JSJYZH*, 2d ed., pt. 3, pp. 106–107.

34 Zhang Jian text in Bastid, *Educational Reform*, 118.

35 Zhang Jian text, translated with small adaptations from ibid., 117–118.

poorer wheat-growing and backward northern prefectures—which had been potentially unstable since the initial establishment of dual administrators for Jiangsu province in 1661–1662. The new province proposed in 1904 derived its name, Jianghuai, from Jiangning and Huai'an prefectures, and its governor was appointed to administer the new entity in January 1905.[36]

Opposition then arose from the governor-general in Jiangning, who anticipated an increased staffing problem in his office in order to oversee the new political unit and worried that a skimpy tax base in the north would require increasing taxes to a level that would soon generate resistance from Jianghuai residents. Zhang Zhidong in Wuhan, with substantial experience in Jiangning, agreed. The province and its governor were recalled in May 1905.[37] The seething conflicts between northern and southern sections of Jiangsu were thereafter left to arbitration within the province.

Parrying Official Claims

After the new Suzhou commissioner of education arrived at his post and read Zhang Jian's letter regarding Southern Quintessence, the conflict between the local educated elite and officials exacerbated. The commissioner's extremely long letter a few months later responded not only to Zhang Jian but also to additional correspondence from the Jiangsu Provincial Educational Association arguing that past gentry donations, even though supplemented by official support, made Southern Quintessence not an official institution, but a community institution (*gongli xingzhi*), with local elite claims to control. The commissioner then raised the proposal by the Beijing Board of Education that Southern Quintessence become a higher normal school, which Zhang Jian's counterproposal had avoided mentioning but was aiming to counteract. Bureaucratic obstructionism followed. If Southern Quintessence became a higher-level school in the humanities, would it not also have to introduce Western humanities? If so, could the current student population possibly study English, French, and German at a level high enough to label the new institution a higher school?[38]

---

[36] Duan Fang, *Duan zongmin gong zougao*, 4, 50–51b; *North China Herald*, February 2, 1905, p. 238; Hummel, *Eminent Chinese*, 920–921; Wang Shuhuai, *Zhongguo xiandai*, 15–22; Jean Chesneaux et al., *China from the Opium Wars to the 1911 Revolution*, 221.

[37] *North China Herald*, April 28, 1905, p. 183.

[38] See Commissioner Mao's letter to the educational association in *JSJYZH*, 3d ed., pt. 2, pp. 209–211.

Commissioner Mao then raised forthrightly the delicate issue of whether or not Southern Quintessence was in any way a community-funded (or public-sphere) institution. If not, the educational association had little right to be discussing the future of an official institution. The commissioner made clear that the provincial director of education, with the active collaboration of Governor-general Zuo Zongtang, had endowed the academy in 1884—an indisputable fact. Then he sharpened the attack. He found the names of the two academy benefactors in the history of the academy from the Guangxu era. This research confused the record of givers and trustees somewhat, but it did correctly identify Yao Wennan, the Shanghai educator, as one of the two men asked by Jiangsu's lieutenant governor in 1888 to assess the value of the polder land that was eventually given to the academy as a gift by Yao and another man. Commissioner Mao raised the serious charge of possible malfeasance. He said Yao Wennan was registered as an expectant Daotai of the second civil service rank at the time, but in fact, he had thereafter become only a county magistrate and then an educator in Shanghai. Thus Yao Wennan was probably never an official of the second rank, and the expectant Daotai rank could have been purchased.

Commissioner Mao concluded that this looked like a case of polder land pettifoggery involving unprincipled lower degree holders. Mao suggested that a forgery, using the better-known name of Yao Wennan's younger brother, Yao Wendong, had possibly occurred. Such misrepresentation would have allowed trusteeship over the donated land and possible private profit. He noted that new public land along the Yangzi had produced a host of public tricksters and dike monopolists, who could have given a minimal rent to the school in the name of a gentry member while keeping most of the tenant's harvests for themselves as secret profits. Therefore the irregularity in Yao Wennan's claimed rank suggested that a scheme for extortion in 1888, not public-minded donations, was part of the history of Southern Quintessence.[39] At least so the commissioner said.

Commissioner Mao's position appeared unassailable. Successfully countering suspicions of malfeasance with claims that Yao had indeed had official status, for example, would have left the academy with the least claim to any community funding in its history. The association tried adroitly to lay the matter of malfeasance to rest and stated that fighting over Southern Quintessence's status as either an

---

[39] See Commissioner Mao's letter to the educational association in ibid., 202–208.

official or a community institution was pointless. At the same time, the association insisted that the commissioner's version of the academy's past history had errors. The response made by the Jiangsu Provincial Educational Association did not, incidentally, carry Zhang Jian's signature, probably because he did not handle daily administrative matters.

Representatives of the Jiangsu Educational Association testified that Yao Wennan and his younger brother, Yao Wendong, had together given the funds in 1888; that there was no forgery of names; and that the elder brother's name, Yao Wennan, was the only one recorded as he had assessed the value of the polder land. Both brothers had the *shengyuan* degree at the time. But the association letter left unanalyzed the status of Yao Wennan's second civil service rank and undiscussed the further question of why Yao Wennan never took higher office.[40]

Because the younger brother, Yao Wendong, was currently an appointed gentry adviser (*xuewu yishen*) to Commissioner Mao's own office (the school reform edicts of 1904 had established this consultant's role), the letter cleverly suggested Commissioner Mao could easily contact him to clear up any suspicions of malfeasance. The association further suggested, with some satire, that another letter of inquiry could easily be written to Shanghai to the Office to Encourage Education that had appointed Yao Wennan director of one school district, as that county Office to Encourage Education was also under the jurisdiction of Commissioner Mao.[41]

The witch-hunt stopped, although the commissioner of education's office never gave up its right to call Southern Quintessence an official institution. In retrospect, the conflict is ironic: the 1884 founder of Southern Quintessence, Huang Tifang, had tried hard to keep gentry interests out of the founding of Southern Quintessence, but its strongest supporters in 1906 wanted to identify it with gentry-based community funding. During the intervening twenty years the large local educated elite produced by the multitude of post-Taiping educational institutions was now trying to defend its own interests without the intercession of the state. Those interests, in the Lower Yangzi case, even included institutions with province-wide objectives and status. The Lower Yangzi educated elite wanted to find evidence in the history of Southern Quintessence, even if it

[40] Ibid., 209.

[41] See reproduction of text of the association's response to Commissioner Mao in ibid., 208–209.

stretched the record somewhat, to defend the provincial institution's autonomy from the demands of control that government officials were making in 1907.

The newly organized provincial-level association of scholars spoke for the impoverished academy in Jiangyin and its students. This expression of group interest could not be made to disappear through accusations of malfeasance—which might have worked on individual gentry figures in say 1864 or in 1884. But the Lower Yangzi educated elite was now organized.[42] In 1908 the Suzhou commissioner of education agreed with Zhang Jian's recommendation to authorize the operation of Southern Quintessence Higher Literary School.

By 1908 there was already a Jiangsu provincial parliament in existence. The commissioner of education in Suzhou then instructed an official to marshal the redefinition of Southern Quintessence through the parliament. For that job the commissioner ended up choosing Chen Qingnian of Zhenjiang, Jiangsu, the former student of Southern Quintessence who had worked under Miao Quansun in a host of intellectual endeavors in post-1900 Jiangning. It is safe to assume that Chen, who remained a disciple of Huang Yizhou until he died, was a broker who defended the lasting interests of his alma mater.[43] In a curious way the Jiangsu Provincial Educational Association was right about the pointless fight over the official versus public-sphere status of Southern Quintessence. Southern Quintessence alumni were spread around in public official positions as well as in local educational associations; and the time had come, no matter what, for the Lower Yangzi educated elite to take charge locally of implementing the region's expanded system of public schools.

In the five years following 1906, the educated elite of the Lower Yangzi assumed much local power. Formal societies institutionalizing that power were forming just as the vertical pole of nonlocal status represented by the provincial director of education was extracted from the province. After 1906 national educational administrators in

---

[42] Professor Min Tu-ki has identified many of the Lower Yangzi literati's spokesmen who—through nationalistic slogans of people's rights (*min quan*)—organized political opposition to the court. What is clear from developments I am citing is that figures such as Tang Shouqian and Zhang Jian spoke for a social stratum that had achieved effective social power by 1906, a stratum that had risen rapidly since 1865, gradually dominating local education, and that was taking charge of provincial education by 1906. See Min Tu-ki, *National Polity*, 209–218.

[43] See Commissioner Mao's implementation document to the Board of Education of Guangxu 34/X/5 (*JSXW*, *ce* 1). See also Chen Xunci, p. 31, n. 154.

Jiangsu appeared all but dysfunctional. Status no longer was allocated from them to candidates inside the province. Instead of cooperation and collaboration, the relationship of the official commissioners of education to the local educated elite was plagued with disputes over jurisdiction.

Following 1906 the local elite was gradually and by default allowed to run the local administration of education in the Lower Yangzi. Besides being school district directors, they filled posts as principals and teachers. Beyond those jobs they formed a variety of educational associations and societies, promoting the expansion of new schools as well as supporting institutions such as teacher-training schools and thereby gradually institutionalizing the self-interest of the educated elite. The Jiangsu Provincial Educational Association coordinated that elite throughout the province in an extrabureaucratic organization with unprecedented power.

The new power gradually formalized by the Lower Yangzi educated elite did not carry with it economic power, apart from working within government tax initiatives. The producer class did not easily trust the *shenjin* stratum, and conflicts with farmers and other local groups erupted when tax money was needed for school expansion. Tax resistance from farmers found alliance with tax resistance from merchants who were organizing as well, and they were both joined by resistance from religious groups offended by government confiscation of temples for schools.[44]

At the upper limits of its exercise of power, the new organization of the educated elite bumped into the official bureaucracy. The Southern Quintessence identity crisis of 1906 demonstrated that the Lower Yangzi educated elite could challenge official interests. The Jiangsu Educational Association took on the battle to determine the future of a provincial-level educational institution. It contended as an equal and came out with a result defending the interests of the organized educated elite.

---

[44] Wang Shuhuai, *Zhongguo xiandai hua*, 259–268; Abe, "Shimmatsu no kigaku," 1288–129.

Conclusion

A paradox within academy expansion after 1864 was that the crisis of reconstruction faced by leading Qing officials made them seek collaboration with eminent scholars who themselves had often rejected or been rejected by officialdom. Yet these scholars were willing to meet the most basic demand of the officials: that revitalized classical education remain relevant to the present. Zeng Guofan and Zuo Zongtang valued Confucian practicality in national reconstruction. The scholars they supported at academies could agree that political and social policy should reflect a hard-nosed evaluation of present realities and that this was possible only if contemporaneous research itself was committed to practical learning. The three elite Lower Yangzi academies studied here successfully developed practical and substantial learning (*shi xue*), achieving this common objective of the official sponsors and the scholar-directors.

The scholars who rose to the call for academy reconstruction did nonetheless bring with them their own demands and interests. The bylaws of Longmen Academy in Shanghai were written by scholars who insisted that institutional autonomy from official interest in training for the civil service examination be made explicit in order to assure the lasting quality of this new institution. In the end the scholars largely got what they wanted. Academy directors spearheaded the publication of significant syntheses of Confucian learning, including the impressive Southern Quintessence compilation of studies defining the history of classical scholarship itself in 1,430 volumes. The officials, from their side, revived academy education and committed thousands of Lower Yangzi families to pursuing its benefits.

The accomplished military strategist Zuo Zongtang became governor-general in Jiangning in the early 1880s. Yet he quickly donated a Yangzi naval installation to Huang Tifang to build a classical academy. The Japanese bombed that academy site into rubble in World War II because the location was still a strategic promontory on the Yangzi. Zuo Zongtang and Huang Tifang had their own strategic—albeit nonmilitary—objectives. These objectives targeted what they felt was the abdication of moral and intellectual purpose in earlier modernization efforts. In addition, the cadre of Confucian scholars produced by Southern Quintessence Academy after 1884 unquestionably attained the lofty aims of Confucian research scholarship that men such as Tao Zhu, Hu Peihui, and Feng Guifen had been trying to establish in the Lower Yangzi since the 1840s.

The most significant effects of reviving academy education, however, were not foreseen by its architects, be they officials or scholars. These effects were social, and they eventually carried political implications. Local educational institutions expanded in two time periods in the late Qing, both fostered by government policy. Tongzhi Restoration policy first vigorously expanded the number of charitable public schools and local academies during the decade 1864–1874, and the effects continued beyond these years. The second expansion, which accelerated the social effects of the first, began in earnest with the New Policies reforms of 1901 and continued until the fall of the dynasty in 1911. Fostered by these policies, subcounty social composition in the Lower Yangzi following 1864 developed a growing stratum of academy-educated *shengyuan* who faced underemployed.

The founders of the Tongzhi educational institutions were men with the conviction that the new schools and academies would help restore social order and educational opportunity in postwar society. The reestablishment of the authority of the central government was an objective that was assumed to follow naturally. Governor-general Zeng Guofan and his inspired associates in the Jiangsu Restoration such as Daotai Ying Baoshi and Tu Zongying shared this assumption. So did Governor Ding Richang, the censured scholar Sun Qiangming, and the Jiangsu provincial director of education in 1884, Huang Tifang.

Reopened and newly founded academies in post-Taiping Jiangsu produced a large cohort of academy-educated students. The number of such students increased for nearly four decades, reaching a total of about thirty thousand by 1900. These young men had studied a classical curriculum that focused on the basic texts of Neo-Confucian education. But in an era when the examination route to office was compromised by the sale of degrees, ranks, and posts, most of these students ended up returning to their native places to form an overeducated, underemployed stratum of local society. They became members of the local educated elite, and their numbers were significantly larger than in the first half of the nineteenth century.

After 1895 the right to organize associations of educators and also the right of nonofficials to manage the plethora of newly founded public educational institutions were assumed by the local educated elite in the Lower Yangzi and largely unopposed by the state. At some points these initiatives by the local elite were taken because the state proved incapable, because of national crises, to carry out public responsibilities. And yet, the central government still attempted to assert supervisory authority over the rapid institutionalization of local education up to 1911.

The new managerial role assumed by the organized local elite represented a clear social evolution in the Lower Yangzi from 1864 to 1911. In the 1860s Governor Ding Richang had provided the seed money for new public charitable schools and academies. Ding's energy in founding schools was unparalleled in the succeeding forty years. But what he would not have recognized at all in the second great expansion of schools after 1901 was the 1906–1907 negotiations between officials in Jiangsu and a new organization coordinating the interests of the educated elite of the province, the Jiangsu Provincial Educational Association.

By 1906 the Lower Yangzi educated elite had formalized a hitherto informal gentry duty over local education. China's first subcounty educational administration was created in 1906, and it was not officials, but the local educated elite who staffed not only supervisor positions, but also the county offices of education and the boards of trustees of specific schools and who supplied the principals and teachers in each school as well.

As the new public school system replaced the civil service examinations, it was even possible for leading institutions to resist further government supervision. Tang Shouqian resigned in 1904 from Longmen Academy in opposition to directives from the central government disregarding his local authority. And the Southern Quintessence identity crisis of 1906 pitted the united and well-organized elite of Jiangsu as an equal in negotiations against the Jiangsu commissioner of education.

At the turn of the century the men who became the intellectual leadership of Jiangning city and Shanghai city had been trained by the leading academy directors such as Liu Xizai at Longmen Academy, Sun Qianming at both Zhongshan Academy and Longmen Academy, and Huang Yizhou at Southern Quintessence Academy. Networking within this academic elite continued as had been the pattern since at least the 1840s. The students of these renowned academy directors were, however, ready to accept a different vision of the relationship of education to the state than had prevailed in the Tongzhi Restoration. Miao Quansun, Chen Qingnian, and Liu Yizheng in Jiangning and Zhang Jian, Shen Enfu, and Yao Wennan in Shanghai—although all embued with the ethos of classical academy training—presided over the disestablishment of state education. Official sponsorship of classical academies ended in the first decade of the twentieth century. The swollen educated elite produced by then was already organizing. Local and provincial educational organizations were preparing to fend for themselves among the many other new groups competing for local and regional resources and power—with little attention to what just forty years before had been the pervasive power of the state.

Epilogue

After 1912 Jiangning city became Nanjing city. It also became a center of "national essence" scholarship thanks to the intellectual leadership of several former Southern Quintessence students and to many Zhongshan Academy students who settled there. Meanwhile in Shanghai, former Longmen Academy students quietly staffed many organizations representing the interests of the educated elite in the city.

Hu Shi, a proponent of some of the most advanced pedagogical methods in the American progressive education movement, was later of the same opinion as the Qing student Shen Xianglong from Longmen Academy's first class in lamenting the end of classical academies. Hu's father, Hu Chuan, had preserved his diaries and other records from his years at Longmen Academy, when he had studied with Liu Xizai for three years, from 1867 to 1870. Hu Chuan recorded many of the teachings of Liu Xizai, and one he retained for his chronological biography was "Proper social usage and military regulations, these studies contain learning of practical value."[1] This precept dovetails nicely with Huang Yizhou's realism a bit later at Southern Quintessence.

In the 1920s Hu Shi singled out Longmen Academy, along with Southern Quintessence Academy and Ruan Yuan's two early 1800s academies, as late models of the best in the Qing tradition of academies. He lamented that, at the turn of the twentieth century, a hundred-year-old German tradition of public schools came to replace a thousand-year-old Chinese tradition, whose pedagogy, at least, was vastly superior.[2]

---

[1] Hu Songping, *Hu Shizhi xiansheng nianpu changpian chugao*, 11–18.

[2] Hu Shi, "Shuyuan zhi de shilue," *Jiaoyu huikan* 1.1 (1924): 1–4; Hummel, *Eminent Chinese*, 722. See an edited recording of this lecture in Hu Shi, "Shuyuan zhi shi lun," *Dongfang zazhi* 21.3 (February 1924): 142–146.

Hu Shi himself initiated a late-1920s intellectual movement to systematically sift the valued traditions from the past and reassert those relevant to China's current needs.[3] Such a position was compatible with John Dewey's Progressive era notions—which Hu Shi had studied—that each generation should write its own history.[4] It was also compatible, however, with the progressive Eastern Zhejiang Historical School's principles and Zhang Xuecheng's writings—which so interested Hu Shi.[5]

Hu Shi's followers, such as Fu Sinian (Z. Mengzhen, 1896–1950), picked up the academy theme in the liberal journal *Duli pinglun* (Independent critic) in the 1930s.[6] A Fu Sinian article published in 1932 denounced as a great loss the conversion of the classical academies in 1902 into new public schools. Fu decried the misconception of reformers that college-level new schools, following the form of European models as interpreted by the Japanese, should simply extend high school education. A specific element that was sacrificed by the reform, Fu Sinian felt—and he included National Peking University in his indictment—was the academy tradition of advancing scholarship. He concluded that the emphasis on the outward form of the evolution of higher education in Europe and America had left twentieth-century Chinese education as superficial as the eight-legged essay formalism of the pre-1901 era.[7]

In the 1930s this liberal criticism was counterattacked in intellectual circles. In 1936 Hu Huaichen, a scholar specializing in Shanghai's cultural history, attacked Hu Shi's praise for academy pedagogy as ignoring the other side of the issue. Hu Huaichen

[3] See Irene Eber, "Hu Shih and Chinese History: The Problem of *Cheng-li kuo-ku*," *Monumenta Serica* 27 (1968): 169–207.

[4] Barry Keenan, *The Dewey Experiment in China: Educational Reform and Political Power in the Early Republic*, 37, 148.

[5] Hu wrote a chronological biography of Zhang Xuecheng in 1922 and published it in Shanghai. See Hu Shi, *Zhang Shizhai xiansheng nianpu*. In 1921 Hu Shi further denounced contemporaneous education as prostituted to warlord power. Such a position was also compatible with the traditions of his father's alma mater, as Longmen Academy achieved some autonomy from government dictation and stressed individualized research. See Keenan, *Dewey Experiment*, 151. See also Hu Shi, "Shuyuan zhi lun," 142–146.

[6] Fu Sinian had entered in the *gu shibian* (discussions on ancient history) critiques of the late 1920, when Hu Shi's group, including the young historian Gu Jiegang (b. 1895), did so much critical scholarship on the validity of the official dynastic version of early Chinese history.

[7] Fu Sinian, "Gaige gaodeng jiaoyu zhong jige wenti," in Fu Sinian, *Fu Mengzhen xiansheng ji*, 6:292–293. I am grateful to Alexander Woodside for this reference.

referred to the anecdote of Longmen's director Sun Qiangming rejecting out of hand the student who had a foreign consul write a letter of reference for him. "Without knowing it, however, Sun thereby actually allowed foreigners to influence the internal affairs of the academy, despite himself."[8]

In the 1930s some of the most refined universities gradually adapted academy pedagogy to their curricula. When the historian Xie Guozhen assessed the Qing academy tradition in the mid-1930s, he demonstrated that the foremost research institutes operating in the 1930s were indebted to the academy tradition. The advanced research institutes of Academia Sinica (Zhongyang yanjiu yuan), established after 1928, as well as Beijing University's Graduate Institute of National Studies, were in a line of descent from the traditions begun by the classical academies. The founding regulations of the Tsing-hua University Graduate Institute of Chinese Studies, established by Wang Guowei and Liang Qichao shortly before they both passed away in the late 1920s, stated the following: "The system of this graduate institute is modeled on that of former academies, and on the English university system, emphasizing individual study under the specialized guidance of professors." At Tsing-hua University, students selected research topics and attended weekly or twice-weekly lectures on subjects such as Chinese cultural history. Then for the rest of the year they conducted in-depth research on their chosen topic.[9]

There was one twentieth-century educational institution that was basically a replica of the best in China's classical academies. It was founded and led by Tang Wenzhi from Taicang department near Shanghai. Tang had entered the opening class at Southern Quintessence Academy at age twenty in January 1885 with his *juren* degree in hand. He was chosen by Director of Education Wang Xianqian to help edit the *Continuation of the Qing Exegesis of the Classics* in 1,430 volumes before he left the academy in 1888. His *jinshi* was awarded in 1892, and he had an official career in the Bureau of Foreign Affairs. In 1903 he was appointed to the new Board of Commerce in Shanghai where he promoted the development of the Chinese economy for four years. He then ran the Shanghai Industrial School (Shanghai shiye xuexiao) and finally settled back in Wuxi city and there founded, in 1920, an institution of learning that he headed for thirty years.[10]

---

[8] Hu Huaizhen, "Xuexiao sheng," 162–163.

[9] Xie Guozhen, *Jindai shuyuan*, 24–26; quotation, 25.

[10] A Zhejiangese named Shi Xingzhi is also called a founder of Wuxi guoxue

The Wuxi National Studies Institute (Wuxi guoxue zhuanxiu guan) was an institution using classical academy pedagogy. The curriculum set by Tang focused on the same masterworks of the great tradition as were read at Southern Quintessence Academy or at Longmen Academy or at Zhongshan Academy. As they were read in thread-bound editions, with little use made of modern anthologies, the library was crucial. Tang collected voraciously and stocked some 200,000 volumes of old editions of these works and more than double that number of more recent editions. He promoted in his students the ability to study them independently. The historian and bibliographer Gu Shi commented that this library reminded him of the Southern Quintessence collection he had known fifty years earlier.[11]

Most important, learning at Wuxi Institute proceeded through a teacher-disciple relationship. This academy trait meant tutorial attention for the student. Care and personal attention brought with them strict learning and rigor. Wuxi Institute, in fact, sought to recapture what Ruan Yuan considered a crucial element of Zheng Xuan's pedagogical legacy.[12] For the Latter Han to establish specialists to interpret individual classics recalled the vital interpretive role Confucius himself established with his personal disciples. Ruan Yuan meant to reestablish this method of learning in the early 1800s, and the best post-Taiping academies in the Jiangnan region emulated the model.

At Wuxi Institute Tang Wenzhi taught explication of texts. He drew out the subtle meaning of phrases in front of the students. He also required students to master many texts through oral recitation reminiscent of Zhu Xi's injunctions against the mechanical mastery of

---

zhuanxiu guan. In his own writing, however, the thirty-year director termed himself the founder. See Chen Qichang et al., "Tang Wenzhi zhuanlue," in *Zhongguo xiandai shehui kexue jia zhuanlue*, 358; Tang Wenzhi, "Chen jun shanyu muzhiming," 123:420.

[11] Chen Qichang, "Tang Wenzhi he guoxue juanxiu guan," in *Jiangsu wenshi ziliao xuan ji*, 177, citing Gu Shi, "Shiwu nian lai zhi mulu xue" (Bibliographical study in the past fifteen years); Chen Qichang et al., "Tang Wenzhi zhuanlue," 366–367.

[12] See Alexander Woodside, "Relations between Chinese Academies and Their External World, 1700–1840," paper presented at American Historical Association panel (San Francisco, 1983), p. 9, citing Ruan Yuan, "Zengzi shibian zhushi xu" (An introduction to the ten sections of Zengzi with commentary and explanation), *Yanjing shi ji* (Collection from the study for the examination of the classics) (composed 1798), 1st collection, 2:12b–14b.

textbook learning.[13] As the institute prepared to open in 1920, Tang invited Chen Qingnian, his fellow student and disciple of Huang Yizhou at Southern Quintessence and a mentor of Liu Yizheng, to give some lectures and set the tone for the institution. This was the man who, after 1908, brokered the interests of the former academy in the Jiangsu provincial parliament. The invitation was similar to Zeng Guofan's 1860s invitation to Wu Tingdong to lecture in the former Taiping capital so that orthodox values embodied in a model figure could be emulated. But Chen Qingnian wrote back that he was too ill to travel and, indeed, died soon thereafter. It was Tang Wenzhi himself who, for the next thirty years, would represent the standard of classical learning in this replica of China's last classical academies. In that time, more than 1,700 students were trained at Wuxi National Studies Institute.[14]

[13] Chen Qichang et al., "Tang Wenzhi zhuanlue," 366–367. See Zhu Xi, *Sage*, 138.

[14] Tang Wenzhi, "Chen jun Shanyu muzhiming," 123:420; Chen Qichang, "Tang Wenzhi zhuanlue," 367–368.

Glossary

Aiguo nü xuexiao 愛國女學校
Aiguo xueshe 愛國學社
Bao Huanzhu (Z. Puqing) 鮑還珠 (字: 浦青)
Bao Yuanshen (Z. Huatan) 鮑源深 (字: 花潭)
bian 辨
bianzhi 辨志
Bianzhi wenhui 辨志文會
boxue 博學
boxue yueli 博學約禮
buzheng shi 布政使
Cang Jie 倉頡
Changjiang shuishi jingkou ying youji shu 長江水師京口營游擊署
Changyin shuyuan 常陰書院
Changzhou 堂州
Chen Ai (Z. Huchen) 陳艾 (字: 虎臣)
Chen Li (Z. Lanfu) 陳澧 (字: 蘭甫)
Chen Qingnian (Z. Shanyu) 陳慶年 (字: 善餘)
cizhang 詞章
congshu 叢書
cungu xuetang 存古學堂
da xuetang 大學堂
Dai Zhen 戴震
Daliang shuyuan 大梁書院
dao 道
daoli 道理
Daonan shuyuan 道南書院
Daoxiang shuyuan 道鄉書院
daoxue 道學
de qi jinghua zhe 得其菁華者
Deda dian 德大典
difang shenshi 地方紳士
Ding Fubao 丁福保
Ding Lijun 丁立鈞
Ding Quzhong (Z. Guochen; H. Yunwu) 丁取忠 (字: 果臣, 號: 雲梧)
Ding Richang (Z. Yusheng) 丁日昌 (字: 雨生)
dongshi 董事
Fan Benli 范本禮
Fang Zongcheng (Z. Cunzhi) 方宗誠 (字: 存之)
fashang shengxi 發商生息
Fei Nianci 費念慈
Fei Xuezeng 費學曾
Feng Lifan (Z. Jie'an) 馮禮蕃 (字: 介菴)
Feng Xu (Z. Menghua) 馮煦 (字: 夢華)
Fengchi shuyuan 鳳池書院
fu 賦

Fu Sinian (Z. Mengzhen) 傅斯年 (字: 孟真)
Gangmu 綱目
gaodeng xuetang 高等學堂
Gaoping shuyuan 高平書院
Gaoshan shuyuan 高山書院
gong 公
gongli 公立
gongli xingzhi 公立性質
gongsheng 貢生
Gongtongchang 公同昌
Gu Guangyu (H. Fangxi) 顧廣譽 (號: 訪溪)
Gu shibian 古史辨
Gu Yan 顧言
guancha 觀察
Guangya shuyuan 廣雅書院
Gujing jingshe 詁經精舍
guocui 國粹
Guoxue shuju 國學書局
guwen 古文
guxue 古學
Hanlin yuan 翰林院
Hanxue 漢學
He Changling (Z. Ougeng) 賀長齡 (字: 耦庚)
he dao 河道
He Guizhen 何桂珍
He Shenxiu (Z. Zicheng) 何慎修 (字: 子丞)
He Yikun 何貽焜
Hong Rukui 洪汝奎
Hu Chuan (Z. Dunfu) 胡傳 (字: 鈍夫)
Hu Linyi (Z. Kuangsheng) 胡林翼 (字: 貺生)
Hu Shi 胡適
Hu xuehui 滬學會
Huainan zi 淮南子
Huang Shisan (Z. Weixiang) 黃式三 (字: 薇香)
Huang Tifang (Z. Shulan) 黃體芳 (字: 漱蘭)
Huang Yizhou (Z. Yuantong) 黃以周 (字: 元同)
Huang Zongxi (Z. Taizong) 黃宗羲 (字: 太冲)
Huangqing jingjie xubian 皇清經解續編
Jia Fengzhen 賈豐臻
jiandu 監督
Jianghuai 江淮
Jiangnan zhengshu wendu 江南徵書文牘
Jiangning 江寧
Jiangning fu 江寧府
jiangshe 講社
Jiangsu anchashi 江蘇按察使
Jiangsu jiaoyu zonghui 江蘇教育總會
Jiangsu xuewu zonghui 江蘇學務總會
Jiangsu sheng 江蘇省
Jiangsu sheng jiaoyu hui 江蘇省教育會
Jiang-Chu bianyi ju 江楚編譯局
Jiangyin 江陰
jiansheng 監生
jiaoyu 教育
Jiaoyu yanjiu hui 教育研究會
Jin Songchen 金松岑
jinghua 精華
jingji 經濟
jingxue 經學
Jingxun biyi 經訓比義
Jingye shuyuan 敬業書院
jingyi 經義
Jinling shuju 金陵書局
jinshi 進士
Jinsi lu 近思錄
Jintai shuyuan 金臺書院
Jiyang shuyuan 暨陽書院
Jizi zha 季子札

Junli sima fa 軍禮司馬法
junzi boxue yu wen, yue zhi yi li 君子博學於文, 約之以禮
Jupo shuyuan 菊坡書院
juren 舉人
kai 楷
kaishu 楷書
kaoju 考據
kekao 科考
Kuiguang shuyuan 奎光書院
Kunshan 崑山
li 禮
Li Duanfen (Z. Xinchen) 李端棻 (字: 信臣)
li qi wei wo bei she 禮豈爲我輩設
Li Shenqi (Z. Zhaoluo) 李申耆 (字: 兆洛)
Li wei zhong xin zhi bo 禮爲忠信之簿
Li Yanshou 李延壽
Liang Dingfen (Z. Xin[Xing]hai) 梁鼎芬 (字: 心[星]海)
lieshen 劣紳
Liji 禮記
lijin 釐金
Lin Shoutu (Z. Yingshu) 林壽圖 (字: 穎叔)
Linjin shuyuan 臨津書院
Liu Quan (Z. Fengyuan) 柳泉 (字: 逢原)
Liu Shipei (Z. Shenshu) 劉師培 (字: 申叔)
Liu Shouzeng (Z. Zhiyun) 劉壽曾 (字: 芝雲)
Liu Xingen (Z. Binshu) 柳興恩 (字: 賓叔)
Liu Xizai (H. Rongzhai) 劉熙載 (號: 融齋)
liu yi ren yangzi 留一人樣子
Liu Yizheng (Z. Yimou) 柳詒徵 (字: 翼謀)
Liu Yusong (Z. Boshan) 劉毓崧 (字: 伯山)
Liyan shuyuan 禮延書院
lizhi 禮致
Longmen shuyuan 龍門書院
Lu Longqi (Z. Jiashu) 陸隴其 (字: 稼書)
Lu Shiyi 陸世儀
Lu Wenchao (H. Baojing) 盧文弨 (號: 抱經)
Meixi xuetang 梅溪學堂
Miao Quansun (H. Yifeng) 繆荃孫 (號: 藝風)
min 民
minquan 民勸
mu 畝
mufu 幕府
nanfang zhi xue de qi jinghua zhe 南方之學得其精華者
Nanjing congshu 南菁叢書
Nanjing jingjie 南菁經解
Nanjing zhaji 南菁札記
Nantong shifan xuetang 南通師範學堂
Nanyang gongxue 南洋公學
Niehai hua 孽海花
Niu Yongjian 鈕永建
Pu Liang 溥良
puxue 朴學
Qian Daxin 錢大昕
Qian Yanshi 錢衍石
Qiang shu xuetang 強恕學堂
Qin Chengye (Z. Buzhi; H. Yitang) 秦丞業 (字: 補之; 號: 易堂)
Qingliu 清流
qingyi 清議
qu 區
Quan xue pian 勸學篇
Quan Zuwang (Z. Shaoyi) 全祖望 (字: 紹衣)
quanxue suo 勸學所

quanxue yuan 勸學員
Rizhi lu 日知錄
Ruan Yuan 阮元
Ruizhu shuyuan 蘂珠書院
Sanjin shuyuan 三近書院
Shanghai xian jiaoyu hui 上海縣教育會
shatian 沙田
shen 紳
Shen Enfu (Z. Xinqing) 沈恩孚 (字: 信卿)
Shen Xianglong (Z. Yuezhai) 沈祥龍 (字: 約齋)
shendong 紳董
shengjian 生監
shengyuan 生員
shenjin 紳襟
shexue 社學
shi 師
Shi jing 詩經
shi xue 實學
shifan xuetang 師範學堂
shishen 士紳
shiwen 時文
shixing 實行
shixue 實學
shiyong 實用
Shu jing 書經
Sishu 四書
Songjiang fu 松江府
Songxue 宋學
Su bao 蘇報
suikao 歲考
Sun Hanyai (Z. Kuijun) 孫漢厓 (字: 揆均)
Sun Qiangming (H. Qutian) 孫鏘鳴 (號: 渠田)
Sun Yirang 孫詒讓
Sun Yiyan 孫詒言
Susongtai beibing 蘇松太備兵
Suzhou fu 蘇州府
Taicang zhou 太倉州
Tang Jian (Z. Queshen) 唐鑑 (字: 確愼)
Tang Shouqian (H. Zhixian; Z. Zhen) 唐壽潛 (號: 蟄仙; 字: 震)
Tang Wenzhi (Z. Rujing) 唐文治 (字: 茹經)
Tao Zhu (Z. Zishuang) 陶澍 (字: 子霜)
ti 體
tifu zhi 堤覆制
ting 廳
tixue shi 堤學使
Tongcheng 桐城
Tongjian 通鑑
tongnian 同年
Tu Zongying (H. Langxuan) 涂宗瀛 (號: 郎軒)
Wan Huquan (Z. Qingxuan) 萬斛泉 (字: 清軒)
Wan Sida (Z. Chongzong) 萬斯大 (字: 充宗)
Wan Sitong (Z. Jiye) 萬斯同 (字: 季野)
Wang Xianqian 王先謙
Weng Taofu (Z. Binsun) 翁弢夫 (字: 斌孫)
wenke gaodeng xuetang 文科高等學堂
Wenyou shuyuan 文游書院
Wenzheng shuyuan 文正書院
Woren 倭仁
Wu Dacheng (Z. Qingqing) 吳大澂 (字: 清卿)
Wu Jizha 吳季札
Wu Tingdong (H. Zhuru) 吳廷棟 (號: 竹如)
Wu Zhihui 吳稚暉
Wuxi guoxue zhuanxiu guan 無錫國學專修館
Xia Riao (Z. Langyun) 夏日璈 (字: 琅雲)

xian 縣
xian shixue 縣視學
xiang 鄉
Xiang Wenrui 項文瑞
xiangyue 鄉約
Xianyang shuyuan 峴陽書院
Xiao xue 小學
xiaoxue tang 小學堂
Xijiao shuyuan 西郊書院
Xinan shuyuan 溪南書院
xingli 性理
xingli xue 性理學
xingli zhushu 性理諸書
xiucai 秀才
xiushen 修身
Xu Shen 許慎
xue bu 學部
Xue heng zazhi 學衡雜誌
Xue shi lu 學仕錄
xuehui 學會
xueshi shenshi 學師紳士
xueshu bu ming er zhishu bi 學術不明而治術敝
xuetang 學堂
xuewu gonghui 學務公會
xuewu gongsuo 學務公所
xuewu yishen 學務議紳
xuezheng 學政
xundao 訓導
xungu 訓詁
Yan Yan 言偃
Yan Zi 言子
Yang Deheng (Z. Zhongqian) 揚德享 (字: 仲乾)
Yang Yi (Z. Rongpu) 揚頤 (字: 蓉溥)
yangwu yundong 洋務運勤
yangxian guan 養賢館
Yao Chun (Z. Chunmu) 姚椿 (字: 春木)
Yao Nai (Z. Xibao) 姚鼐 (字: 惜抱)
Yao Wennan (Z. Zirang) 姚文楠 (字: 子讓)
Yi tong zhi 一統志
yili 義理
Yin Baoxian 殷葆諴
Ying Baoshi (Z. Minzhai) 應寶時 (字: 敏齋)
Yinghua shuyuan 英華書院
yishu 義塾
yiwen zhi 藝文志
yixue 藝學
yong 用
Yongjia 永嘉
Yu Yue (Z. Quyuan) 俞越 (字: 曲園)
Yuan Chang (H. Shuangqiu) 袁昶 (號: 爽秋)
Yuan Shuxun (Z. Xiangting) 袁樹勛 (字: 香亭)
Yuan Xitao (H. Guanlan) 袁希濤 (號: 觀瀾)
Yuanhe 元和
yuankao 院考
Yuanxiang dian 袁祥典
Yucai xuetang 育才學堂
Yudingtai 郁鼎泰
yulu 語錄
Zeng Guofan 曾國藩
Zeng Pu 曾樸
zhaji cezi 劄記冊子
Zhang Huanlun (Z. Jingfu) 張煥綸 (字: 經甫)
Zhang Jian (Z. Jizhi) 張謇 (字: 季直)
Zhang Jizhi (Z. Qinruo) 章際治 (字: 琴若)
Zhang Luxiang (Z. Kaofu) 張履祥 (字: 考夫)
Zhang Qiyun 張其昀
Zhang Wenhu (Z. Mengbiao) 張文虎 (字: 孟彪)
Zhang Xuecheng (Z. Shizhai)

張學誠 (字: 實齋)
Zhang Zhidong 張之洞
Zhendan xueyuan 震旦學院
Zheng Banqiao 鄭板橋
zheng lian ming 正廉明
Zheng Xuan 鄭玄
Zhengmeng shuyuan 正蒙書院
Zhengyi shuyuan 正誼書院
Zhenjiang fu 鎮江府
zhi 志
zhishi 治事
zhiyong 致用
Zhongguo jiaoyu hui 中國教育會
Zhongguo tushu gongsi 中國圖書公司
Zhongni 仲尼
zhongxing 中興
zhou 州
Zhou Shumo 周樹模
Zhouli 周禮
zhu jing 主敬
Zhu Kongzhang (Z. Zhongwo) 朱孔彰 (字: 仲我)
Zhu Xiaotang (Z. Xianting) 朱小唐 (字: 獻庭)
zhu zhi ci 竹枝詞
zhusheng 諸生
Zhuxi shuyuan 竹西書院
zijin 紫金
Ziyang shuyuan 紫陽書院
Ziyu 子游
Zizhi tongjian 資治通鑑
Zong Yuanhan (Z. Xiangwen) 宗源瀚 (字: 湘文)
Zuo Zongtang 左宗棠

Bibliography

Gazetteers

Abbreviations used in this section are:

XZ (*Xianzhi*) 縣志
FZ (*fuzhi*) 府志

Baoshan XZ 寶山 1882 ed.
Baoshan xian xu zhi 寶山縣續志 1921 ed.
Changshao hezhi gao 常昭合志稿 1974 reprint of 1904 ed.
Changzhou FZ 常州 1886 ed.
Chuansha tingzhi 川沙廳志 1975 reprint of 1879 ed.
Chuansha tingzhi 川沙廳志 1974 reprint of 1937 ed.
Congming XZ 崇明 1975 reprint of 1930 ed.
Congming XZ 崇明 1926 rev. ed. of 1881 original
Dantu XZ 丹徒 1970 reprint of 1878 ed.
Danyang XZ 丹陽 1961 reprint of 1927 ed.
Danyang xian xuzhi 丹陽縣續志 1974 reprint of 1927 ed.
Fengxian XZ 奉賢 1970 reprint of 1878 ed.
Gaochun XZ 高淳 1881 ed.
Huating XZ 華亭 1970 reprint of 1878 ed.
Jiading xian xu zhi 嘉定縣續志 1930 ed.
Jiading XZ 嘉定 1881 ed.
(Xu zuan) Jiangning FZ 續纂江寧 1970 reprint of 1880 ed.
Jiangpu beicheng 江浦埤乘 1891 ed.
Jiangyin xianzhi xuzhi 江陰縣志續志 1970 reprint of 1921 ed.
Jiangyin XZ 江陰 1968 reprint of 1878 ed.
Jinshan XZ 金山 1974 reprint of 1878 ed.
Jintan XZ 金壇 1885 ed.
(Xu zuan) Jurong XZ 續纂句容 1974 reprint of 1904 ed.
Kunxin liang xian xuxiu hezhi 崑新兩縣續修合志 1970 reprint of 1880 ed.
Lishui XZ 溧水 1970 reprint of 1905 ed.

Liuhe XZ 六合 1883 ed.
Liyang xian xuzhi 溧陽縣續志 1971 reprint of 1899 ed.
Lou xian xuzhi 婁縣續志 1974 reprint of 1979 ed.
Nanhui XZ 南匯 1970 reprint of 1927 ed.
Qingpu xian xuzhi 青浦 1975 reprint of 1934 ed.
Qingpu XZ 青浦 1970 reprint of 1879 ed.
Shanghai xian xuzhi 上海縣續志 1970 reprint of 1918 ed.
Shanghai XZ 上海 1975 reprint of 1882 ed.
Shangjiang liangxian zhi 上江兩縣志 1970 reprint of 1876 ed.
Songjiang fu xuzhi 松江府續志 1974 reprint of 1884 ed.
Suzhou FZ 蘇州 1970 reprint of 1883 ed.
Taicang zou zhi 太倉州志 1975 reprint of 1919 ed.
Wu XZ 吳 1970 reprint of 1933 ed.
Wujiang xian xuzhi 吳江縣續志 1879 ed.
Wujin Yanghu XZ 吳進陽湖 1968 reprint of 1906 ed.
Wuxi Jinkuei XZ 無錫金匱 1970 reprint of 1910 ed.
(Jiaqing chongxiu) Yitong zhi 嘉慶重修一統志 1966 reprint of 1844 rev. ed. of 1820 ed.
Yixing Jingxi xian xin zhi 宜興荆溪縣新志 1974 reprint of 1882 ed.
Yixing xuzhi 宜興續志 1970 reprint of 1920 ed.
Zhenyang XZ 鎮洋 1975 reprint of 1919 ed.

Articles and Books

Abe Hiroshi 阿部洋. "Shimmatsu no kigaku bōdō" 清末の毀學暴動 (Antischool riots at the end of the Qing). In Taga Akigoro 多賀秋五郎, ed., *Kindai Ajia kyōiku kenkyu* 近アジア教育史研究 (Studies in modern Asian educational history). Tokyo, 1975.

———. "Shimmatsu no kindai gakkō Kōsei-shō o chūshin ni" 清末の近代學校一江西省を中心に (Modern schools in late Qing times—mainly in Jiangxi province). *Rekishi hyōron* 173:47–60 (Jan. 1965); 175:56–66 (Mar. 1965).

Aries, Philippe. "Introduction." In *A History of Private Life*, vol. 3: *Passions of the Renaissance*, ed. Roger Chartier. Cambridge: Harvard University Press, 1989.

Ayers, William. *Chang Chih-tung and Educational Reform in China*. Cambridge: Harvard University Press, 1971.

Ban Shuge 班書閣. "Shuyuan xing fei kao" 書院興廢考 (The administration and pedagogy of academies). *Nushi xueyuan qikan* 女師學院期刊 (Women Normal University periodical), 1.2:1–22 (1933).

Bao Yuanshen 鮑源深. "Qing gou kan jing shi shu" 請購刊經世疏 (To

petition the reprinting of books on the classics and history). In Sheng Kang 盛康, *Huang chao jingshi wen bian xubian* 皇朝經世文編續編 (Supplement to writings on imperial statecraft), 841:371–372. Rpt., Taibei: Wenhai, 1966.

Barnett, Suzanne Wilson. "Biographical Notices and Modern Education in Local Gazetteers of Nineteenth-Century Foochow." *Hanxue yanjiu* 3.2:771–796 (1985).

Bastid, Marianne. *Aspects de la réforme de l'enseignement en Chine au début du 20e siècle: d'après des écrits de Zhang Jian*. Paris: Mouton, 1971.

———. *Educational Reform in Early Twentieth-Century China*. Trans. Paul J. Bailey. Ann Arbor: Center for Chinese Studies, University of Michigan, 1988.

———. "*Qingyi* and the Self-strengthening Movement," in *Qingji ziqiang yundong yentao hui lunwen ji* 清季自強運動研討論文集 (Papers from the conference on the Qing self-strengthening movement). Taibei, 1988.

Bastid-Bruguiere, Marianne. "Currents of Social Change." In John K. Fairbank and Kwang-ching Liu, eds., *The Cambridge History of China*, vol. 11, no. 2. Cambridge: Cambridge University Press, 1980.

Bays, Daniel. *China Enters the Twentieth Century: Chang Chih-tung and the Issues of a New Age, 1895–1909*. Ann Arbor: University of Michigan, 1978.

Biggerstaff, Knight. *The Earliest Modern Government Schools in China*. Ithaca, N.Y.: Cornell University Press, 1961.

Boorman, Howard. *Biographical Dictionary of Republican China*. 4 vols. New York: Columbia University Press, 1967.

Borthwick, Sally. *Education and Social Change in China: The Beginnings of the Modern Era*. Stanford, Calif.: Hoover Institution Press, 1983.

Boyer, Paul, and Stephen Nissenbaum. *Salem Possessed: The Social Origins of Witchcraft*. Cambridge: Harvard University Press, 1974.

Brunnert, H. S., and V. V. Hagelstrom. *Present Day Political Organization in China*. Trans. A. Beltchenko and E. E. Moran. Shanghai: Kelly and Walsh, 1912.

Chan, Wing-tsit. "The *Hsing-li ching-i* and the Ch'eng-Chu School of the Seventeenth Century." In Wm. Theodore DeBary, ed., *The Unfolding of Neo-Confucianism*. New York: Columbia University Press, 1975.

———, ed. *Chu Hsi and Neo-Confucianism*. Honolulu: University of Hawaii Press, 1986.

Chang, Carsun. *The Development of Neo-Confucian Thought*. 2 vols. New York: Bookman Associates, 1962.

Chang, Chih-tung. *China's Only Hope: An Appeal by Her Greatest Viceroy, Chang Chih-tung with the Sanction of the Present Emperor Kwang Su*. New York: Fleming H. Revell, 1900.

Chang, Ch'i-yun (Zhang Qiyun). "The Political Thought and Institutions of Ancient China: An Interpretation of the *Chouli*." *Chinese Culture* 1.2:6–14 (Oct. 1957).

Chang, Chung-li. *The Chinese Gentry*. Seattle: University of Washington Press, 1970.

Chang, Hao. "The Anti-foreignist Role of Wo-jen (1804–1871)." (Harvard) *Papers on China* 14:1–29 (1960).

———. *Chinese Intellectuals in Crisis: Search for Order and Meaning (1890–1911)*. Berkeley: University of California Press, 1987.

———. *Liang Ch'i-ch'ao and Intellectual Transition in China, 1890–1907*. Cambridge: Harvard University Press, 1971.

Chen Daosheng 陳道生. "Zhongguo shuyuan jiaoyu xin lun" 中國書院教育新論 (New views on education at Chinese academies). *Shida jiaoyu yanjiu suo jikan diyi ji* 師大教育研究集刊第一輯, 1958, pp. 113–138.

Chen Dongyuan 陳東原. "Qingdai shuyuan fengqi zhi bianqian" 清代書院風氣之變遷 (The shift in the style of academies in the Qing period). *Xuefeng* 學風 (Currents of scholarship), 3.5:15–20 (1933).

Chen Qichang 陳其昌. "Tang Wenzhi he guoxue zhuanxiu guan" 唐文治和國學專修館 (Tang Wenzhi and the Institute of National Studies). In *Jiangsu wenshi ziliao xuan ji* 江蘇文史資料選輯 (Selection of sources on Jiangsu literature and history), 165–177 (1983).

——— et al. "Tang Wenzhi zhuanlue" 唐文治傳略 (Biographical sketch of Tang Wenzhi). In *Zhongguo xiandai shehui kexue jia zhuanlue* 中國現代社會科學家傳略 (Biographical sketches of contemporary Chinese social scientists). Shanxi, 1985.

Chen Tao 陳弢, comp. *Tongzhi zhongxing jingwai zouyi yuepian* 同治中興京外奏議約編 (Memorials from outside Beijing during the Tongzhi Restoration). 8 vols. 1875. Rpt., Beijing, 1985.

Chen Xunci 陳訓慈. "Qingdai zhedong zhi shixue" 清代浙東之史學 (Eastern Zhejiang School of History in the Qing period). *Shixue zazhi* 史學雜誌 (Journal of history), 2.6:1–42 (April 1931).

Chen Yuanhui 陳元暉等 et al. *Zhongguo gudai de shuyuan zhidu* 中國古代的書院制度 (The academy system in Chinese antiquity). Shanghai, 1981.

Chesneaux, Jean, et al. *China from the Opium Wars to the 1911 Revolution*. New York: Pantheon Books, 1976.

Chien, Yu-wen. *The Taiping Revolutionary Movement*. New Haven, Conn.: Yale University Press, 1973.

Chu, Samuel. *Reformer in Modern China: Chang Chien, 1853–1926*. New York: Columbia University Press, 1965.

Couvreur, S. *Dictionnaire classique de la langue chinoise*. Taibei, 1963.

Dai Zhaochen, 戴肇辰 ed. *Xue shi lu* 學仕錄 (Records of scholar-officials). 16 vols. N.p., 1867.

DeBary, Wm. Theodore. "Chinese Despotism and Confucian Ideals: A Seventeenth-Century View." In John K. Fairbank, ed., *Chinese Thought and Institutions*. Chicago: University of Chicago Press, 1967.

———. *Message of the Mind in Neo-Confucianism*. New York: Columbia University Press, 1989.

DeBary, Wm. Theodore, and John W. Chaffee, eds. *Neo-Confucian Education: The Formative Stage*. Berkeley: University of California Press, 1989.

Dian Yuan 點元. "Keyuan cangshu jishi" 可園藏書紀實 (An account of the Ke garden collection). *Jiangsu wenxian* 江蘇文獻 (Jiangsu documents), 1.3–4:53–67 (May 1944).

Ding Lijun 丁立鈞. "Nanjing wenchao sanji xu" 南菁文鈔三集敘 (Preface to the third collection of writings from Southern Quintessence Lyceum). In *Nanjing jiangshe wenji: disan ji* 南菁講舍文集: 第三集 (The third collection of writings from Southern Quintessence Lyceum). Jiangyin, 1901.

Ding Richang 丁日昌. *Ding Zhongcheng zhengshu* 丁中丞政書 (The political papers of Ding Richang). In *JDSL*, series 3, 761–765.

"Dinghai Huang shi fuzi zhuan, Shisan, Yizhou" 定海黃氏父子傳, 式三, 以周 (Biographies of Shisan, Yizhou, father and son, of the Huang family from Dinghai). In *Qingdai puxue dashi liejuan* 清代樸學大師列傳 (Biographies of Confucian masters). In *QDZJ* 012:344–347 (1985).

Duan Fang 端方. *Duan zhongmin gong zougao* 端忠敏公奏稿 (Memorial of Duan Fang). 16 *juan*. 1918.

Dzung Zung (Zheng Jun). "Two Whites: The Future Policy of Nan-tsin School." *Nanjing* 7:3–7 (1924).

Eastman, Lloyd. *Throne and Mandarins: China's Search for a Policy during the Sino-French Controversy, 1880–1885*. Cambridge: Harvard University Press, 1967.

Eber, Irene. "Hu Shih and Chinese History: The Problem of *Cheng-li kuo-ku*." *Monumenta Serica* 27.8:169–207 (1968).

Elman, Benjamin. "The Evolution of Civil Service Examinations in Late Imperial China." *Newsletter for Modern Chinese History*, no. 11:65–89 (1991).

———. *From Philosophy to Philology: Intellectual and Social Aspects of*

Change in Late Imperial China. Cambridge: Harvard University Press, 1984.

———. "Imperial Politics and Confucian Societies in Late Imperial China: The Hanlin and Donglin Academies." *Modern China* 15.4:379–418 (1989).

Elvin, M. "The Administration of Shanghai, 1905–1914." In Mark Elvin and G. William Skinner, eds., *The Chinese City between Two Worlds*, pp. 239–262. Stanford, Calif.: Stanford University Press, 1974.

———. "Market Towns and Waterways: The County of Shanghai from 1480 to 1910." In G. William Skinner, ed., *The City in Late Imperial China*. Stanford, Calif.: Stanford University Press, 1977.

Esherick, Joseph W., and Mary Backus Rankin, eds. *Chinese Local Elites and Patterns of Dominance*. Berkeley: University of California Press, 1990.

Fang, Chao-ying. "Ting Jih-ch'ang." In Arthur Hummel, *Eminent Chinese of the Ch'ing Period*. Washington, D.C.: Government Printing Office, 1943.

Feng Guifen 馮桂芬. "Gaijian, Zhengyi shuyuanji" 改建正誼書院記 (A record of the renovation of Zhengyi Academy). In Feng Guifen, *Xuzhi tang ji*.

———. "Xiyin shushe wushen keyi xu" 惜陰書舍戊申課藝序 (Preface to the 1848 curriculum of Xiyin study). In Feng Guifen, *Xuzhi tang ji*.

———. *Xuzhi tang ji* 顯志堂集 (Collection from the Hall of Manifest Aspirations). 1876. Rpt., Taibei, 1967.

Feng Xu 馮煦. *Hao'an suibi* 蒿菴隨筆 (Varied writings from a grass hut). Taibei, 1966.

Fincher, John H. *Chinese Democracy: The Self-government Movement in Local, Provincial and National Politics, 1905–1914*. Canberra: Australia National University Press, 1983.

Franke, Wolfgang. *The Reform and Abolition of the Traditional Chinese Examination System*. Cambridge: Harvard University East Asian Research Center, 1968.

Fu Sinian 傅斯年. "Gaige gaodeng jiaoyu zhong jige wenti" 改革高等教育中幾個問題 (Some issues in reforming higher education). In Fu Sinian 傅斯年, ed., *Fu Mengzhen xiansheng ji* 傅孟眞先生集 (Collected works of Fu Sinian). 6 vols. Taibei, 1952.

FWGD. *Fuwu gongdu* 撫吳公牘 (Official papers from Ding Richang's governorship of Jiangsu). 1878 preface. 3 vols. Rpt., Taibei, n.d.

Gan Xi 甘熙. *Baixia suoyan* 白下瑣言 (Fragmented notes on Nanjing city). Taibei, 1970.

Grimm, Tilemann. "Academies and Urban Systems in Kwangtung." In

G. William Skinner, ed., *The City in Late Imperial China*. Stanford, Calif.: Stanford University Press, 1977.

Hail, William J. *Tseng Kuo-fan and the Taiping Rebellion: With a Short Sketch of His Later Career*. 1926. Rpt., Taibei, 1964.

Hayashi Tomoharu 林友春. "Shincho no shoin kyoiku" 清朝の書院教育 (Academy education in the Qing period). *Gakushuin Daigaku Bungakubu Kenkyu Nenpo* 學習院大學文部研究年報 (Annual research bulletin of the humanities section of Gakushuin University), 6:177–197 (1959).

He Guanbiao 何冠彪. *Mingmo Qingchu xueshu sixiang yanjiu* 明末清初學術思想研究 (Research on scholarly thought in the late Ming, early Qing era). Taibei, 1991.

Hong Huanqun 洪煥椿. *Zhejiang wenxian congkao* 浙江文獻叢考 (A collection of reprinted Zhejiang source materials). Hangzhou, 1983.

Hsiao, Kung-ch'uan. *Rural China: Imperial Control in the Nineteenth Century*. Seattle: University of Washington Press, 1967.

Hsieh, Andrew Cheng-kuang. "Tongzhi nianjian de Jinling shuju" 同治年間的金陵書局 (Jinling publication bureau in the Tongzhi period). *Dalu zazhi* 大陸雜誌 (Mainland magazine), 37.1–2:46–55 (1968).

———. "Tseng Kuo-fan, a Nineteenth-Century Confucian General." Ph.D. dissertation, Yale University, 1975.

Hsu, Immanuel C. Y. "Late Ch'ing Foreign Relations, 1866–1905." In John K. Fairbank and Kwang-ching Liu, eds., *The Cambridge History of China*. Vol. 11, no. 2. Cambridge: Cambridge University Press, 1980.

Hu, C. T. "The Historical Background: Examinations and Control in Pre-Modern China." *Comparative Education* 20.1:7–26 (1984).

Hu Chuan 胡傳. "Dunfu nianpu" 鈍夫年譜 (Chronological biography of Hu Chuan). In Hu Shi, *Sishi zishu* (Autobiography at forty). Taibei, 1991.

———. *Taiwan riji yu pinqi* 臺灣日記與稟啓 (Taiwan diaries and records). 2 vols. Taibei, 1960.

Hu Huaichen 胡懷琛. "Xuexiao shenghuo yu shuyuan shenghuo" 學校生活與書院生活 (School life and academy life). In *Shanghai yanjiu ziliao* 上海研究資料 (Shanghai research materials), 1935. Rpt., Taibei, 1973.

Hu Peihui 胡培翬. "Xiyin shuyuan bie zhusheng wen" 惜陰書院別諸生文 (On Xiyin Academy's other government students). In Hu Peihui, *Jiu liu shi wenchao, buyi* 研六室文鈔補遺 (Posthumous supplement to the study of the six classics literary collection). 10 vols. N.p., 1880.

Hu Shi 胡適. *Hu shi koushu zizhuan* 胡適口述自傳 (Hu Shi's oral history autobiography). Tang Degang yizhu 唐德剛譯註 (Translated with commentary by Tang Degang). Taibei, 1986.

———. "Shuyuan zhi di shilue" 書院制的史略 (A historical sketch of the academy system). *Jiaoyu huikan* 教育彙刊 (Education periodical), 2.1:4 (1924).

———. "Shuyuan zhi shi lun" 書院制史略. (An outline history of the academy system). *Dongfang zazhi* 東方雜誌 21.3:142–146 (Feb. 1924).

———. *Sishi zishu* 四十自述 (Autobiography at forty). Taibei, 1991.

———. *Zhang Shizhai xiansheng nianpu* 章實齊先生年譜. (Zhang Xuecheng's chronological biography). Taibei, 1973.

Hu Shi xiansheng nianpu changbian chugao 胡適先生年譜長編初稿 (Draft of chronicle of Mr. Hu Shi). Hu Songping 胡頌平, ed. Taibei, 1984.

Huang, Boyle (Baoyu) 黃寶瑜. Interview with the artist, architect, and calligrapher Huang Baoyu. Toronto, Canada, Aug. 15, 1990.

Huang Liuhong 黃六鴻. *A Complete Book Concerning Happiness and Benevolence: Fu-hui ch'uan-shu*. 1699. Ed. and tr. Djang Chu 章楚. Tucson: University of Arizona Press, 1984.

"Huang Shisan zi Yizhou" 黃式三子以周 (Huang Shisan and his son Yizhou). In *Rulin Zhuan, xia* 儒林傳下 (Biography of Confucians, part two). In *QDZJ* 104:646–652.

Huang Tifang 黃體芳. "Nanjing shuyuan bei ji" 南菁書院碑記 (The Southern Quintessence Academy stele inscription). Jiangyin, stele inscription, ninth lunar month, 1885.

———. "Shulan shiqi" 漱蘭詩葺 (Shulan's poetry sheaths). In *Oufeng zazhi huikan*, vol. 1.

———. "Xuezheng Tifang wei chuangjian Nanjing shuyuan shaoshi bei" 學政體芳爲創建南菁書院曉示碑 (Proclamation stele by Provincial Director of Education Tifang upon founding Southern Quintessence Academy). Jiangyin, stele inscription, Oct. 1885.

Huang Wei 黃葦. *Zhongguo difang zhi cidian* 中國地方志詞典 (Dictionary of Chinese gazetteers). Hefei, 1986.

"Huang xianchen yizhou" 黃先生以周 (Mr. Huang Yizhou). In *Qing Ruxue an xiaozhuan* 清儒學案小傳 (Brief biographies of Confucians in the Qing danasty). In *QDZJ* 7:146–149 (1985).

Huang Yanpei 黃炎培. "Shen Xinqing xiansheng zhuan" 沈信卿先生傳 (Biography of Mr. Shen Xinqing). *Renwen fukan* 人文复刊 (Humanities supplement), 1.2:1–4 (1947).

Huang Yizhou 黃以周. *Jingji zazhu* 儆季雜著 (Miscellany of early admonition). Jiangyin, 1895.

———. *Li shu tonggu* 禮書通故 (Understanding antiquity through the ritual classics). 100 *juan*, 2 vols. Rpt., Taibei: Huashi, 1976.

———. "Lun shuyuan" 論書院 (On academies). In *JJZZ*, 3.4:18a–19b (1895).

———. "Nanjing jiangshe wenji xu" 南菁講舍文集敘 (Preface to collected writings from Southern Quintessence Lecture Hall). Jiangyin, 1889.

———. "Nanjing shuyuan jiangxue bei ji" 南菁書院講學碑記 (Learning at Nanjing Academy). Jiangyin, stele inscription, 1885. Rpt. in *JJZZ* 5.6:22b–24b (1895).

———. "Nanjing shuyuan li zhu yi" 南菁書院立主義 (Establishing masters at Southern Quintessence Academy). In *JJZZ* 5.6:32b–33b (1895).

"Huang Yizhou" 黃以周 (Huang Yizhou). In Cai Guanluo 蔡冠洛, ed., *Qingdai qibai mingren zhuan* 清代七百名人傳 (Biography of four hundred celebrities in the Qing period). In *QDZJ* 196:276–278.

Huangchao xu wenxian tongkao 皇朝續文獻通考 (Continuation of collection of imperial documents). Comp. Liu Jinzao 劉錦藻. 400 vols. Shanghai, 1936.

Hummel, Arthur W.,ed. *Eminent Chinese of the Ch'ing Period (1644–1912)*. Washington, D.C.: Government Printing Office, 1943.

Ichiko, Chuzo. "Political and Institutional Reform, 1901–1911." In JohK. Fairbank and Kwang-ching Liu, eds., *The Cambridge History of China*. Vol. 11, pt. 2. Cambridge: Cambridge University Press, 1980.

JDSL. *Jindai zhongguo shiliao congkan* 近代中國史料叢刊 (Collections of historical materials on modern China). Series 1, 1966; series 2, 1974; series 3, 1986. Rpt., Taibei: Wenhai.

Jiang Weiqiao 蔣維喬. *Jiangsu jiaoyu xingzheng gaikuang* 江蘇教育行政概況 (Jiangsu educational administration). Shanghai, 1924.

Jiang Zanchu 蔣贊初. *Nanjing shihua* 南京史話 (The story of Nanjing). Nanjing, 1981.

"Jiangnan sheng gaodeng ji fuxue xianxue tang shiban zhangcheng" 江南省高等及府學縣學堂試辦章程 (Regulations for county, prefectural, and higher schools in Jiangnan province). In *Jiaoyu xiao ce huiji* 教育小冊彙輯 (Collection of essays on education), 34 *ce*, 1902.

Jiangning fu chongxiu puyu sitang zhi 江寧府重修普育四堂志 (Jiangning's gazetteers of the renovation of four schools for the needy). Ed. Tu Zongying 涂宗瀛. Rev. ed., Sun Yunjing 孫雲錦. 6 *juan*. 1886. Rpt., Jiangning, 1936.

Jiangning fu chongjian puyu tang zhi 江寧府重建普育堂志 (Jiangning's gazetteer of the reconstructed school for the needy). Ed. Tu Zongying 涂宗瀛. 8 *juan*. 1871.

Jiangsu 江蘇 (Jiangsu journal). 1903–1904.

Jiangsu jiaoyu gongbao 江蘇教育公報 (Bulletin of Jiangsu education), 1918–1926.

Jiangsu shengli (1869–1904) 江蘇省例 (Jiangsu provincial regulations). Suzhou: Jiangsu shuju, c. 1904.

Jiangsu shengli dier shifan xuexiao 江蘇省立第二師範學校. *Jiangsu shengli dier shifan xuexiao ershi zhou nian ce* 江蘇省立第二師範學校二十周年冊 (The twentieth anniversary book of the number two normal school in Jiangsu province). Shanghai, 1925.

Jiangsu wenxian 江蘇文獻 (Jiangsu documents). 1942–1943.

"Jiaoyu hui wei mintuan zhi jichu" 教育會爲民團之基礎 (Educational associations as a base for organizing people). *Jiangsu* 江蘇 (Jiangsu journal), 3:13–19 (1903).

Jiaoyu xiao ce huiji 教育小冊匯輯 (A collection of small pamphlets on education). 34 vols. Kent Hall Library, Columbia University.

Jinshi Zhongguo jingshi sixiang yantao hui lunwen 近世中國經世思想研討會論文集 (Proceedings of the conference on the theory of statecraft of modern China). Ed. Zhongyang yanjiu yuan jindai shi yanjiu so 中央研究院近代史研究所 (The Institute of Modern History of Academia Sinica). Taibei, 1984.

JJZZ. *Jingji zazhu*. See Huang Yizhou.

Johnson, David; Andrew J. Nathan; and Evelyn S. Rawski, eds. *Popular Culture in Late Imperial China*. Berkeley: University of California Press, 1985.

Jones, Susan Mann, and Philip A. Kuhn "Dynastic Decline and the Roots of Rebellion." In John K. Fairbank and Kwang-ching Liu, eds., *The Cambridge History of China*. Vol. 10, pt. 1. Cambridge: Cambridge University Press, 1978.

JSJYGB. *Jiangsu jiaoyu gongbao* 江蘇教育公報 (Jiangsu education bulletin). 1918–1926.

JSJYZH. *Jiangsu jiaoyu zonghui* 江蘇教育總會 (Jiangsu education association). 1st ed., 1906; 2d ed., n.d.; 3d ed., 1908; 4th ed., 1908; 6th ed., 1911.

JSXW. *Jiangsu xuewu gongdu* 江蘇學務公牘 (Documents on educational affairs in Jiangsu). Ed. Jiangsu xuewu gongsuo 江蘇學務公所 (Educational bureau of Jiangsu). 4 parts. Suzhou, 1906–1911.

JYXZXZ. *Jiangyin xianzhi xuzhi* 江陰縣志續志 (Jiangyin district gazetteer). 1921.

Keenan, Barry. *The Dewey Experiment in China: Educational Reform and Political Power in the Early Republic*. Cambridge: Council on East Asian Studies, Harvard University, 1977.

Keisei bumpen somokuroku 經世文編總目錄 (Comprehensive index to

essays on statecraft). Ed. Kindai Chugoku Kenkyu Iinakai 近代中國研究委員會 (Committee on research on modern China). 3 vols. N.p., 1956.

Kojima Yoshio 小島淑男. "Shinmatsu no hyoson toji ni tsuite: soshūfu no ku, to tō o chūshin ni" 清末の郷村統治について: 蘇州府の區, 圖董を中心に (On late Qing rural management: focusing on precinct and *qu* managers in Suzhou prefecture). 史潮 *Shichō* (Historial tide), no. 88:16–30 (1964).

Kuhn, Philip. "The Development of Local Government." In John K. Fairbank and Albert Feuerwerker, eds., *The Cambridge History of China*. Vol. 13. Cambridge: Cambridge University Press, 1986.

———. "Local Self-government under the Republic: Problems of Control, Autonomy, and Mobilization." In Frederic Wakeman and Carolyn Grant, eds., *Conflict and Control in Late Imperial China*. Berkeley: University of California Press, 1975.

———. *Rebellion and Its Enemies in Late Imperial China: Militarization and Social Structure, 1796–1864*. Cambridge: Harvard University Press, 1970.

Kuo, Ting-yee, and Liu Kwang-ching. "Self-strengthening: The Pursuit of Western Technology." In John K. Fairbank, ed., *The Cambridge History of China*. Vol. 10, pt. 1. Cambridge: Cambridge University Press, 1978.

Kupfer, Carl F. *Sacred Places in China*. Cincinnati, Ohio: Western Methodist Book Concern, 1911.

Legge, James. *Confucius*. New York: Dover, 1971.

Leonard, Jane. *Wei Yuan and China's Redicovery of the Maritime World*. Cambridge: Council on East Asian Studies, Harvard University, 1984.

Leung, Angela Ki Che. "Elementary Education in the Lower Yangtze Region in the 17th and 18th Centuries." Paper presented at the American Council of Learned Societies Conference on Education and Society in Late Imperial China, Montecito, California, June 8–14, 1989.

Leung, Man-kam. "Juan Yuan (1764–1849): The Life, Works, and Career of a Chinese Scholar-Bureaucrat." Ph.D. dissertation, University of Hawaii, 1977.

Levenson, Joseph. "T'i and Yung—'Substance and Function'." In Joseph Levenson, *Confucian China and Its Modern Fate: The Problem of Intellectual Continuity*. Berkeley: University of California Press, 1965.

Li, Chien-nung. *The Political History of China, 1840–1928*. Trans. and ed. Ssu-yu Teng and Jeremy Ingalls. Stanford, Calif.: Stanford University Press, 1967.

Li Dingfang 李鼎芳. *Zeng Guofan ji qi mufu renwu* 曾國藩及其幕府人物 (Zeng Guofan and the personnel in his private bureaucracy). Hong Kong, 1967.

Li Xibi 李希泌 and Zhang Shuhua 張椒華. *Zhongguo gudai cangshu yu jindai tushuguan shiliao* 中國古代藏書與近代圖書館史料 (China ancient books and historical materials on modern libraries). Beijing, 1982.

Liang, Qichao. *Intellectual Trends in the Ch'ing Period*. Cambridge: Harvard University Press, 1970.

Liang Qizi (Angela Leung). "Mingmo Qingchu minjian cishan huodong de xingqi—yi Jiang-Zhe diqu weili" 明末清初民間慈善活動的興起 (The rise of charitable institutions in the late Ming–early Qing era). *Shihuo yuekan* 食貨月刊 (Shihuo monthly), 15.6–7:52–79 (1986).

"Liangjiang zongdu Liu Kunyi zouchen chouban Jiangnan ge xuetang zhe" 兩江總督劉坤一奏陳籌辦江南各學堂折 (A memorial on Jiangnan's new schools from Liangjiang governor-general Liu Kunyi). In Zhu Youhuan 朱有瓛, ed., *Zhongguo jindai xuezhi shiliao* 中國近代學制史料 (Historical materials on school systems of modern China), 785–787.

Lin, Man-houng. "Currency and Society: The Monetary Crisis and Political-Economic Ideology of Early Nineteenth-Century China." Ph.D. dissertation, Harvard University, 1989.

"Lin Shoutu" 林壽圖 (Mr. Lin Shoutu). In *Beizhuanji bu* 碑傳集補 (Supplement to stone memorial biographies). In *QDZJ* 121:152.

Liu Boji 劉伯驥. *Guangdong shuyuan zhidu* 廣東書院制度 (The academy system in Guangdong). Taibei, 1978.

Liu Dingsheng 柳定生. "Liu Yizheng zhuan lue" 柳詒徵傳略 (A biographical sketch of Liu Yizheng). In *Zhongguo dangdai shehui kexue jia* 中國當代社會科學家 (Social scientists in contemporary China). Beijing, 1982.

Liu, Kwang-ching. "The Ch'ing Restoration." In John K. Fairbank, ed., *The Cambridge History of China*. Vol. 10, pt. 1. Cambridge: Cambridge University Press, 1978.

———. "On Ch'ing Scholarship, Education and Morality." Printed comments on AHA panel papers, American Historical Association, Jan. 1, 1984.

———, ed. *Orthodoxy in Late Imperial China*. Berkeley: University of California Press, 1990.

Liu Qi 劉琪. "Ruan Yuan jiaoyu shijian shuping" 阮元教育實踐述評 (An account of Ruan Yuan's educational practice). *Huadong shifan daxue xuebao* 華東師範大學學報 (East China Normal University journal), Mar. 1986: 67–76.

Liu Shiji 劉石吉. *Ming-Qing shidai Jiangnan shizhen yenjiu* 明清時代江南市鎮研究 (Studies in urban Jiangnan in the Ming-Qing period). Shanghai, 1987.

Liu Shipei 劉師培. *Liu Shenshu xiansheng yishu* 劉申叔先生遺著 (Bequeathed works of Liu Shenshu). 4 vols. Taibei, 1975.

———. "Nanbei xuepai butong lun" 南北學派不同論 (Differences in northern and southern scholarly factions). In Liu Shipei 劉師培, *Liu Shenshu xiansheng yishu*.

"Liu Xingen" 柳興恩 *Qingshi gao liezhuan* 清史稿列傳 (Classified biography in the draft Qing history). In *QDZJ* 1985: 94–620.

Liu Yizheng 柳詒徵. "Guoxue shuju benmo" 國學書局本末 (National studies publishing house—from beginning to end). *Jiangsu shengli guoxue tushuguan disan nian-kan* 江蘇省立國學圖書館第三年刊 (Jiangsu sinological library, 3d yearly edition), 1–16 (1930).

———. "Jiangsu shuyuan zhi chugao" 江蘇書院志初稿 (Draft gazetteer of Jiangsu academies). *Jiangsu shengli guoxue tushuguan disi niankan* 江蘇省立國學圖書館第四年刊 (Jiangsu sinological library, 4th annual), 1–92 (1930).

———. "Jiangsu yixue shexue zhi" 江蘇義學社學志 (Jiangsu gazetteer of private and community schools). *Jiangsu wenxian* 江蘇文獻 (Jiangsu documents), 1:71–87; 2:70–80 (1943).

———. *Liu Yimo xiansheng wenlu* 柳翼謀先生錄 (Professor Liu Yimo's writings). Taibei, 1970.

———. "Liu Yizheng zizhuan ji zishu" 柳詒徵自傳及自述 (Autobiography and personal narrative by Liu Yizheng). *Wenxian* 文獻 (Documents), 7:121–130 (1981).

———. "Qingji jiaoyu zhi guochi" 清季教育之國恥 (The national disgrace of education in the Qing era). *Guofeng banyue kan* 國風半月刊 (National spirit bimonthly), 8.1:7 (Jan. 1935).

———. *Ri you huibian* 日游彙編 (Compiled records of a visit to Japan). Jiangyin, 1903.

———. "You guan Taiping Tianguo de liangze shiliao" 有關太平天國的兩則史料 (Two pieces of historical material on the Taiping Heavenly Kingdom). *Jianghai xuekan* 江海學刊 (Jianghai academic journal), 2:73–74 (1983).

———. *Zhongguo wenhua shih* 中國文化史 (A cultural history of China). 3 vols. Taibei, n.d.

Liu Zhufeng 劉祝封. "Qianfei jilue" 錢匪紀略 (A brief account of the Gold Coin rebels). In *Oufeng zazhi huikan* 甌風雜誌彙刊 (Collected issues of *Wenzhou Miscellany*). Collection 1. Ruian, Zhejiang: Oufengshe, 1934.

Lojewski, Frank A. "Reform within Tradition: Feng Kuei-fen's Proposal for Local Administration." *Ch'ing-hua hsueh pao*, n.s. 11, 1.2:147–159 (1975).

———. "Ting Jih-ch'ang in Kiangsu: Traditional Methods of Surmounting Dysfunction in Local Administration during the Late-Ch'ing Period." *Jindai shi yanjiu suo qikan* 近代史研究所期刊 (Bulletin of the Institute of Modern History, Academia Sinica), 8 (1979).

Longmen shuyuan. *Xuding Shanghai longmen shuyuan kecheng liuze* 續定上海龍門書院課程六則 (Six provisions of the revised curriculum of Longmen Academy in Shanghai). Shanghai, c. 1870.

———. *Xuding Shanghai longmen shuyuan zhangcheng liuze* 續定上海龍門書院章程六則 (Six provisions of the revised bylaws of Longmen Academy in Shanghai). Shanghai, c. 1870.

Lu Baoqian 陸寶千. *Qingdai sixiang shi* 清代思想史 (A history of Qing-period thought). Taibei, 1983.

Lui, Adam Y. C. "The Academies (*shu-yuan*) under the Ch'ing." *Journal of Asian History* 7.1:54–68 (1973).

"Lun Shanghai Longmen shuyuan Jingye ge shuyuan yi gaishi shiwu" 論上海龍門書院敬業各書院宜改試時務 (That Longmen Academy and Jingye Academy and others should introduce current affairs). In *Zhongwai wenxian celun huihai* 中外文獻策論匯海 (Current affairs documents from China and overseas). Shanghai, 1901.

Luo Yudong 羅玉東. *Zhongguo lijin shi* 中國釐金史 (A history of *lijin* in China). Hong Kong, 1977.

Ma, Amy Fei-man. "Local Self-government and the Local Populace in Ch'uan-sha, 1911." *Select Papers from the Center for Far Eastern Studies*, no. 1:47–84 (1975–76).

Ma Fengchen 馬奉琛. *Qingdai xingzheng zhidu yanjiu cankao shumu* 清代行政制度研究參考書目 (Bibliography of reference works on the administrative system in the Qing period). Taibei, 1974.

MacKinnon, Stephen R. *Power and Politics in Late Imperial China: Yuan Shi-kai in Beijing and Tianjin, 1901–1900*. Berkeley: University of California Press, 1980.

Mair, Victor H. "Language and Ideology in the Written Popularizations of the Sacred Edict." In David Johnson et al., eds., *Popular Culture in Late Imperial China*. Berkeley: University of California Press, 1985.

Mann, Susan. *Local Merchants and the Chinese Bureaucracy, 1750–1950*. Stanford, Calif.: Stanford University Press, 1987.

Mao Xianglin 毛祥麟. "Ji Longmen shuyuan" 記龍門書院 (A record of Longmen Academy). In Zhu Xingui 璩鑫圭, *Zhongguo jindai jiao-*

yu shi ziliao huibian.

Mayers, S. F. *List of the Higher Metropolitan and Provincial Authorities of China.* Shanghai: Kelly and Walsh, 1907.

Meng Xiancheng 孟憲承 et al. *Zhongguo gudai jiaoyu shi ziliao* 中國古代教育史資料 (Sources on the history of ancient Chinese education). Beijing, 1980.

Meskill, John. *Academies in Ming China: A Historical Essay.* Tucson: University of Arizona Press, 1982.

Miao Quansun 繆荃孫. "Chu zhou fu xue jiaoshou Huang xiansheng muzhiming" 處州府學教授黃先生墓志銘 (Funerary inscription of Huang Yizhou). In *YFTXJ* 1:13a–15b.

———. "Qing gu shilang xian Hanlin yuan shidu xueshi Sun Xiansheng muzhi ming bei" 清故侍郎銜翰林院侍讀學士孫先生墓志銘碑 (Funerary inscription of Sun Qiangming). In *QDZJ* 120:545–548.

———. *Yifeng Tang wen xu ji* (*YFTXJ*) 藝風堂文續集 (Collected works from the Artistic Breeze Studio). 8 *juan*. N.p., 1909.

———. *Yifeng Tang youpeng shuza* 藝風堂友朋書札 (Correspondence with friends of Yifeng Tang). 2 vols. Shanghai, 1981.

———. "Zhongshu xian chu zhou fu xue jiaoshou Huang xiansheng muzhiming" 中書銜處州府學授黃先生墓志銘 (Funerary inscription of Huang Yizhou). In *QDZJ* 119:320–323.

———. "Zhoupan xian houxuan taodao Zhang xiansheng muzhi ming" 州判銜候選訓導張先生墓志銘 (Funerary inscription of Zhang Wenhu). In *YFTXJ* 1:16a–16b.

Min Tu-ki. *National Polity and Local Power: The Transformation of Late Imperial China.* Cambridge: Council on East Asian Studies, Harvard University, 1989.

Miyazaki, Ichisada 宮崎市定. "Mindai So-Shō chihō no shitaifu to minshō 明代蘇松地方の士大夫と民衆 (The gentry and the common people in the Suzhou-Sungjiang region during the Ming period). In Miyazaki Ichisada, *Ajia shi kenkyu* アジア史研究 (Research on Asian history). 5 vols. Vol. 4, pp. 321–360. Kyoto: Dōhōsha, 1980.

Najita, Tetsuo. *Visions of Virtue in Tokugawa Japan: The Kaitokudō Merchant Academy of Osaka.* Chicago: University of Chicago Press, 1987.

Nanjing 南菁. (Southern Quintessence). Jiangyin, 1925.

———. (Southern Quintessence). Jiangyin, 1935.

Nanjing daxue 南京大學. *Nanjing daxue xiao shi ziliao xuanji* 南京大學校史資料選輯 (Selected materials on the history of Nanjing University). Nanjing, 1982.

Nanjing jiangshe wenji 南菁講舍文集 (Collected writings from Southern Quintessence Lyceum). Jiangyin. *Diyi ji* 第一集 (First collection), 1889. *Er ji* 第二集 (Second collection), 1894. *Disan ji* 第三集 (Third collection), 1901.

Nanjing shizhi 南京史志 (Nanjing historical gazetteer).

Nanjing shuyuan liushi zhounian jinian ce 南菁書院六十周年紀念冊 (Southern Quintessence Academy's sixtieth anniversary). Shanghai, 1941.

Nanjing wenxian 南京文獻 (Nanjing documents). 24 *ce*. Nanjing, 1948.

Nanjing xiaoshi ziliao 南菁校史資料 (Nanjing school history documents). Jiangyin, 1982.

Nanjing xueyue 南菁學約 (Curriculum of Southern Quintessence). Jiangyin, 1904.

Niehai hua ziliao 孽海花資料 (Source materials on *Niehai hua*). Ed. Wei Shaochang 魏紹昌. Shanghai, 1982.

Nivison, David. *The Life and Thought of Chang Hsueh-ch'eng (1738–1801)*. Stanford, Calif.: Stanford University Press, 1966.

North China Herald and Supreme Court and Consular Gazette. Feb. 2, 1905–May 19, 1905.

Ocko, Jonathan. *Bureaucratic Reform in Provincial China: Ting Jih-ch'ang in Restoration Kiangsu, 1867–1870*. Cambridge: Council on East Asian Studies, Harvard University, 1983.

Ogawa Yoshiko 小川嘉子. "Shindai ni okeru gigaku setsuritsu no kiban" 清代に於ける義學設立の基盤 (The basis for charitable school foundings in the Qing). In Tomoharu Hayashi 林友春, ed., *Kinsei Chugoku kyōiku shi kenkyu* 近世中國教育史研究 (Research on Chinese education in the modern era). Tokyo, 1958.

Okubo, Eiko 大久保英子. *Min Shin jidai shoin no kenkyu* 明清時代書院の研究 (A study of academies in the Ming and Qing periods). Tokyo, 1976.

———. "Shindai kosetsu chihō no shoin to shakai" 清代江浙地方の書院と社會 (Academies and society in the Jiangche region in the Qing period). In Taga Akigorō 多賀秋五郎, ed., *Kinsei to Ajia kyoiku shi kenkyu* 近令アジア教育史研究 (Research on the history of education in East Asia in modern times). Tokyo, 1970.

Orb, Richard. "Chihli Academies and Other Schools in the Late Ch'ing: An Institutional Survey." In John Schrecker and Paul Cohen, eds., *Reform in Nineteenth-Century China*. Cambridge: Harvard University Press, 1976.

Pan Minde 潘敏德. *Zhongguo jindai diandangye zhi yanjiu 1644–1937* 中國近代典當業之研究 (A study of the modern Chinese pawnshop, 1644–1937). Monograph series, no. 13. Taibei: Institute of History, National Taiwan Normal University, 1985.

Peake, Cyrus. *Nationalism and Education in Modern China*. New York: Columbia University Press, 1932.

Polacheck, James. "Gentry Hegemony: Soochow in the T'ung-chih Restoration." In Frederic Wakeman and Carolyn Grant, eds., *Conflict and Control in Late Imperial China*. Berkeley: University of California Press, 1975.

———. *The Inner Opium War*. Cambridge: Council on East Asian Studies, Harvard University, 1991.

Porter, Jonathan. *Tseng Kuo-fan's Private Bureaucracy*. China Research Monograph, no. 9. Berkeley: Center for Chinese Studies, University of California, 1972.

QDZJ. *Qingdai zhuanji congkan* 淸代傳記叢刊 (Collectanea of Qing biographies). 206 vols. Taibei, 1985.

"Qian Jiangsu xunfu Nie Jigui zouchen gaishe xuetang zhe" 前江蘇巡撫聶緝槼奏陳改設學堂折 (Former Governor Nie's edict on schools). In Zhu Youxian 朱有瓛, ed., *Zhongguo jindai xuezhi shiliao* 中國近代學制史料, 454–455.

Qian Mu 錢穆. *Tongcheng pai wenxue shi* 桐城派文學史 (The literary history of the Tongcheng school). Hong Kong, 1975.

Qingdai zhiguan nianbiao 淸代職官年表 (A chronological table of Qing officials). Ed. Qian Shipu 錢實甫. 4 vols. Beijing, 1980.

Qingding daqing huidian shili 欽定大淸會典事例 (Records in the official Qing encyclopedia). 24 vols. 1899. Rpt., Taibei, 1963.

"Qingmo xiaoxue jiaoyu zhi yanbian" 淸末小學教育之演變 (The evolution of elementary education in the late Qing). Ed. Dong Zhenjia 佟振家. *Shida yuekan* 師大月刊 (Teachers' college monthly), 25:130–182 (Feb. 1936).

Qingshi lunwen suoyin 淸史論文索引 (Index of historical essays on the Qing dynasty). Beijing, 1984.

QSG. *Qingshi gao*. See Zhao Ersun.

"Quanguo jiaoyu xingzheng huiyi ge shengqu baogao huilu: quanguo jiaoyu xingzheng huiyi jilu" 全國教育行政會議各省區報告彙錄: 全國教育行政會議記錄 (National educational administration conference, collection of reports by province). In *JDSL*, 1916. Rpt., Taibei.

Rankin, Mary. *Early Chinese Revolutionaries*. Cambridge: Harvard University Press, 1971.

———. *Elite Activism and Political Transformation in China: Zhejiang Province, 1865–1911*. Stanford, Calif.: Stanford University Press, 1986.

———. "The Origins of a Chinese Public Sphere: Local Elites and

Community Affairs in the Late Imperial Period." *Etudes Chinoises* 9.2:13–60 (Automne 1990).

———. "Public Opinion and Political Power: *Qingyi* in Late Nineteenth Century China." *Journal of Asian Studies* 41.3:453–484 (1982).

Rankin, Mary; John K. Fairbank; and Albert Feuerwerker. "Introduction: Perspectives on Modern China's History." In John K. Fairbank and Albert Feuerwerker, eds., *The Cambridge History of China*. Vol. 13. Cambridge: Cambridge University Press, 1986.

Rankin, Mary Backus, and Joseph W. Esherick. "Concluding Remarks." In Joseph W. Esherick and Mary Backus Rankin, eds., *Chinese Local Elites and Patterns of Dominance*. Berkeley: University of California Press, 1990.

Rawski, Evelyn S. *Education and Popular Literacy in Ch'ing China*. Ann Arbor: University of Michigan Press, 1979.

Rhoads, Edward. *China's Republican Revolution: The Case of Kwangtung, 1895–1913*. Cambridge: Harvard University Press, 1975.

Rowe, William. "Education and Empire in Southwest China: Ch'en Hung-mou in Yunnan, 1733–38." Paper presented at the ACLS Conference on Education and Society in Late Imperial China, Montecito, California, June 8–14, 1989.

———. "The Public Sphere in Modern China." *Modern China* 16.3:309–329 (July 1990).

Schneider, Laurence. "National Essence and the New Intelligentsia." In Charlotte Furth, ed., *The Limits of Change: Essays on Conservative Alternatives in Republican China*. Cambridge: Harvard University Press, 1979.

Schoppa, Keith R. *Chinese Elites and Polical Change: Zhejiang Province in the Early Twentieth Century*. Cambridge: Harvard University Press, 1982.

———. "Power, Legitimacy, and Symbol: Local Elites and the Jute Creek Embankment Case." In Joseph W. Esherick and Mary Backus Rankin, eds., *Chinese Local Elites and Patterns of Dominance*. Berkeley: University of California Press, 1990.

Schrecker, John E. "The Reform Movement of 1898 and the *Qingyi* Reform as Opposition." In John E. Schrecker and Paul Cohen, eds., *Reform in Nineteenth-Century China*. Cambridge: Harvard University Press, 1976.

Shanghai xian jiaoyuhui huiyuan xingming lu 上海縣教育會會員姓名錄 (Index of names of members of Shanghai education association). Ed. Shanghai xian jiaoyu ju 上海縣教育局 (Shanghai education bureau). Shanghai, 1917.

Shanghai xian quanxuesuo diaocha ge xuetang yilan biao 上海縣勸學所調查各學堂一覽表 (Chart of schools surveyed by Shanghai *quanxuesuo*). Ed. Shanghai quanxueso 上海勸學所 (Shanghai quanxueso). N.p., n.d.

Shanghai xu xianzhi 上海續縣志 (Continuation of the Shanghai district gazetteer). 1918.

"Shanghai xuetang yiban" 上海學堂一般 (Shanghai schools). *Jiangsu* 江蘇 (Jiangsu journal), 3:159–165 (1903).

Shen Enfu 沈恩孚. "Shanghai Longmen shuyuan jilue" 上海龍門書院紀略 (A sketch of Shanghai's Longmen Academy). *Renwen yuekan* 人文月刊 (Humanities monthly), 8.9:4 (Dec. 1937).

———. "Shen Enfu zizhuan" 沈恩孚自傳 (Autobiography). *Renwen fukan* 人文復刊 (Humanities supplement), 1.2:3–4 (July 1947).

Shen, Han-yin Ch'en. "Tseng Kuo-fan in Peking, 1840–1852: His Ideas in Statecraft and Reform." *Journal of Asian Studies* 27:1 (Nov. 1967).

Shen Songqiao 沈松僑. *Xueheng pai yu wusi shiqi de fan xin wenhua yundong* 學衡派與五四時期的反新文化運動 (The *Critical Review* group: A consevative alternative to the new culture movement in the May Fourth era). Taibei, 1984.

Shen Xianglong 沈祥龍. "Tandong zashi" 潭東雜識 (Miscellaneous points from the eastern Tan). *Wenyi zazhi* 文藝雜誌 (Arts magazine), 7 (1914), 9 (1915).

Sheng Langxi 盛朗西. *Zhongguo shuyuan zhidu* 中國書院制度 (China's academy system). Taibei, 1977.

"Sheng Long" 盛隆 (Sheng Long). In *Qingdai Piling mingrenxiaozhuan* 清代毗陵名人小傳 (Famous persons from Changzhou in the Qing period). In *QDZJ* 197:243–245.

"Sheng shixue Jiang Gongchen shicha Jiangning xian jiaoyu zhuangkuang baogao shu" 省視學蔣拱視察江寧縣教育狀況報告書 (Reports of provincial inspector of education on education conditions in Jiangning by Jiang Gongchen). *JSJYGB* 6:17–21 (1922).

"Sheng shixue Zhang Weigao shicha Jiangning xian jiaoyu zhuangkuang baogao shu" 省視學章慰高視察江寧縣教育狀況報告書 (Reports of provincial inspector of education on education conditions in Jiangning by Zhang Weigao). *JSJYGB* 7:1–5 (1921).

Shoudu zhi 首都志 (Capital gazetteer). Ed. Ye Chucang 葉楚傖 and Liu Yizheng 柳詒徵 . 2 vols. Nanjing, 1935.

SHSTZG. *Shanghai shi tongzhi guan qikan* 上海市通志館期刊 (The journal of the provincial gazetteer office of Shanghai city). Ed. Shanghai shi tongzi guan 上海市通志館 (The provinicial gazetteer office of Shanghai city). 1933–34. Rpt., Hong Kong, 1967.

Sima Qian 司馬遷. *Shiji* 史記 (Records of the historian). Taibei, 1978.

Su Yunfeng 蘇雲峰. "Guangya shuyuan (1888–1902)" 廣雅書院 (Guangya Academy). *Jindai shi yanjiu suo jikan* 近代史研究所期刊 (Bulletin of the Institute of Modern History), 13:239–304 (1984).

———. *Zhang Zhidong yu Hubei jiaoyu gaige* 張之洞與湖北教育改革 (Zhang Zhidong and the reform of Hubei education). Taibei, 1976.

Sun Qiangming 孫鏘鳴. "Xiyin shuyuan dongzhai keyi xu" 惜陰書院東齋課藝序 (Preface to the curriculum of the Eastern Studio of Xiyin Academy). In Zhu Xingui, ed., *Zhongguo jindai jiaoyu shi ziliao huibian.*

Taga Akigorō 多賀秋五郎, comp. *Kindai Chūgoku kyōiku shi shiryō* 近代中國教育史資料 (Materials on the history of education in modern China). 4 vols. 1972. Rpt., Taibei, 1976.

Tang Wenzhi 唐文治, comp. "Chen jun Shanyu muzhiming" 陳君善餘墓誌銘 (Funerary inscription of Chen Shanyu). In *Bei zhuan bu* 碑傳補 (Supplement to stone memorial biography). In *QDZJ* 123:415–421.

Tang Zhijun 湯志鈞. *Jindai jingxue yu zhengzhi* 近代經學與政治. Beijing, 1989.

———. *Wuxu bianfa shi* 戊戌變法史 (A history of the 1898 reform movement). Beijing, 1984.

———. "Wuxu bianfa shiqi Shanghai di chuban jie" 戊戌變法時期上海的出版界 (Publications in Shanghai during the 1898 reform period). *Lishi jiaoxue wenti* 歷史教學問題 (Problems in history teaching), 10–14 (Apr. 1982).

Tao Zhu 陶澍 "Zhongshan shuyuan keyi xu" 鍾山書院課藝序 (Preface to the curriculum of Zhongshan Academy). In Tao Zhu 陶澍 *Tao Wenyi gong chuanji* 陶文毅公全集 (The complete works of the honorable Tao Wenyi). Taibei: Wenhai, 1966.

Ten Years of the Kiangsu Provincial Educational Association. Shanghai, n.d.

Teng, Ssu-yu, and Knight Biggerstaff. *An Annotated Bibliography of Selected Chinese Reference Works.* Rev. ed. Cambridge: Harvard University Press, 1969.

Thompson, Roger. "Statecraft and Self-government: Competing Visions of Community and State in Late Imperial China." *Modern China* 14.2:156–188 (April 1988).

———. "Visions of the Future, Realities of the Day: Local Administrative Reform, Electoral Politics, and Traditional Chinese Society on the Eve of the 1911 Revolution." Ph.D. dissertation, Yale University, Department of History, 1985.

"Tianjin fu zizhi ju shiban diaocha jian zhang" 天津府自治局試辦調查簡章 (Brief regulations for surveys of Tianjin's self-government bureau). *Dongfang zazhi* 東方雜志 (Eastern miscellany), 4.4:172–176 (1907).

Till, Barry. *In Search of Old Nanking*. Hong Kong: Joint Publishing Company, 1982.

"Tu Zongying" 涂宗瀛 (Tu Zongying). In *Shengqing yuanyuan lu* 聖清淵源錄 (Record of Qing origins). In *QDZJ* 4:895–896.

Wakeman, Frederic. "Localism and Loyalism during the Ch'ing Conquest of Kiangnan." In Frederic Wakeman and Carolyn Grant, eds., *Conflict and Control in Late Imperial China*. Berkeley: University of California Press, 1975.

———. "The Price of Autonomy: Intellectuals in Ming and Ch'ing Politics." *Daedalus* 102.2:35–70 (1972).

Wang Deyi 王德毅. *Qingdai bieming zihao suoyin* 清代別名字號索引 (Index of personal names in the Qing dynasty). Taibei, 1985.

Wang Ermin 王爾敏. *Wanqing zhengzhi sixiang shi lun* 晚清政治思想史論 (Historical essay on late Qing political thought). Taibei, 1976.

Wang Qizhong 王氣中. *Liu Xizai he Yigai* 劉熙載和藝概 (Liu Xizai and the *Yigai*). Shanghai: Guji chubanshe, 1981.

Wang Shiduo 汪士鐸. "Dali siqing Li gong muzhi ming" 大理寺卿李公墓誌銘 (Funerary inscription for director of the Court of Judicature and Revision, the Honorable Li). In *QDZJ* 120:546–547.

———. *Wang Huiweng yibing riji* 汪悔翁乙丙日記 (Wang Shiduo's diary of the yibing year). Ed. Deng Zhicheng 鄧之誠. In *JDSL* series 1, no. 126.

Wang Shuhuai 王樹槐. "Qingmo Minchu Jiangsu sheng de xinshi jiaoyu" 清末民初江蘇省的新式教育 (New-style education in late Qing and early Republican Jiangsu). In *Zhongyang yanjiu yuan guoji Hanxue huiyi lunwen ji* 中央研究院國際漢學會議論文集 (Collected essays from the international sinology conference of Academia Sinica). Taibei: Zhongyang yanjiu yuan guoji Hanxue huiyi lunwen ji, 1981.

———. *Zhongguo xiandai hua diqu yanjiu: Jiangsu sheng 1860–1916* 中國現代化地區研究: 江蘇省 1860–1916 (Regional studies on Chinese modernization: Jiangsu province 1860–1916). Taibei, 1984.

Wang Xianqian 王先謙. "Nanjing congshu xu" 南菁叢書序 (Preface to Nanjing collectanea). In *Xushou tang* 虛受堂 (Xushou studio). Rpt., Taibei, 1972.

———. "Nanjing shatian ji" 南菁沙田記 (The polder fields of Southern Quintessence). Jiangyin, stele, 1889.

Wang Xiyu 王希玉. "Zhang Qinruo shengsheng zhuan" 章琴若先生傳

(A biography of Zhang Qinruo). In *Jiasi zhai shiwen jinyu* 駕絲齋詩文燼餘 (Remnants of poetry and prose from the Jiasi studio). Taibei, 1985.

Wang, Yeh-chien. "The Impact of the Taiping Rebellion on Population in Southern Kiangsu." (Harvard) *Papers on China* 19:120–158 (1965).

Wang Zhongmin 王重民. *Qingdai wenji bianmu fenlei soyin* 清代文集篇目分類索引 (A topical classified index to Qing essay collections). Beijing, 1965.

Watters, Thomas. *A Guide to the Tablets in a Temple of Confucius*. Shanghai: American Presbyterian Mission Press, 1879.

Wei Shaochang, ed. 魏紹昌. *Niehai hua ziliao* 孽海花資料 (Source materials on Niehai hua). Shanghai, 1982.

Wei Xiumei 魏秀梅. *Tao Zhu zai Jiangnan* 陶澍在江南 (Tao Zhu in Jiangnan). Taibei, 1985.

Whelan, T. S. *The Pawnshop in China*. Ann Arbor: University of Michigan Press, 1979.

Woodside, Alexander. "Relations between Chinese Academies and Their External World, 1700–1840." American Historical Association panel paper, San Francisco, 1983.

———. "State, Scholars, and Orthodoxy: The Ch'ing Academies, 1736–1839." In Kwang-ching Liu, ed., *Orthodoxy in Late Imperial China*.

Woren 倭仁. "Da Tu Langxuan" 答涂朗軒 (Answering Tu Langxuan). In *Wo Wenduan gong yishu* 倭文端公遺書 (The bequeathed works of Woren). 2 vols. Taibei, 1968.

Wright, Mary. *The Last Stand of Chinese Conservatism: The T'ung-Chih Restoration, 1862–1974*. New York: Atheneum, 1969.

Wu Daren 吳大任. *Liang Jiean xiansheng nianpu* 梁節庵先生年譜 (Chronological biography of Liang Jiean). Taibei, 1979.

Wu Jingheng 吳敬恒. "Hanyai shiji xu" 寒涯詩集序 (The Preface to the collection of poems of Hanyai). In *Wu Zhihui xiansheng wencui* 吳稚暉先生文粹 (Works of Mr. Wu Zhihui). 4 vols. Shanghai, 1928.

Wu Xinlei 吳新雷. "Nanjing shuyuan de xueshu yanjiu ji qi dui wenhua jie de gongxian" 南菁書院的學術研究及其對文化界的貢獻 (Scholarly research at Southern Quintessence Academy and its cultural contribution). *Nanjing daxue xuebao* 南京大學學報 (University of Nanjing journal), 2:15–23 (1985).

Wu Yun, 吳雲 ed. *De yi lu* 得一錄 (Charitable deeds). 1869. Rpt., Taibei, 1969.

"Wu Zhihui xiansheng nianpu jianbian" 吳稚暉先生年譜簡編 (Select chronological biography of Wu Zhihui). In Lo Jialun 羅家倫 et al., eds., *Wu Zhihui xiansheng quanji* 吳稚暉先生全集 (Complete works of Wu Zhihui). 18 vols. Taibei, 1969.

Wu Zhihui xiansheng quanji 吳稚暉先生全集 (Complete works of Wu Zhihui). Ed. Luo Jialun 羅家倫 et al. 18 vols. Taibei, 1969.

"Xiangyue" 鄉約 (Rural compact). In *Nanhui xianzhi* 南匯縣志 (District gazetteer of Nanhui), 1879.

Xiao Mu 蕭穆. "Liu Rongzhai zhongyun biezhuan" 劉融齋中允別傳 (A biography of Liu Rongzhai). *Jingfu leigao* 敬孚類稿 (Classified drafts of respectful sincerity). Guangzhou, 1889.

Xiao Yishan 蕭一山. *Qingdai tongshi* 清代通史 (A complete history of the Qing era). 5 vols. Taibei, 1980.

Xie Guozhen 謝國楨. *Jindai shuyuan xuexiao zhidu bianqian kao* 近代書院學校制度變遷考 (Analysis of the transformation of academies into schools in modern times). 1937. Rpt., Taibei, *JDSL* vol. 66, 1974.

Xinhai geming shiqi qikan jieshao 辛亥革命時期期刊介紹 (An introduction to periodicals of the 1911 revolution period). 3 vols. Beijing, 1982.

Xue Shiyu 薛時雨. "Xiyin shuyuan xizhai keyi xu" 惜陰書院西齋課藝序 (Preface to the curriculum of the Western Studio of Xiyin Academy). In Zhu Xingui, *Zhongguo jindai jiaoyu shi ziliao huibian.*

"Xuebu da ge sheng xuexi fenshi xuewu renyuan wu de wen ganshe waishi" 學部劄各省學習分飭學務人員毋得干步涉外事文 (On not permitting intervention in outside activities by educational personnel—a response from the Board of Education to the commissioners of education of each province). In Taga, 1:674.

Xuebu zongwu si 學部總務司. *Xuebu zouci jiyao* 學部奏咨輯要 (A compilation of the proclamations of the Board of Education). 1908. Rpt., Taibei, *JDSL*, vol. 96, 1986.

———, ed. *Diyi ci jiaoyu tongji tubiao* 第一次教育統計圖表 (The first statistical tables on education). 1907. Rpt., Taibei, *JDSL*, vols. 93–95, 1986.

Xueshi lu 學仕錄 (Record of scholars). Ed. Dai Zhaochen 戴肇辰. Guangzhou, 1866.

Xuewu gongsuo 學務公所. *Jiangsu xuewu wendu* 江蘇學務文牘 (Documents on educational affairs in Jiangsu). 4 sets. Suzhou, 1906–1911. See *JSXW*.

"Xuexiao kao qi" 學校考、七 (On schools, seven). In *Huangchao xu wenxian tongkao* 皇朝續文獻通考 (Continuation of collection of imperial documents). Comp. Liu Jinzao 劉錦藻. 400 vols. Vol. 100:8589–8593.

Xuezheng quanshu 學政全書 (Complete guide for the provincial director of education). 2 vols. Rpt., Taibei, 1974.

Yan Zhen 嚴辰. "Fei Youting guancha" 費幼亭觀察 (Inspector Fei Youting). *Mohua yin quan gan jiu huai ren ji* 墨花吟館感舊懷人集 (A collection of warm memories of people from the Mohuayin hall). In *QDZJ* 29:482–483.

"Yang Deheng" 楊德享 (Yang Deheng). In *Rulin zhuan* 儒林傳 (Biography of Confucians). In *QDZJ* 104:343.

Ye Erkai 葉爾愷. "Huang Tifang juan" 黃體芳傳 (Biography of Huang Tifang). In *Jiangnan zhengshu wendu* 江南徵書文牘 (Documentary evidence on Jiangnan publications). In Huang Qun 黃群, ed., *Jingxiang lou congshu* 敬鄉樓叢書 (Collectanea from Jingxiang Hall). 1931.

Ye Weishan 葉惟善. *Archive of Student Notebooks while at Southern Quintessence Higher School, 1902–1905*. Rare book collection, National Central Library, Taibei.

YFTXJ. *Yifeng tang wen xu ji*. See Miao Quansun.

Yifeng laoren nianpu 藝風老人年譜 (Chronological biography of the venerable Yifeng). Ed. Xia Suntong 夏孫桐. Beijing, 1936.

Yin Baoxian 殷葆諴. *Zhui yi lu* 追憶錄 (Recollections). Shanghai, c. 1930.

Ying Baoshi 應寶時. "Xundao Ying Baoshi Longmen shuyuan ji" 巡道應寶時龍門書院記 (Daotai Ying Baoshi's account of Longmen Academy). *Shanghai xianzhi* 上海縣志 (Shanghai gazetteer), 9 (1870).

Yu, Ying-shih. "Some Preliminary Observations on the Rise of Ch'ing Confucian Intellectualism." *Tsing Hua Journal of Chinese Studies* 2:105–146 (1975).

Yu Yue 俞樾. "Yu Ying Minzhai tongnian" 與應敏齋同年 (To Ying Minzhai who passed the examinations in the same year as myself). In Yu Yue 俞樾, ed., *Chunzai tang quanshu* 春在堂全書 (Complete works from the arrival of Spring Hall). 8 vols. Taibei, 1968.

———. "Zuochunfang zuozhongyun Liu jun mu pei" 左春坊左中允劉君墓碑 (Funerary inscription of Liu Xizai). In Yu Yue, ed., *Chunzai tang quanshu*.

"Yuan Chang" 袁昶. In *Qingshi liezhuan* 清史列傳 (Classified biographies from the Qing history). In *QDZJ* 103:740–751.

Yuan Chang 袁昶. "Zhongjing jiangyuan jianli jingyi zhishi liangzhai zhangcheng" 中江講院建立經誼治事兩齋章程 (Zhongjiang Academy establishes regulations for classics and statemanship divisions). 2 parts. Wuhu, Anhui, 1895–1896.

Zeng Guofan 曾國藩. "Fu Ding Guochen" 覆丁果臣 (In response to Ding Guochen). *ZWZQJ* 33:15526–27.

———. "Fu Li Gongbao" 覆李公保 (In response to Li Gongbao).

ZWZQJ, 24 *juan*, 1974.

———. "Fu Wu Zhuru Shilang" 覆吳竹如侍郎 (In response to vice-president Wu Zhuru). *ZWZQJ* 33:15900–03.

———. "Jiangning fuxue ji" 江寧府學記 (A record of Jiangning's *fuxue*). *ZWZQJ*, 4 *juan*, 1974.

———. "Ouyang Sheng wenji xu" 歐陽生文集序 (The preface to the collected writings of Ouyang Sheng). *ZWZQJ*, 3:12721–25.

———. "Tang Queshen gong muzhi ming" 唐確慎公墓志銘 (Funerary inscription of Tang Queshen). *ZWZQJ*, 4 *juan*, 1974.

———. "Zhi Li Xiaohu dali" 致李小湖大理 (To the honorable Li Xiaohu). *ZWZQJ*, 29 *juan*, 1974.

Zeng Wenzheng 曾文正. *Zeng Wenzheng gong (Guofan) quanji* (*ZWZQJ*) 曾文正公 (國藩) 全集 (Complete works of Zheng Wenzheng). Taibei, 1974.

Zhang Bingmi 章炳麟. "Huang Xiansheng zhuan" 黃先生傳 (Biography of Mr. Huang Yizhou). In *Beizhuan ji, sanbian* 碑傳集三編 (Collection of stele biography, 3d. ed.). In *QDZJ* 126:139–142 (1985).

Zhang Daxiang 張達驤 and Li Shisun 李石孫. "Zhang Zhidong shiji shuwen" 張之洞事蹟述聞 (Oral traces of Zhang Zhitong). In *Wen shi ziliao xuanji* 文史資料選輯 (Selections of source materials on literature and history), no. 99 collection. Beijing, 1984.

Zhang Jizi jiu lu 張季子九錄. (Records of Zhang Jian on nine subjects). Ed. Zhang Yizu 張怡祖. Taibei, 1983.

Zhang Kaiyuan 章開沅. *Kaituo zhe de zuji: Zhang Jian zhuan gao* 開拓者足跡張謇傳稿 (Footprints of a pioneer: a draft biography of Zhang Jian). Shanghai, 1986.

———. "The 1911 Revolution and the Jiang-zhe Bourgeoisie." *Chinese Studies in History* 18.3–4:83–133 (Spring–Summer 1985).

Zhang Qiyun 張其昀. "Wu shi Liu Yimo xiansheng" 吾師柳翼謀先生 (My teacher Professor Liu Yimo). *Zhuanji wenxue* 傳記文學 (Biographical literature), 12.2:39–41 (1968).

Zhang Shouyong 張壽鏞 et al., comps. *Huang chao zhanggu huibian* 皇朝掌故彙編 (Encyclopedic records of imperial management). Rpt. Taibei, *JDSL*, vol. 128, 1986.

Zhang Weixiang 張維驤. *Qingdai Biling mingjen xiaozhuan* 清代毗陵名人小傳 (Brief biographies of famous persons from Changzhou in the Qing period). 2 vols. Shanghai, 1944.

Zhang Wenhu 張文虎. "Nanjing shuyuan chongji Han Gaomi Zheng shi Song Xinan Zhu zi" 南菁書院崇祀漢高密鄭氏宋新安朱子 (Southern Quintessence Academy's veneration of Mr. Zheng from Gaomi district in the Han dynasty, and Master Zhu from

Xinan district in the Song dynasty). In *Shurang yushu* 鼠壤餘疏 (Additions from the land of plentiful rodents). Vol. 10, 1:9a–10a. In *Fupou ji* 覆瓿集 (Collection of jar covers). 12 vols. 1887.

———. "Nanjing shuyuan ji" 南菁書院記 (A record of Southern Quintessence Academy). Jiangyin, stele inscription, 1883.

Zhang Xuecheng 章學誠. *Wen shi tongyi* 文史通義 (Principles of literature and history). Collated by Ye Ying 葉瑛. Taibei, 1973.

Zhang Yin 張崟. "Gujing jingshe chugao" 詁經精舍初稿. (A preliminary draft of the Gujing Retreat). *Wenlan xuebao* (Wenlan journal of studies), 2.1:1–47 (Mar. 1936).

Zhang Yufa 張玉法. Qingji di lixian tuanti 清季的立憲團體 (Constitutional associations in the Qing period). Taibei, 1985.

Zhang Zhengfan 張正藩. "Qing dai shuyuan shuyue" 清代書院述略 (An account of Qing-period academies). *Guoli bianyi guankan* 國立編譯館刊 2.3:223–234 (Dec. 1973).

Zhang Zhidong. *China's Only Hope: An Appeal*. Trans. Samuel Woodbridge. New York: Revell, 1900.

Zhao Chunnian 趙椿年. "Tanyan zhai shiyou xiaoji (bu)" 覃研齋師友小記 (A brief record of teachers and friends of Tanyan studio—with supplement). *Zhonghe yuekan* 中和月刊 (Harmony monthly), 2.4:2–18 (1941).

Zhao Ersun 趙爾巽. *Qingshigao* (*QSG*) 清史稿 (A draft history of the Qing dynasty). Beijing, 1977.

Zhao Quancheng 趙泉澄. *Qingdai dili yange biao* 清代地理沿革表 (A table of geographical changes in the Qing period). Shanghai, 1955.

Zhongguo difang zhi lian he mulu 中國地方志聯合目錄 (Bibliography of China regional gazetteers). Beijing, 1985.

Zhongguo dixue lunwen suo yin 中國地學論文索引 (Index of essays of Chinese gazetteers). 2 vols. Taibei, 1970.

Zhonghe yuekan shihao xuanji 中和月刊史料選集 (Selected historical materials from *Zhonghe* monthly). In *JDSL*, vol. 600, 1966.

Zhonghua minguo disan ci jiaoyu tubiao 中華民國第三次教育圖表 (The third educational statistics in the Republic of China). Ed. Jiaoyu bu 教育部 (Ministry of Education). 1915. Rpt. Taibei, *JDSL*, vols. 98–99, 1986.

Zhonghua mingguo Taiwan diqu gong cang fangzhi mulu 中華民國台灣地區公藏方志目錄 (Index to gazetteers held in the Republic of China, Taiwan). Ed. Wang Deyi 王德毅. Taibei, 1985.

Zhongshan shuyuan zhi 鍾山書院志 (Zhongshan Academy gazetteer). Ed. Jian Chang 建昌 and Tang Qunnian 湯椿年. 4 vols. 1725.

Zhu Xi 朱熹. *Learning to Be a Sage: Selections from the Conversations of*

Master Chu, Arranged Topically. Trans. Daniel Gardner. Berkeley, University of California Press, 1990.

———. "Pingjiang fu Changshou xianxue Wu gong ciji" 平江府常熟縣學吳公祠記 (A record of the venerable Wu's shrine at Changshou xianxue in Pingjiang prefecture). *Zhu Wengong wenji* 朱文公文集 (Collection of writings of Zhu Xi), *ce* 1, 2:1456–1457. In *Sibu congkan zhengbian* 四部叢刊正編 (Formal editions of the four books series). 100 vols. Taibei, 1979.

———. *Reflections on Things at Hand: The Neo-Confucian Anthology*. Comp. Chu Hsi and Lu Tsu-Ch'ien. Trans. with notes, Wing-tsit Chan. New York: Columbia University Press, 1967.

Zhu Xingui 璩鑫圭. *Zhongguo jindai jiaoyu shi ziliao huibian* 中國近代教育史資料彙編 (Collected source materials on modern Chinese educational history). Shanghai, 1990.

Zhu Ying 朱英. Xinhai geming shiqi xinshi shangren shetuan yanjiu 辛亥革命時期新式商人社團研究 (Research on new-style merchant associations in the era of the 1911 revolution). Beijing: Renmin daxue chubanshe, 1991.

Zhu Youxian 朱有瓛, ed. *Zhongguo jindai xuezhi shiliao* 中國近代學制史料 (Historical materials on modern China's system of study). The first collection in two parts. Shanghai, 1986.

Zi, Etienne. *Pratique des Examens Littéraires en Chine*. Shanghai: Imprimerie de la mission catholique, 1894.

Zong Yuanhan 宗源瀚. *Yiqing quan wenquo ji* 頤情館聞過集 (Collected materials from the Yiqing studies). Preface dated 1877. 12 *juan*. N.p.

Zuo Zongtang 左宗棠 "Jiang tang" 講堂 (Lecture hall). Jiangyin, stele inscription, 1883. Rpt. *Nanjing* 南菁 (Nanjing), 35 (1935). Also rpt. as "Nanjing Shuyuan ti e bawei" 南菁書院題額跋尾 (Inscription naming Southern Quintessence Academy). In Zuo Zongtang, *Zuo Wenxiang gong quanji*. Vol. 6, "wenji" (collected writings) section, p. 2633.

———. "Jiangyin chuangjian Nanjing shuyuan dongfa jianbiao xiangxia yinliang pian" 江陰創建南菁書院動撥鹽標項下銀兩片 (Authorization to disperse funds to establish Southern Quintessence Academy in Jiangyin). In Zuo Zongtang, *Zuo Wenxiang gong quanji*. 5:2455.

———. *Zuo Wenxiang gong quanji* 左文襄公全集 (Complete works of Zuo Wenxiang). Ed. Yang Shulin 楊書霖. 9 vols. Taibei: Wenhai: 1979.

ZWDCD. *Zhongwen da cidian* 中文大辭典 (The encyclopedic dictionary of the Chinese language). 10 vols. Taibei, 1973.

ZWZQJ. *Zeng Wenzheng gong (Guofan) quanji*. See Zeng Wenzheng.

Index

INSTITUTE OF EAST ASIAN STUDIES PUBLICATIONS SERIES

CHINA RESEARCH MONOGRAPHS (CRM)

36. Suzanne Pepper. *China's Education Reform in the 1980s: Policies, Issues, and Historical Perspectives*, 1990
sp. Phyllis Wang and Donald A. Gibbs, eds. *Readers' Guide to China's Literary Gazette, 1949–1979*, 1990
38. James C. Shih. *Chinese Rural Society in Transition: A Case Study of the Lake Tai Area, 1368–1800*, 1992
39. Anne Gilks. *The Breakdown of the Sino-Vietnamese Alliance, 1970–1979*, 1992
sp. Theodore Han and John Li. *Tiananmen Square Spring 1989: A Chronology of the Chinese Democracy Movement*, 1992
40. Frederic Wakeman, Jr., and Wen-hsin Yeh, eds. *Shanghai Sojourners*, 1992
41. Michael Schoenhals. *Doing Things with Words in Chinese Politics: Five Studies*, 1992
sp. Kaidi Zhan. *The Strategies of Politeness in the Chinese Language*, 1992
42. Barry C. Keenan. *Imperial China's Last Classical Academies: Social Change in the Lower Yangzi, 1864–1911*, 1994
43. Ole Bruun. *Business and Bureaucracy in a Chinese City: An Ethnography of Private Business Households in Contemporary China*, 1993
44. Wei Li. *The Chinese Staff System: A Mechanism for Bureaucratic Control and Integration*, 1994
45. Ye Wa and Joseph W. Esherick. *Chinese Archives: An Introductory Guide*, 1996
46. Melissa Brown, ed. *Negotiating Ethnicities in China and Taiwan*, 1996
47. David Zweig and Chen Changgui. *China's Brain Drain to the United States: Views of Overseas Chinese Students and Scholars in the 1990s*, 1995
48. Elizabeth J. Perry, ed. *Putting Class in Its Place: Worker Identities in East Asia*, 1996
sp. Phyllis L. Thompson, ed. *Dear Alice: Letters Home from American Teachers Learning to Live in China*, 1998
49. Wen-hsin Yeh, ed. *Landscape, Culture, and Power in Chinese Society*, 1998
50. Gail Hershatter, Emily Honig, Susan Mann, and Lisa Rofel, comps. and eds. *Guide to Women's Studies in China*, 1999
51. Wen-hsin Yeh, ed. *Modern Chinese Literary and Cultural Studies: Theoretical Issues*, 2000
52. Marilyn A. Levine and Chen San-ching. *The Guomindang in Europe: A Sourcebook of Documents*, 2000
53. David N. Keightley. *The Ancestral Landscape: Time, Space, and Community in Late Shang China*, 2000
54. Peter M. Worthing. *Occupation and Revolution: China and the Vietnamese August Revolution of 1945*, 2001

KOREA RESEARCH MONOGRAPHS (KRM)

13. Vipan Chandra. *Imperialism, Resistance, and Reform in Late Nineteenth-Century Korea: Enlightenment and the Independence Club*, 1988
14. Seok Choong Song. *Explorations in Korean Syntax and Semantics*, 1988
15. Robert A. Scalapino and Dalchoong Kim, eds. *Asian Communism: Continuity and Transition*, 1988
16. Chong-Sik Lee and Se-Hee Yoo, eds. *North Korea in Transition*, 1991
17. Nicholas Eberstadt and Judith Banister. *The Population of North Korea*, 1992
18. Hong Yung Lee and Chung Chongwook, eds. *Korean Options in a Changing International Order*, 1993
19. Tae Hwan Ok and Hong Yung Lee, eds. *Prospects for Change in North Korea*, 1994
20. Chai-sik Chung. *A Korean Confucian Encounter with the Modern World: Yi Hang-no and the West*, 1995
21. Myung Hun Kang. *The Korean Business Conglomerate: Chaebol Then and Now*, 1996
23. Lewis R. Lancaster and Chai-shin Yu, eds. *Buddhism in the Early Chosŏn: Suppression and Transformation*, 1996

24. Lewis R. Lancaster and Richard K. Payne, eds. *Religion and Society in Contemporary Korea*, 1998
25. Jeong-Hyun Shin. *The Trap of History: Understanding Korean Short Stories*, 1998
26. Hyung Il Pai and Timothy R. Tangherlini, eds. *Nationalism and the Construction of Korean Identity*, 1999

JAPAN RESEARCH MONOGRAPHS (JRM)

8. Yung H. Park. *Bureaucrats and Ministers in Contemporary Japanese Government*, 1986
9. Victoria V. Vernon. *Daughters of the Moon: Wish, Will, and Social Constraint in Fiction by Modern Japanese Women*, 1988
10. Steve Rabson, trans. *Okinawa: Two Postwar Novellas* by Ōshiro Tatsuhiro and Higashi Mineo. Introduction and afterword by Steve Rabson. 1996 (2d printing, corrected and updated [1989])
12. James W. White. *The Demography of Sociopolitical Conflict in Japan, 1721–1846*, 1992
13. Winston Davis. *The Moral and Political Naturalism of Baron Katō Hiroyuki*, 1996
14. Michael H. Gibbs. *Struggle and Purpose in Postwar Japanese Unionism*, 2000

RESEARCH PAPERS AND POLICY STUDIES (RPPS)

24. Joyce K. Kallgren, Noordin Sopiee, and Soedjati Djiwandono, eds. *ASEAN and China: An Evolving Relationship*, 1988
29. Richard Holton and Wang Xi, eds. *U.S.-China Economic Relations: Present and Future*, 1989
30. Sadako Ogata. *Normalization with China: A Comparative Study of U.S. and Japanese Processes*, 1989
32. Leo E. Rose and Kamal Matinuddin, eds. *Beyond Afghanistan: The Emerging U.S.-Pakistan Relations*, 1990
33. Clark Neher and Wiwat Mungkandi, eds. *U.S.-Thailand Relations in a New International Era*, 1990
34. Robert Sutter and Han Sungjoo, eds. *Korea-U.S. Relations in a Changing World*, 1990
35. Harry H. Kendall and Clara Joewono, eds. *Japan, ASEAN, and the United States*, 1990
36. Robert A. Scalapino and Gennady I. Chufrin, eds. *Asia in the 1990s: American and Soviet Perspectives*, 1990
37. Chong-Sik Lee, ed. *In Search of a New Order in East Asia*, 1991
38. Leo E. Rose and Eric Gonsalves, eds. *Toward a New World Order: Adjusting U.S.-India Relations*, 1992
39. Harumi Befu, ed. *Cultural Nationalism in East Asia: Representation and Identity*, 1993
40. Yufan Hao. *Dilemma and Decision: An Organizational Perspective on American China Policy Making*, 1997
41. Frederic Wakeman Jr. and Wang Xi, eds. *China's Quest for Modernization: A Historical Perspective*, 1997
42. Loraine A. West and Yaohui Zhao, eds. *Rural Labor Flows in China*, 2000
43. Shalendra D. Sharma, ed. *The Asia-Pacific in the New Millennium: Geopolitics, Security, and Foreign Policy*, 2000

INDOCHINA RESEARCH MONOGRAPHS (IRM)

1. William J. Duiker. *China and Vietnam: The Roots of Conflict*, 1986
2. Allan E. Goodman. *The Search for a Negotiated Settlement of the Vietnam War*, 1986
3. Tran Tri Vu. *Lost Years: My 1,632 Days in Vietnamese Reeducation Camps*, 1989
4. Ta Van Tai. *The Vietnamese Tradition of Human Rights*, 1989
5. Douglas Pike, ed. *The Bunker Papers: Reports to the President from Vietnam, 1967–1973*, 3 vols., 1990
6. Judith Banister. *Vietnam Population Dynamics and Prospects*, 1993

These are new and selected publications. Write for a complete list and prices.
E-mail: easia@uclink.berkeley.edu

INTERNATIONAL AND AREA STUDIES

David K. Leonard, Dean

International and Area Studies at the University of California, Berkeley, comprises four groups: international and comparative studies, area studies, teaching programs, and services to international programs.

INSTITUTE OF EAST ASIAN STUDIES
UNIVERSITY OF CALIFORNIA, BERKELEY

The Institute of East Asian Studies, now a part of Berkeley International and Area Studies, was established at the University of California at Berkeley in the fall of 1978 to promote research and teaching on the cultures and societies of China, Japan, and Korea. It amalgamates the following research and instructional centers and programs: the Center for Chinese Studies, the Center for Japanese Studies, the Center for Korean Studies, the Group in Asian Studies, and the East Asia National Resource Center.

www.ingramcontent.com/pod-product-compliance
Ingram Content Group UK Ltd.
Pitfield, Milton Keynes, MK11 3LW, UK
UKHW012150200826
474546UK00002B/12

9 781557 290410